Frank Tillyard

**Banking and Negotiable Instruments**

A Manual of Practical Law

Frank Tillyard

**Banking and Negotiable Instruments**
*A Manual of Practical Law*

ISBN/EAN: 9783744669528

Printed in Europe, USA, Canada, Australia, Japan

Cover: Foto ©Suzi / pixelio.de

More available books at **www.hansebooks.com**

# BANKING

AND

# NEGOTIABLE INSTRUMENTS

A MANUAL OF PRACTICAL LAW

BY

FRANK TILLYARD, B.A.

OF THE MIDDLE TEMPLE, BARRISTER-AT-LAW, LATE VINERIAN SCHOLAR
OXFORD UNIVERSITY

LONDON
ADAM AND CHARLES BLACK
1891

# PREFACE

THE object of this small book is to deal concisely and simply with the practical legal questions which arise in the course of a banker's business. With this end in view, a considerable part of the book has been devoted to the consideration of the various kinds of securities that a customer, wishing to borrow money from his bankers, may present to them. No book on Banking has heretofore dealt with this aspect of the subject. The author, while intending the book primarily for men of business, has sought to make it useful to lawyers, by giving the name of the principal or best authority for the propositions enunciated by him; starting from such authority, subordinate and analogous cases will readily be found. The author, in several chapters, and particularly in Chapter XVII, has had to discuss questions on which the leading lawyers of the day have disagreed, and if he appears unduly dogmatic, he must plead the view of the client who is said to have preferred a wrong opinion to no opinion at all.

F. T.

11 OLD SQUARE, LINCOLN'S INN,
*August* 1891.

# CONTENTS

| | PAGE |
|---|---|
| ABBREVIATIONS . . . . . . . . | ix |
| LIST OF CASES CITED . . . . . . | xi |

| CHAP. | |
|---|---|
| 1. INTRODUCTORY . . . . . . . | 1 |
| 2. BANKING LEGISLATION . . . . . . | 4 |
| 3. MONEY . . . . . . . . | 15 |
| 4. BANKS AND BANKING COMPANIES . . . . | 37 |
| 5. POWERS OF A BANK AND ITS OFFICERS . . . | 43 |
| 6. BRANCH BANKS . . . . . . . | 53 |
| 7. BANKER AND CUSTOMER . . . . . | 56 |
| 8. BANKERS AND THIRD PERSONS . . . . . | 67 |
| 9. BANKERS' ACCOUNTS . . . . . | 71 |
| 10. APPROPRIATION OF PAYMENTS . . . . . | 75 |
| 11. SPECIAL CUSTOMERS . . . . . . | 79 |
| 12. BANKER AS BAILEE OF VALUABLES . . . . | 92 |
| 13. BANKER AS PAYER OF CHEQUES AND BILLS . . | 95 |
| 14. BANKER AS COLLECTOR OF CHEQUES AND BILLS . | 108 |
| 15. BANK INSTRUMENTS . . . . . . | 120 |
| 16. PERSONAL SECURITY . . . . . . | 129 |
| 17. NEGOTIABILITY . . . . . . . | 137 |
| 18. BILLS OF EXCHANGE . . . . . . | 146 |
| 19. MISCELLANEOUS SECURITIES . . . . . | 166 |
| 20. THE FACTORS' ACTS . . . . . . | 181 |
| 21. SECURITY FOR FLOATING BALANCES . . . | 185 |

## CONTENTS

| | PAGE |
|---|---|
| 22. Shares and Debentures . | 190 |
| 23. Criminal Law . | 203 |
| 24. Scotch Law . | 207 |
| 25. Irish Banks . | 210 |

## APPENDIX

| | |
|---|---|
| Banking Partnerships Act . | 211 |
| Bank Notes (Licence, Etc.) Act . | 228 |
| Bank Charter Act . | 236 |
| Bank Incorporation Act . | 254 |
| Leeman's Act . | 275 |
| Coinage Act 1870 . | 277 |
| Bankers' Books Evidence Act 1879 . | 288 |
| Companies Act 1879 . | 291 |
| Companies Act 1862 . | 295 |
| Stamp Duties Act 1870 . | 296 |
| Index . | 297 |

# ABBREVIATIONS USED

| | |
|---|---|
| A. & E. | Adolphus and Ellis |
| B. & Ad. | Barnewall and Adolphus |
| B. & Ald. | Barnewall and Alderson |
| B. & C. | Barnewall and Cresswell |
| Beav. | Beavan |
| Bing. | Bingham |
| Bing. N. C. | Bingham's New Cases |
| Burr. | Burrows |
| C. B. | Common Bench |
| C. B. N. S. | Common Bench New Series |
| C. & M. | Crompton and Meeson |
| C. & P. | Carrington and Payne |
| Camp. | Campbell |
| Cl. & Fin. | Clark and Finelly |
| De G. M. & G. | De Gex, Macnaghten and Gordon |
| E. & B. | Ellis and Blackburn |
| Ex. | Exchequer (Welsby Hurlstone and Gordon) |
| H. & C. | Hurlstone and Coltman |
| H of L. Cas. } H. L. C. } | House of Lords Cases (Clerk) |
| H. & M. | Hemming and Miller |
| H. & N. | Hurlstone and Norman |
| L. J., Bk. | Law Journal, Bankruptcy |
| L. J., Ch. | ,, ,, Chancery |
| L. J., C. P. | ,, ,, Common Pleas |
| L. J., Ex. | ,, ,, Exchequer |
| L. J., Q. B. | ,, ,, Queen's Bench |
| L. R., Ap. Ca. | Law Reports, Appeal Cases |
| L. R., C. P. | ,, ,, Common Pleas |

| | |
|---|---|
| L. R., C. P. D. | Law Reports, Common Pleas Division |
| L. R., Ch. Ap. | ,, ,, Chancery Appeals |
| L. R., Ch. Div. | ,, ,, Chancery Division |
| L. R., E. & I. | ,, ,, English and Irish Appeals |
| L. R., Eq. | ,, ,, Equity |
| L. R., Ex. | ,, ,, Exchequer |
| L. R., P. C. | ,, ,, Privy Council |
| L. R., Q. B. | ,, ,, Queen's Bench |
| L. R., Q. B. D. | ,, ,, Queen's Bench Division |
| L. T. | Law Times |
| Leake | Leake on Contract |
| M. & R. | Manning and Ryland |
| M. & W. | Meeson and Welsby |
| Macq. | Macqueen, House of Lords Cases |
| Man. & G. | Manning and Granger |
| Mer. | Merivale |
| Moore P. C. | Moore's Privy Council |
| Q. B. | Queen's Bench (Adolphus and Ellis) |
| Taunt. | Taunton |
| Times L. R. | Times Law Reports |

# CASES CITED

AGRA and Masterman's Bank, *in re*, 124
Arnold *v.* Cheque Bank, 93, 99
Attorney-General *v.* Birkbeck, 19

BACKHOUSE *v.* Charlton, 86
Bailey *v.* Bodenham, 110
Bailey *v.* Finch, 83
Baker *v.* Nottingham Banking Co., 92
Bank of Australasia *v.* Breillat, 44
Bank of England *v.* Anderson, 12
Bank of Ireland *v.* Evan's Charities, 97
Bank of New South Wales *v.* Owston, 51
Banner *v.* Johnston, 123
Barned's Banking Co., *in re*, 56
Barton *v.* N. Staffordshire Railway Co., 197
Barwick *v.* London Joint-Stock Bank, 49
Beal *v.* Caddick, 77, 86
Bishop, *Ex p.*, 92
Blackburn Benefit Building Society *v.* Brooks, 82
Bodenham *v.* Hoskins, 69
Booth *v.* Bank of England, 12
Bradford Banking Co. *v.* Briggs, 188
Brandao *v.* Barnett, 62
Bridges *v.* Hawkesworth, 34
Burgess *v.* Eve, 132

CAMMIDGE *v.* Allenby, 29
Cavendish *v.* Greaves, 73
Chambers *v.* Miller, 99
Charles *v.* Blackwell, 96, 99
Chartered Bank of India *v.* Evans, 103
Clarke *v.* Birley, 135
Clode *v.* Bailey, 55
Collinson *v.* Lister, 51
Colonial Bank *v.* Cady, 144, 195, 199
Colonial Bank *v.* Hepworth, 195
Colonial Bank *v.* Whinney, 194
Commercial Bank of Scotland *v.* Rhind, 73
Copland *v.* Davies, 210
Coulthart *v.* Clemenson, 132
Crouch *v.* Credit Foncier of England, 200
Cumming *v.* Shand, 76

DARLINGTON District Joint-Stock Bank, *Ex p.*, 86
Devaynes *v.* Noble, 73
Dixon *v.* Bovill, 171

EARL of Sheffield *v.* London Joint-Stock Bank, 89, 91
East of England Banking Co., *in re*, 32
Edmeads *v.* Newman, 33
European Bank, *in re*, 63

FARHALL *v.* Farhall, 87
Farley *v.* Turner, 57

Fine Art Society *v.* Union Bank of London, 169
Firth *v.* Cartland, 68
Foley *v.* Hill, 56, 60
Forster *v.* Wilson, 33
Foster *v.* Green, 50
Fountaine *v.* Carmarthen Railway Company, 200
France *v.* Clark, 191
Fuentes *v.* Montis, 180

GARNETT *v.* Mackewan, 58
General Estates Company, *in re*, 199
General Provident Assurance Company, *in re*, 84, 202
Gibbin *v.* MacMullen, 93
Glyn, Mills, Currie, & Co. *v.* E. & W. India Dock Co., 175
Goodwin *v.* Robarts, 143, 144, 200
Gorgier *v.* Mieville, 138
Gray *v.* Johnston, 60
Gross, *in re*, Kingston, *Ex p.*, 70
Gurney *v.* Behrends, 174

HALLETT'S Estate, *in re*, 68, 78
Hancock *v.* Smith, 68
Hardy *v.* Veasey, 64
Hare *v.* Henty, 109
Hartland *v.* Jukes, 130
Henderson *v.* Bank of Australasia, 44
Hill *v.* Royds, 103
Hill *v.* Smith, 102
Holmes *v.* Bell, 129
Hopkinson *v.* Rolt, 185, 188, 189
Hume *v.* Bolland, 73

IMPERIAL Bank *v.* London and St. Kath. Dock Co., 177
Innes *v.* Stephenson, 86
International Life Assurance Co., *in re*, 81

JOHNSON *v.* Credit Lyonnais, 177
Johnson *v.* Robarts, 117

Kemp, *Ex. p.*, 119
Kilsby *v.* Williams, 78, 109
Kinnaird *v.* Webster, 77, 131

LEASK *v.* Scott, 172
Leeds Bank *v.* Walker, 36
Lichfield Union *v.* Green, 26, 27
Lickbarrow *v.* Mason, 171
Lloyd *v.* Pughe, 80
Locke *v.* Prescott, 88
London and County Banking Co. *v.* London and River Plate Bank, 197
London and County Banking Co. *v.* Radcliffe, 187
Lucas *v.* Dorrein, 64

MACLAE *v.* Sutherland, 44
Magnus *v.* Queensland National Bank, 86
Merchant Banking Co. *v.* Bessemer, 143, 170
Miller *v.* Pace, 15
Moore *v.* Bushell, 67
Morse *v.* Salt, 65, 187

NATAL Investment Co., *in re*, 199

OFFORD *v.* Davies, 131
Ogden *v.* Benas, 97
Orr *v.* Union Bank of Scotland, 121
Overend *v.* Oriental Financial Corporation, 135

PALMER, *in re*, 108
Parker *v.* Mackenna, 47
Partridge *v.* Bank of England, 168
Patent File Company, *in re*, 82
Pedder *v.* Mayor and Corporation of Preston, 58
Picker *v.* London and County Banking Co., 140
Pollard *v.* Bank of England, 111
Pollard *v.* Ogden, 118
Pott *v.* Clegg, 59
Prince *v.* Oriental Bank Corporation, 59, 113

CASES CITED

Raphael v. Bank of England, 34
Robarts v. Tucker, 101
Romford Canal Co., in re, 201

Samuell v. Howarth, 134
Scholey v. Ramsbottom, 100
Sewell v. Burdick, 176
Simmons v. London Joint-Stock Bank, 90, 139
Sims v. Bond, 67
Smith v. Everett, 19
Smith v. Mundy, 26
Société Générale de Paris v. Walker, 193
South Blackpool Hotel Co., in re, 198
Stewart v. Greaves, 9
Strong v. Foster, 134
Suffell v. Bank of England, 35
Swift v. Winterbottom, 9, 50

Tassell v. Cooper, 61

Tatam v. Hasler, 34, 151
Thompson v. Bell, 4
Timmins v. Gibbons, 31
Tondeur, Ex p., 127

Union Bank of Canada v. Cole, 126
United Service Co., in re, 63, 93.

Vagliano Brothers v. Bank of England, 100, 104, 106

Warwick v. Rogers, 113
West of England Bank, in re, 46
Whitaker v. Bank of England, 101
Williamson v. Williamson, 65, 66
Willis v. Bank of England, 53
Woodland v. Fear, 54
Wookey v. Pole, 167

Young v. Grote, 98

## ADDENDA

(1.) The bill referred to at page 17 has now become law.

(2.) An Act (54 & 55 Vict., c. 43) has also been passed this session to enable companies to deal with difficulties arising from forged transfers, the forgery of which has not been discovered until the transferee has been registered as a shareholder. It was commonly known as the Pitt Lewis Bill.

(3.) The Stamp Acts have been consolidated by 54 & 55 Vict., c. 39.

# CHAPTER I

### INTRODUCTORY

The exigencies of modern commerce demand in many cases that one person or body of persons shall fulfil many functions. The banker of to-day is no exception to this rule, and, under stress of competition, has taken upon himself many duties which can conveniently be performed along with the necessary business of a banker. It will always be useful to be able to distinguish those functions which are of the essence of banking, and originally called banking into existence, from those other functions which the banker, once called into existence, has taken upon himself either for the convenience of his customers or his own profit.

The earliest English bankers were goldsmiths, who, in the times of commotion preceding the Commonwealth, were willing to receive the money of customers under a promise to repay it, with interest, upon the demand of their customers. The receipt of money, under a liability to repay it upon demand, is still the basis of banking.

The receipts which the goldsmith gave in return for his customer's money constituted the earliest form of bank note. When the first goldsmith or banker discovered that, on an average, only a small percentage of the money entrusted to him was required at a given time, and that accordingly the possession of a certain amount of gold was enough, while his credit remained good, to enable him to promise to pay on demand very much larger sums, banking was established as a lucrative trade. The issue of promissory notes by a goldsmith or banker by way of loan was the second stage in the development of banking. Roughly speaking, for a hundred years, banking meant the receipt of money, coupled with the issue of bank notes. The most important change that has occurred in the nature of banking was brought about by the invention and adoption of cheques. These came into use about the year 1780; and from about that time London banks, other than the Bank of England, began to discontinue their note issue. Upon the receipt of money from a customer they entered the amount in their books to the credit of the customer, and handed him a cheque-book. These London banks still retained the power of issuing notes, for it was commonly supposed that a deposit bank— that is to say a bank which was forbidden to issue notes— was not a lawful institution; and it was not till fifty years later that any banks were started purely as banks of deposit.

The commercial difference between an old bank of issue, whose issue of notes was unrestricted, and a modern deposit bank is, that on the debtor side of an imaginary balance-sheet of the former the chief item would be, "*Dr.* to bank notes issued," an item which is only limited by the willingness of the general public to keep the notes in circulation; whereas, in the case of the latter, the chief item would be, "*Dr.* to sums due by the bank on current and deposit accounts," an item which is limited by the numbers and wealth of the customers of the particular bank. Bank notes, so far as they are issued by way of advances, constitute an increase of the working capital of the issuing banker, for which he pays nothing beyond the cost of paper and printing, his licence, and the stamp-duty. Accordingly, with an unrestricted issue, there is every temptation for a banker to issue as many notes as possible. The working capital of a deposit bank, consisting as it does mainly of deposits of customers, is charged with the payment of interest to them. As, however, interest is generally paid on minimum balances, and not at all on small balances, this payment does not heavily handicap the deposit banks. For example, the London and County Bank, at the end of the half-year ending June 31st, 1890, owed on deposit and current accounts £33,804,035, and had paid during that period for interest £153,397, or a little less than one per cent. per annum.

Advances are now usually made either directly by a loan of money, or indirectly by the discount of bills of exchange.

Besides the important functions of receiving and lending money, issuing bank notes, and discounting bills of exchange, the modern banker will take charge of securities and valuables, collect dividends, and invest and transmit money for his customers.

This sketch of the main points of the development of banking may enable my readers with more ease to understand the following chapter on banking legislation.

# CHAPTER II

## BANKING LEGISLATION

*Establishment of the Bank of England.*—During the period which saw the establishment of banking as a distinct business, a period extending roughly from the beginning of the Commonwealth up to the Revolution, there was no special legislation dealing with banking. Any person or any number of persons in partnership were free to issue their promissory notes in return for money deposited with them, or by way of loan. It is not probable, however, that any of the evils which free trade in bank notes would now produce were then present, or even imagined. The fact that these promissory notes were novelties, and that doubts were felt whether promissory notes at all were on the same footing as bills of exchange, is enough to show us that they were not at that period money in the sense in which they afterwards became so. The first Banking Act was the Act which established the Bank of England in 1694. William III was at that date in need of cash, and was only too glad to promote the establishment of the bank in return for a loan of £1,200,000. That amount was subscribed within a few hours of the opening of the list. The business of the corporation was confined to banking, as it was expressly forbidden to trade except in bills of exchange, bullion, and goods deposited as security and not redeemed. The bills of the corporation were to be transferable by endorsement under the hand of the holder, and the assignee was to have the right to sue in his own name. The Act did not in express terms give the bank an exclusive privilege of banking, nor was there in that year any apparent need for such privilege. Two years later another scheme was projected, and an Act for the establishment of a National Land Bank was actually passed; but the capital was never subscribed, and the scheme immediately fell through. The Bank of England, alarmed by the prospect of the creation of rival establishments, in the next year secured the privilege of being the only bank which was to "be created or established, permitted, suffered, countenanced, or allowed by Act of Parliament, within this kingdom." The bank was now secured against the competition of similar corporations.

The beginning of Anne's reign saw the settlement of the question of the character of promissory notes, by the passing of an Act in 1704 declaring that promissory notes were like bills of exchange. The effect of this was to make them transferable by delivery, so that a *bonâ fide* holder for value obtained a good title, and could sue in his own name. The promissory note of a banker or a banking firm thus became a highly useful instrument.

*Limitation of Private Banking.*—The Bank of England was, however, threatened with another danger. The statutory privileges of that bank did not protect it against private individuals either alone or in partnership. If a score of the wealthiest merchants united in partnership for the purposes of banking, and issued bank notes secured by their united private fortunes, such a bank might become a serious rival even to so wealthy a corporation as the Bank of England. Accordingly, an Act was passed in the year 1708, in order to secure still further the monopoly of the Bank of England. This Act is the beginning of the curious connection of banking partnerships with the number 6, which is still in existence so far as regards the issue of bank notes. One clause of the Act enacted that it should not be lawful for any body politic or corporate whatsoever, erected or to be erected, other than the Bank of England, or for other persons whatsoever, united or to be united in covenants or partnership exceeding the number of six persons in England, to borrow, owe, or take up any sums of money on their bills or notes payable at demand, or at any less time than six months from the borrowing thereof. For more than a century this, with immaterial alterations, remained law.

*Origin of Deposit Banks.*—For the whole of this period this legislation was successful in dividing banking business between the Bank of England and private partnerships of not more than six partners, though this was not a necessary consequence of the Act. The custom of entering in bank books, to the credit of a customer, money received from him, and giving to him a cheque-book instead of bank notes, which, as before mentioned, grew up about the year 1780, was sufficient to render this legislation almost nugatory; for it enabled banking to be carried on without the use of bank notes, and the monopoly of the Bank of England as a matter of fact only extended to the issue of notes and certain bills. When this was realised—as was the case about the year 1830—there came into existence, under a declaratory Act, a new class of banks, and banking began to assume its modern character.

The exact causes which led banks of issue to give cheque-books instead of notes are not clearly known, but it is obvious that any reduction of the amount of outstanding bank notes on which a bank was liable must have increased its stability. It was not an unknown thing for a bank to collect the notes of a rival bank and present them for payment in quantities sufficient to embarrass or even ruin the bank liable upon them. It is clearly impossible to collect and present customers' cheques in a similar way or with similar consequences.

*Joint-Stock Banks of Issue.*—When this custom of using cheque-books gained acceptance, the London private banks totally discontinued their note issue, and thus there were, in the early part of this century, banks of excellent credit who were able, without the use of bank notes of their own issue, to carry on successfully the functions of a bank of deposit, as such banks are now called. As is well known the liabilities to the public of the leading London joint-stock banks have since become, in several cases, greater than the corresponding liability of the Bank of England. But before we pass on to notice the establishment of the London banking companies we must first notice an important Act which introduced large partnership banks of issue. The feeling of the mercantile world against state-favoured monopolies had steadily grown during the great growth of English commerce, which dates from the latter half of the eighteenth century; and the favoured position of the Bank of England, as the only corporation or large body of persons able to issue bank notes, was, in the early part of this century, beginning to be felt an anomaly. Further, the security of a private bank with not more than six partners had been proved to be miserably inadequate if its issue of notes was unrestricted. In 1801 the value of gold rose to £4, 5s. per oz., or a premium of more than 10 per cent. In 1809 there were seven hundred and twenty-one country banks having a total note issue of £30,000,000, and in that year gold rose to £4, 11s. per oz. In 1813 gold had reached the price of £5, 10s. per oz., or a premium of over 40 per cent. In 1816 eighty-nine country banks stopped payment, and the private note issue of the country was at once reduced one-half. In the next crisis of 1825 there were seventy-six bank failures. In 1826 two Acts were passed, one restricting for three years the issue of bank notes under £5, and the other permitting an extension of banking co-partnerships. The latter Act (Appendix, p. 211) involved a relinquishment by the Bank of England of part of its privileges, but that bank still retained its old rights in London and the surrounding country. It was enacted that it should be lawful for any bodies politic or corporate with more than six members, and for co-partnerships of more than six persons, to carry on business as bankers in England, provided that they had no establishment as bankers in London, or within sixty-five miles of it, and that the liability of all members or partners was unlimited. Such bodies or partnerships were empowered to issue their notes on unstamped paper, on giving security and taking out a licence. A co-partnership or company formed under this Act of 1826 was not a corporation, and had therefore no common seal. It was a co-partnership created by deed or articles of co-partnership for a particular purpose, with certain statutable privileges and liabilities. It could sue and be sued only in the name of one of its public officers, and in all litigious business the company was represented by one of its public officers who must be a member of the company, and individual members could not sue and be sued in respect of transactions with the company till a judgment or decree had been first obtained against the company through one of its public officers. The Act conferred no authority on the public officer to bind the company, but made him the representative of the bank only for litigious purposes; and, although he must be a member of the company, he might have nothing to do with the management of its affairs (*Swift* v. *Winterbotham* L. R., 8 Q. B., 244). Apart from this special procedure, the liabilities of the members were different from those of ordinary partners. At common law, those members only would be liable who were such when the contract was entered into; but, by the Statute, not only those, but all who became members afterwards, and until the bills, notes, or debts were paid, were made liable. At common law, all the goods of the contracting parties and other persons would be liable to immediate execution; but, by the Statute, the goods of the company were liable, and the members for the time being at the period of execution in the first instance, and afterwards those who were so at the time of the contracts being entered into or carried into effect, or when the judgment was obtained thereon. At common law the Statutes of Limitations apply, but by the Statute the members who have ceased to be such for three years were exempt from debts of every description (*Stewart* v. *Greares*, 10 M. & W., 711). The Statute contained no provision as to the manner in which the company should make or sign deeds, contracts, or documents of any description, and it was held (*Swift* v. *Winterbotham*, supra) that it could not affix its signature to documents otherwise than by the hand of some individual or individuals who, by the articles of co-partnership, were appointed to represent the general body in such matters. Under this Act a great many banks, including the National Provincial Bank of England, were formed, and it is just possible there are some of such banks still in existence that have never brought themselves within later Acts.

*The Modern Bank Note.*—By an Act of the year 1828 all issuing banks, if not carrying on business within the city of London or within three miles of it, were allowed, upon obtaining a licence and giving security, to issue on unstamped paper promissory notes for any sum of money amounting to £5 or upwards, and expressed to be payable to bearer on demand. From this time bank notes have not been allowed in England for amounts less than £5, and the county bank note assumed its modern form.

*Origin of the London Joint-Stock Banks.*—It has been already stated that, although the London private banks voluntarily became merely banks of deposit, it was commonly supposed that the privileges of the Bank of England were sufficient to make unlawful the carrying on of any form of banking business by a bank which was forbidden to issue notes. A closer examination of the statutes affecting the Bank of England showed that its monopoly left untouched the acceptance of deposits, but it was not till 1820 or thereabouts that the discovery was made. In 1833 the legal officers of the Crown gave it as their opinion that banks of deposit were lawful at common law, and in the same year the position of such banks was declared and affirmed in a section of an Act of Parliament passed to continue the privileges of the Bank of England. There was now nothing to hinder the formation in London, and other places within sixty-five miles of it, of large co-partnerships intended to act as deposit banks, and from this time dates the rise of the great London banking companies.

*The Bank Charter Act.*—Meanwhile the evils of an unrestricted note issue were not removed by the abolition of small notes, and in the years 1844 and 1845 Sir Robert

Peel made a great attempt to deal with the currency question in all parts of the United Kingdom. The English Act is known as the Bank Charter Act, and was passed in the year 1844. It still regulates the note issue both of country banks and the Bank of England. It would be out of place here to give more than a summary of this very important Act, the text of which is set out in full in the Appendix, p. 236. The Act provides for the restriction of the issues of private banks and of the Bank of England, and for the continuation of the modified monopoly of the latter bank. The chief provisions enact that, after the passing of the Act, there are to be no new banks of issue; but a banker who was on May 6th, 1844, lawfully issuing his own bank notes under a licence according to the Act of 1828, may continue to issue notes to an average amount not exceeding his average issue as determined by the actual issue of his bank for twelve weeks before the passing of the Act. A bank loses its right of issue by ceasing to exercise it, and if consisting of not more than six members, by bringing its number of members above six, and if consisting of more than six members by establishing a place of business in London or within sixty-five miles of it. Bank of England notes are to be issued from a separate department, called the issue department. The issue department may issue against public securities notes to the extent of £14,000,000, and beyond that sum may issue notes to the banking department in exchange for gold coin, or gold or silver bullion. If a banker ceases to issues notes, the Bank of England may be empowered to increase its issue of notes against public securities by two-thirds of the amount of the discontinued issue. The same Act also enables any bank to draw, accept, or indorse bills of exchange, notwithstanding that they are payable at less than six months, so long as they are not payable on demand. This last provision is more important than it at first sight appears to be, and was inserted because the Bank of England had insisted on its strict privileges, to the detriment of the London joint-stock banks. Thus, in the case of *The Bank of England* v. *Anderson* (3 Bing., N. C., 589), it appeared that the Bank of St. Albans received £25 from a customer and gave him a bill for £25 drawn by them on their London agents, the London & Westminster Bank, payable twenty-one days after date. The London & Westminster Bank had sufficient funds of the Bank of St. Albans to meet the bill. In an action by the Bank of England against the London & Westminster Bank, it was held that the acceptance of the bill at twenty-one days was an infringement of the privileges of the Bank of England. It was then sought to evade the privileges of the Bank of England by having such bills drawn on the managers of the London agents, under the guarantee of the London bank to pay the same. But this arrangement was held by the House of Lords to be illegal, as being a colourable evasion of the Act (*Booth* v. *Bank of England*, 6 Bing. N. C., 415). The insertion of the above section enabled the great London joint-stock banks to act as agents for country banks in the same way that a private bank could.

*Incorporated Banks.* — Legislation since the Bank Charter Act down to the present time has been directed towards the development of joint-stock banking. The Act of 1826, as we have seen, did not attempt to incorporate the partners of the banks formed under it. The year 1844 saw the passing of a second Banking Act (Appendix, p. 254), which enacted that no future partnership of more than six partners should be formed unless incorporated under the provisions of that Act.

Such corporations were, by their very nature, able to sue and be sued in their own names. Execution was to be issued against the property and effects of the Company before resort was made to the present or past shareholders, whose liability was practically the same as under the Act of 1826. If, however, execution was levied on a shareholder, the directors were bound to make a call on the other shareholders within three weeks, in order to reimburse him.

*Banks with Limited Liability.*—The principle of limited liability was first applied to banks in 1858, but the Act of that year is not important, as the Companies Act of 1862 swept away all former Acts relating to joint-stock companies of any sort. The provisions of that Act cannot be dealt with in this volume, but it should be noticed that under that Act the liability of a past shareholder is extinguished at the end of a year from the date of his ceasing to be a member. Further, ten instead of six, a change introduced in an Act of 1857, is maintained as the maximum number of partners permissible in an unregistered banking partnership formed after the commencement of the Act. New or old companies availing themselves of the Act have the option of registering, either with or without limited liability; but, as far as the liability of an old company on its notes is concerned, no limit to its liability can be gained by registration as a limited company.

The principle of limited liability was not *per se* found to be very suitable to banking companies. Uncalled capital was always liable to be called up or to be mortgaged for the benefit of creditors other than depositors. The failure of the Glasgow Bank in 1878 attracted people's attention very forcibly to the dangerous position, both of shareholders whose liability was unlimited and of depositors who might for years have been trusting an insolvent bank. The Companies Act 1879 (Appendix, p. 291) was framed to enable banks to limit their liability and at the same time to ensure publicity of accounts, and a certain amount of stability. This Act enables banks and other companies to register under the Companies Acts, as limited companies with shares partly paid up, and then to provide that the unpaid balance shall only be called up upon the Company going into liquidation; and further provides, in the case of banking companies registering under it, for a compulsory independent audit of the bank accounts. All the leading joint-stock banks have taken advantage of that Act.

This sketch does not intend to deal exhaustively with legislation as to banks but merely to indicate the policy of the State from time to time with regard to them. As this is in course of writing it seems possible that the Chancellor of the Exchequer may attempt an amendment of the Bank Charter Act with reference to the issue of bank notes, and may also, either directly or indirectly, compel banks to keep a larger reserve of cash or money at call to meet their current liabilities.

# CHAPTER III

## MONEY

THE simplest function of a banker is to receive his customer's money.

*Definition.*—By money is meant either metallic money or paper money. Money is sometimes called currency, because it passes freely from hand to hand or passes current. The term money is preferable to the term currency, because, while persons have been found to argue that paper currency includes cheques and bills of exchange, they have never gone so far as to call cheques and bills of exchange money. Popular practice and banking customs alike regard money as consisting either of coins or bank notes. Bank notes obtained the position of money more than a century ago, for in deciding the case of *Miller* v. *Race* (1 Burr., 452) Lord Mansfield said: "Bank notes are not goods nor securities, nor documents for debts, nor are so esteemed; but are treated as money, as cash in the ordinary course and transaction of business, by the general consent of mankind, which gives them the credit and currency of money to all intents and purposes. They are as much money as guineas themselves are, or any other current coin that is used in common payments as money or cash; . . . . . they are never considered as securities for money but as money itself. On payment of them receipts are always given as for money, not as for securities or notes."

*Metallic Money.*—British money is coined from three different metals—gold, silver, and copper; but gold is the only standard metal. Legal coins are issued from the Mint, and from no other source. The Coinage Act 1870 (Appendix, p. 277) empowered the Queen in Privy Council to establish branch mints in the Colonies, and under this power large numbers of sovereigns have been and still are coined in Australia.

The coins which the Mint have power to issue are contained in a schedule to the Coinage Act, which sets out the standard and minimum legal weights, and the standard of fineness. The Queen in Privy Council has power to change the device and the denomination of coins. It was under this power that, in 1887, the new jubilee device was adopted and the double florin issued to the public.

Under the same Act every person has the right to have gold bullion, if of sufficient fineness, coined at the Mint, free of any charges for assaying the metal, coining it, or for waste in coinage, at the rate of £3, 17s. $10\frac{1}{2}$d. per ounce of standard gold. This right does not extend to silver or copper bullion. This privilege is not of great practical importance, as the owner of the gold loses the use of it when it is being coined, and there is an alternative right conferred by the 3rd section of the Bank Charter Act. Under that section every person has the right to exchange bullion, subject to the expense of melting and assaying it, at the issue department of the Bank of England for Bank of England notes, at the rate of £3, 17s. 9d. per ounce of standard gold. The bank notes can be at once exchanged for sovereigns in the banking department.

*As Legal Tender.*—As long as coins are of the full legal

weight they are a legal tender, if made of gold, up to any amount, if of silver up to forty shillings, if of copper up to a shilling.

A new sovereign weighs 123·27447 grains and remains a legal tender until reduced by wear below a weight of 122·5 grains, a diminution of about three-fourths of a grain. The 7th section of the Coinage Act gives any person power to smash a light coin, but it is a matter of everyday knowledge that light coins are never smashed, and pass current for all ordinary purposes at places other than the Bank of England. In fact it was with the greatest difficulty that the Government were able to call in pre-Victorian sovereigns and half-sovereigns, and a short Act, called the Coinage Act 1889, had eventually to be passed, which enacted that pre-Victorian gold coins would for a certain period be taken at their nominal value, if there was no evidence that they had been illegally diminished in weight. If a sovereign or half-sovereign was four grains short, that fact was to be *primâ facie* evidence of such illegal treatment. A bill on similar lines dealing with light Victorian coins is now before Parliament.

*Paper Money.*—English paper money consists of bank notes. The distinguishing characteristics of English bank notes are that they are not issued by the Government, and are strictly convertible.

A bank note may be defined, for practical purposes, as an unconditional promise, written or printed on unstamped paper, made by a bank to pay on demand to the bearer of the paper the sum mentioned therein, such sum not being less than £5.

We shall find it convenient to make four divisions of the subject dealing with (*a*) Banks of issue, (*b*) Amount of issue, (*c*) Stamp duties, (*d*) Legal qualities of notes.

### (a) *Banks of Issue*

The history of banks of issue, and incidentally certain aspects of their character, have already been dealt with, but here we are concerned with the whole law relating to them, as it now stands. There are three local rings, with London as centre, in which the rights of issue differ—first, the City of London and three miles round, in which the Bank of England has a complete monopoly; secondly, the district more than three, but within sixty-five miles of London, in which the monopoly is divided between the Bank of England and banking firms of less than six members lawfully issuing notes on May 6th, 1844; lastly, the district more than sixty-five miles from London, in which the monopoly is divided between the Bank of England and banking firms of six or more or less members, lawfully issuing notes on May 6th, 1844 (see *Lindley on Partnership*, p. 186 n.).

*Transmission of Right of Issue.*—It seems probable that a private bank issue will ultimately cease to exist. No fresh bank can gain a right to issue notes, and the old banks often go out of existence, or lose their right of issue. In the first place a bank loses its right of issue by coming to London, as in the case of the National Provincial Bank, or if composed of more than six partners by coming within the sixty-five mile radius. Secondly, if an issuing banker becomes bankrupt, or ceases to carry on the business of a banker or discontinues the issue of bank notes, either by agreement with the Bank of England or otherwise, he ceases to have the right to issue notes. Again, if a bank with not more than six partners increases the number of its partners above six, it becomes unlawful for such bank to issue notes, and it is immaterial whether such bank is within or without the sixty-five mile radius. Lastly, if two banks unite so that the total number of partners exceeds six, the united bank, instead of being able to issue the aggregate amount of their previous issues, forfeits the right to issue any notes. Subject to these rules the right to continue to issue notes is not prejudiced or affected by any change in the personal composition of the banking company or partnership, either by the transfer of any shares or share therein, or by the admission of any new partner or member thereto, or by the retirement of any present partner or member therefrom. As the right to issue bank notes is of some value, two examples will be given, the first to show what is a permissible device for transmission of such right, and the second to show what is not a permissible device. In the first case (*Smith* v. *Everett*, 29 L. J., Ch., 236), it appeared that two partners, Everett and Smith, established a bank in Salisbury in 1811. They issued notes, and under the Bank Charter Act were entitled to issue them to the extent of £15,695. By the year 1856 both partners were getting advanced in years, and in July of that year Smith died. There then survived to Everett the sole and exclusive right of issuing notes. Had he then sold the business straight out the right of issuing notes would have disappeared. The right was, however, perpetuated by Everett giving the purchasers the benefit of his services, and allowing them to use his name for eleven months under a very stringent indemnity against loss.

In the second case (*Attorney-General* v. *Birkbeck*, L. R., 12 Q. B. D., 605) there was an attempt to transfer the right to issue notes from a private firm, Birkbeck & Co., known as the Craven Bank, to a limited company, under the name of the Craven Bank, Limited. The bank had been started in Yorkshire in 1791, and the extent of its authorised note issue was about £60,000. In 1880, Birkbeck & Co. transferred their business to the Limited Company as a going concern, with the goodwill, but with a reservation to the vendors of their right to issue their own bank notes, the benefit of which issue was to be included in the sale by the following provisions:—The notes were to be issued in the old form, *i.e.* in the name of the firm, but through the officers of the company only. The company was to pay £2 per cent. per annum interest on the amount of notes in circulation. The rights of the firm as to issue were not to be assigned, and the admission of new partners to perpetuate the right was to be made only with the consent of the company. When the business was taken over, the notes in circulation were treated as a liability which the company had to meet, and the amount of that liability was deducted from the purchase-money paid to the firm. As the outstanding notes were presented for payment they were cashed by the company; and they were again issued by the company to persons who had to receive cash from them, and who chose to take it in that form. The firm and the company were sued for penalties under the Stamp Act for unlawfully issuing unstamped bank notes. The Court held, on the above facts, that the company had obtained the whole benefit of the privilege of issuing the notes and the sole power of issuing them, and that was in substance and truth a transfer of the privilege. As the company were not carrying on business and issuing notes on May 6th, 1844, they were contravening the Bank Charter Act. As for the firm, the Court held that, on the making of the agreement of 1880, they had ceased to carry on the business of bankers, and had become shareholders and directors of the company. As they had ceased to carry on the business of banking, by the terms of the Bank Charter Act they had lost the right to issue bank notes. Both the company and the firm were, therefore, liable to pay the penalties sued for.

*Limited Bank of Issue.*—A joint-stock banking company, which was lawfully issuing its own notes on May 6th, 1844, may incorporate itself by registration under the Companies Acts either as a limited or unlimited company. But it cannot limit its liability upon its notes. The law on this point is now contained in the Companies Act 1879, s. 6, which enacts that "A bank of issue registered as a limited company, either before or after the passing of this Act, shall not be entitled to limited liability in respect of its notes; and the members thereof shall continue liable in respect of its notes in the same manner as if it had been registered as an unlimited company; but in case the general assets of the company are, in the event of the company being wound up, insufficient to satisfy the claims of both the note-holders and the general creditors, then the members, after satisfying the remaining demands of the note-holders, shall be liable to contribute towards payment of the debts of the general creditors a sum equal to the amount received by the note-holders out of the general assets of the company." Thus, if the liability to note-holders is £100,000 and to general creditors is £500,000, and the assets of the company are £150,000, its realisable uncalled capital another £150,000, the general assets will be £300,000, of which the note-holders will take £50,000 and the general creditors £250,000. The shareholders will then have to pay the note-holders £50,000, and afterwards the general creditors another £50,000, on account of that amount taken by the note-holders from the general assets. Unless all the share holders are reduced to bankruptcy the general creditors will take the whole of the £300,000. Subject to that exception the note-holders will always be paid in full, and the general creditors will get the same dividend as if there had been no liabilities to the note-holders, and the company had been an ordinary limited company. If, however, all the shareholders are reduced to bankruptcy by the calls, the following is the order of payment away of the assets as realised. Assets other than uncalled capital are divided rateably between the note-holders and the general creditors. The uncalled capital is divided in the same way. Any sum realised by further calls is then paid to the note-holders; when they are satisfied, the general creditor will take a further amount not exceeding the share of the note-holders in the general assets. Thus if, in the example given above, the calls on the shareholders only produce £200,000, the note-holders will be paid in full, but the general creditors will only receive £250,000 instead of £300,000.

## (b) *Amount of Issue*

The Bank of England has the right to issue bank notes up to the amount of £14,000,000 on the credit of securities to that value transferred to the issue department of the bank. The Queen in Privy Council may increase the amount which may be issued by the bank on the credit of securities, to an extent not exceeding two-thirds of the amount which other bankers may have ceased to issue under other provisions of the Act. The total amount which the bank is now authorised to issue on the credit of securities is about £15,000,000. On a transfer of gold or silver bullion or gold coin from the banking to the issue department, the issue department may issue notes on the credit of such bullion or coin to an amount equal to their aggregate value. The amount of silver bullion must never exceed in value one-fourth of the gold coin and bullion.

The maximum amount of the issue of a bank, other than the Bank of England, is the amount certified by the Commissioners of Stamps and Taxes as being the average amount of the bank notes of such bank in circulation during a period of twelve weeks preceding April 27th, 1844. To speak more strictly, the amount so certified is not a maximum, but a maximum average amount for periods of four weeks at a time. A banker has to send in weekly accounts, showing the amount of his bank notes in circulation on every day of the week, and the weekly average. At the end of each successive period of four weeks, there must be a further account of the average for such period. Such average is to be arrived at by adding the totals for each business day, and dividing by the number of days. The penalty for exceeding the certified average is the amount of the excess. The Commissioners of Stamps and Taxes are empowered to cause the books of bankers, containing an account of their bank notes in circulation, to be inspected for the purpose of testing and verifying the accounts rendered. For further details the reader is referred to the Bank Charter Act, ss. 13, 17, 18, 19, and 20, printed in the Appendix, at p. 236.

## (*c*) *Stamp Duty and Licences*

The Bank of England has the right to issue notes without taking out a licence, and without the payment of any stamp duty or any composition in lieu thereof.

A bank of issue may issue notes either on stamped or unstamped paper, but, as a matter of practice, bank notes are always unstamped. Unstamped bank notes may be issued on obtaining a licence from the Commissioners of Stamps, and giving a bond to secure the payment of a composition for the stamp duties which would otherwise have been payable on the notes issued. The licence is annual, bearing a £30 stamp, and expiring on the 10th October in each year. A separate licence has to be taken out for each town or place at which a bank issues notes; but as, before the Bank Charter Act, four licences were sufficient to authorise issues at any number of places, there is a proviso in that Act that bankers who were, at the date of that Act, issuing notes at more than four places under four licences, may continue to issue notes at the same places with only four licences. In other words, a banker opening a fresh branch, and issuing notes thereat, must take out a fresh licence for such new place of issue. The composition is payable twice a year upon accounts delivered within the first half of January and July. These accounts are to show the amount of notes in circulation on each Saturday in the preceding half-year, with a special provision for notes that are less than seven days in circulation, and on the average circulation so found the composition has to be paid at the rate of 3s. 6d. for every one hundred pounds. For further details the reader is referred to the Statute 9 Geo. IV, c. 23, printed in the Appendix at p. 228, and to the Bank Charter Act, s. 22.

The provisions of the Stamp Act 1870, relating to bank notes are as follows:—

"The term 'banker' means and includes any corporation, society, partnership, and persons, and every individual person, carrying on the business of banking in the United Kingdom.

"The term bank note includes—

"(1) Any bill of exchange or promissory note issued

by any banker, other than the governor and company of the Bank of England, for the payment of money not exceeding one hundred pounds to the bearer on demand.

"(2) Any bill of exchange or promissory note so issued which entitles or is intended to entitle the bearer or holder thereof, without indorsement, or without any further or other indorsement than may be thereon at the time of the issuing thereof, to the payment of money not exceeding one hundred pounds on demand, whether the same be so expressed or not, and in whatever form, or by whomsoever such bill or note is drawn or made.

"A bank note issued duly stamped, or issued unstamped by a banker duly licensed or otherwise authorised to issue unstamped bank notes, may be from time to time re-issued without being liable to any stamp duty by reason of such re-issuing.

"If any banker, not being duly licensed or otherwise authorised to issue unstamped bank notes, issues, or causes or permits to be issued, any bank note not being duly stamped, he shall forfeit the sum of fifty pounds.

"If any person receives or takes any such bank note in payment or as a security, knowing the same to have been issued unstamped, contrary to law, he shall forfeit the sum of twenty pounds."

For the amount of stamp duty, see the Appendix, p. 296.

### (d) *Legal Qualities of Bank Notes*

*Tender.*—A Bank of England note, so long as the bank continues to pay gold on demand for its notes, is a legal tender. But the other requirements of a legal tender must be complied with—as, for instance, that the exact sum must be tendered without requiring change. It follows that a Bank of England note cannot legally be tendered in payment of a debt less than £5.

The Bank of England cannot make a legal tender of its notes in payment of its own debts.

Country notes are also a legal tender, unless, at the time of the tender, objection is made to the receipt of them on the ground that, strictly speaking, they are not cash, but only promissory notes (*Lichfield Union* v. *Greene*, 1 H. & N., 884).

*Cutting in halves.*—A bank note may be cut in halves, and the halves sent separately through the post or otherwise. In such a case there is no change of property until the second half has got into the possession of the person holding the first half (*Smith* v. *Mundy*, 29 L. J., Q. B., 172).

*How different from Promissory Notes.*—There are certain manifest differences between a bank note and a promissory note payable on demand not issued by a banker. Shortly, they are that bank notes issued on unstamped paper cannot be for a sum less than £5, can only be issued up to a restricted aggregate amount by any particular bank, and, lastly, are popularly treated as cash. Chiefly for the first and last reasons the common law drew a distinction between bank notes and other negotiable instruments as regards cash payments in cases of purchase and sale. The law as to English negotiable instruments in general was codified and amended in the Bills of Exchange Act 1882, but where that Act is silent the rules of the common law still apply. That Act is silent as to the presumption to be drawn from the acceptance by a creditor of a bank note, or other negotiable instrument, instead of cash, and accordingly the rules of the common law as to that presumption are still in force.

As to forged or altered bank notes, other than Bank of

England notes, the Bills of Exchange Act 1882, s. 64, introduces an important change, which will be noted in its proper place.

It has been thought possible that bank notes were not intended to be touched by the Bills of Exchange Act, but, though they are not anywhere specially included in the Act, the definition of a promissory note in s. 83 (1) manifestly includes them, and the proviso in favour of the Bank of England in s. 97 (3) (c) would be meaningless if the Act was to be construed, even without that section, so as to exclude Bank of England notes.

Practical questions as to bank notes arise in three cases —(a) when the issuing bank refuses to honour its own notes; (b) when a bank note has been lost or stolen; (c) when a bank note has been forged or altered.

*Dishonoured Notes.*—We shall consider the remedy of a holder of a dishonoured note, first against previous holders and then against the bank issuing it.

It is quite legal to transfer a note by indorsement and delivery, as well as by delivery. In such a case a *bonâ fide* holder for value can recover the amount of the note from any indorsee, and such indorsee can, in his turn, recover its amount from a prior indorsee. Where a note is a legal tender the person to whom it is offered cannot oblige the person offering it to indorse it, but in all other cases he can exact indorsement as a condition upon which he will receive the note in payment.

A person who is the holder of a bank note will in ordinary cases part with it in one of four ways—he will either buy something with it, or pay a debt with it, or pay it into his banking account, or get some one to change it for him. Between the first two cases the common law draws a distinction which it does not recognise in the case of other negotiable instruments (see *Lichfield*

*Union* v. *Greene*, 1 H. & N., 884). When a person pays for goods at the time of their purchase, or pays a past debt by a negotiable instrument—as, for instance, by a cheque—the presumption is that the creditor takes such negotiable instrument as a payment, conditional on the instrument being honoured. If the instrument is not honoured, and the creditor has not been in fault, the debt is revived. But when goods are purchased and paid for at the time of purchase by bank notes, the seller is presumed to take upon himself the risk of the notes being dishonoured, and the purchaser is released. But the purchaser must, of course, be acting in good faith, and if he knew at the time of the purchase that the maker of the note had stopped payment, he would not be allowed to impose upon the seller (see Bills of Exchange Act 1882, s. 58 [3]). This exceptional rule as to payment by bank notes only applies to payments made at the actual time of the purchase and sale, and subsequent payments are treated as payments of past debts, and are presumed to be only conditional. When a person pays a bank note into his banking account, it is more than probable that he will get the same form of receipt as if he had paid in coin. Nevertheless, the banker, unless he has been in fault, is not accountable for the amount of the note if afterwards dishonoured. Lastly, a person getting as a favour change for a bank note is liable to refund the value of the note on its being afterwards dishonoured, if the transferee has not been in fault.

We must now explain what is meant by being in fault. The holder of a bank note, being the holder of an instrument payable on demand, has a duty cast upon him of presenting the note for payment within a reasonable time, or within a like time of transferring it to some one else, *i.e.* of circulating it. Let us take an extreme example.

A person pays his butcher's bill with a bank note on Monday, and the bank stops payment on the following Friday. If the butcher has chosen to keep the note till Saturday, the loss must fall on him, as on Tuesday he could have either paid one of his own debts with it, or got cash for it from the bank. A reasonable time for presentment or circulation is not later than the day after its receipt. If there is a chance of the notes being paid by the bank, in order to charge the transferor, presentment must be made at the bank by the transferee before he tenders back the note to the transferor and asks for his money back again. Where the bank, the maker of the note, has actually stopped payment it is not necessary to present the notes before applying to the transferor. Notice of the dishonour of a note must always be given by the transferee to the transferor within a reasonable time, that is, in general within the day after the transferee is in a position to give such notice. If this were not so the remedies of the transferee might be seriously prejudiced by delay.

My readers will now be in a position to appreciate the two actual cases now given to exemplify this summary of the law. The first case is that of *Cammidge* v. *Allenby* (6 B. & C., 373), in which it appeared that the plaintiff had sold some corn to the defendant on the morning of a Saturday in York. The defendant paid the plaintiff on the same day at three o'clock in the afternoon by certain promissory notes of the bank of D. & Son, at Huddersfield, payable to bearer on demand. D. & Son stopped payment on the same day at eleven o'clock in the morning, and never afterwards resumed their payments; but neither of the parties knew of the stoppage, or of the insolvency of D. & Son. The vendor never circulated the notes, or presented them to the bankers for payment; but, on the following Saturday, required the vendee to take back the notes, and to pay him the amount, which the latter refused. Bayley J. said: "If the notes had been given to the plaintiff at the time when the corn was sold, he could have had no remedy upon them against the defendant. The plaintiff might have insisted upon payment in money. But if he consented to receive the notes as money, they would have been taken by him at his peril. If, indeed, he could show fraud or knowledge of the maker's insolvency in the payer, then it would be wholly immaterial whether they were taken at the time of sale or afterwards. Here the notes were given to him in payment subsequently, and the question is, whether they operate as a discharge of the debt due to the plaintiff in respect of the corn. The rule as to all negotiable instruments is, that if they are taken in payment of a pre-existing debt they operate as a discharge of that debt, unless the party who holds the instruments does all that the law requires to be done in order to obtain payment of them. Then the question is, what it was the duty of the plaintiff to do in order to obtain payment of these notes. They were intended for circulation. But I think that he was not bound *immediately* to circulate them, or to send them into the bank for payment; but he was bound, within a reasonable time after he had received them, either to circulate them or present them for payment. Now here it is conceded that if there had not been any insolvency of the bankers, the notes should have been circulated or presented for payment on Monday. It is clear that the plaintiff on that day might have had knowledge that the bankers had stopped payment, and having that knowledge, if presentment was unnecessary, he had then another duty to perform. In consequence of the negotiable nature of the instruments, it became his duty to give notice to the party who paid him the notes that the bankers had become insolvent, and that he, the plaintiff, would resort to the defendant for payment of the notes; and it would then have been for the defendant to consider whether he could transfer the loss to any other person; for, unless he had been guilty of negligence, he might perhaps have resorted to the person who paid him the notes. That party would, however, be discharged if he received no notice of non-payment, or of the insolvency of the bankers till a week after he had paid them to the defendant. The neglect, therefore, on the part of the plaintiff to give to the defendant notice of the insolvency of the bankers may have been prejudicial to the defendant." Judgment was therefore given for the defendant.

The second case is that of *Timmins* v. *Gibbons* (18 Q. B., 722), of which the facts and decision were as follows: M. W. deposited with a banking company £80, of which £65 was made up of country bank notes. The receipt given was as follows: "Received of M. W., £80, for which we are accountable. £80 at 3%, with 14 days' notice." The company sent the notes on the same day to their agents in London, who presented them on the following day, when they were dishonoured. The agents sent them back by that evening's post to the company who, on the following day, gave notice of dishonour to M. W. M. W. gave fourteen days' notice of withdrawal, whereupon the company tendered the notes back, and M. W. refused them. The country bank, the maker of the notes, was about five miles from the office of the company, and had stopped payment from the close of the day on which the notes were deposited. M. W. sued the company for the £65, as being either money lent to them, or as money had and received by them. The Court held that the company, as transferees of the notes, had not been in any way in fault, and held that M. W. could not recover the sum claimed.

We may sum up these rules by saying that the transferee of a bank note, which is subsequently dishonoured, can recover the amount of the note from the transferor, provided that the transferee has not been negligent, or has not accepted the note as part of a bargain and sale of goods for cash.

The holder of a dishonoured note who wishes to proceed against the bank that issued it must present it for payment in some form or other. No particular form of demand is required by the law merchant. In the case of a banking company, it has been held that the sending in of a claim along with the note to the liquidator was a sufficient demand; and 5 per cent. interest was allowed on the claim as from such date (In re *East of England Banking Co.*, L. R., 4 Ch. Ap., 14).

A customer who is indebted to a bank, which has stopped payment of its notes, may set off against his debt any notes of the bank which are in his hands at the time at which he receives notice of an act of bankruptcy on the part of the bank, and in this way he may secure payment in full of such notes. So also, until notice of an act of bankruptcy, a customer may collect notes for the purpose of setting them off against a debt to the bank, but he cannot set off notes of which he is merely a trustee for others. Thus, where a firm, being customers of a bank with an overdrawn account, received from persons dealing with them on the day on which the bank stopped payment and the day following, but without notice of the act of bankruptcy, certain £5 notes of the bank in part payment of antecedent debts, on the condition that they were to debit themselves with so much only as they should receive from the assignees for such notes, and also other notes for which they paid nothing, but were to pay so much only as they should receive from the assignees for such notes, it was held that the firm had a beneficial interest in the first class of notes, and were therefore entitled to set them off, but not the second class, as they held them merely as trustees for others (*Forster* v. *Wilson*, 12 M. & W., 191). Where two bankers hold each other's notes, the only debt that can be sued for is the difference of the amounts of such holdings (*Edmeads* v. *Newman*, 1 B. & C., 418).

*Lost or Stolen Notes.*—A bank note being a negotiable instrument, a person can, by delivery of it, give to a *bonâ fide* transferee for value a better title than he himself has. Thus, if A loses a £5 Bank of England note, which B finds and uses to pay his rent to C, if C takes the note without notice that it is a lost one, C becomes absolutely entitled to it, and A cannot recover either the note or its value from C. The same rule holds good in favour of a *bonâ fide* holder for value in the case of stolen notes. It should, however, be noticed that while a thief has no title to a note stolen by him, the innocent finder of a note is in the position of an owner as against the whole world, except the person who lost it. He can sue the maker upon it, and so also can persons deriving their title from him, even with notice of the loss. But the finder of a lost note, and all persons taking with notice of the loss, can be sued by the true owner to recover either the note or its value.

The finder of a lost note, and not the person on whose property it is found, is the person entitled to possession of the note. This was decided in a case where a person entered a shop and found on the floor a bundle of bank notes, which had been accidentally dropped there. The finder handed them for safe custody to the shopkeeper, and, as the true owner could not be found, demanded them back. The Court held that the finder was entitled to them and not the shopkeeper (*Bridges* v. *Hawkesworth*, 21 L. J., Q. B., 75).

Bank notes which have been stolen come within the Bills of Exchange Act 1882, s. 30 (2), which enacts that "every holder of a bill is deemed to be a holder in due course; but if, in an action on a bill, it is admitted or proved that the acceptance, issue, or subsequent negotiation of the bill is affected with fraud, duress, or force and fear, or illegality, the burden of proof is shifted, unless and until the holder proves that, subsequent to the alleged fraud or illegality, value has in good faith been given for the bill." Under this enactment it has been decided that when fraud is proved, the burden of proof is on the holder, to prove both that value has been given, and that it has been given in good faith without notice of the fraud (*Tatam* v. *Hasler*, L. R., 23 Q. B. D., 345).

The effect of "stopping" bank notes is not to make the note valueless; it is only an intimation to the banker not to pay without full inquiry. In the case of Bank of England notes it is a means of advertising the fact that the notes have been lost or stolen, for the numbers of stopped notes are circulated from time to time amongst money-changers and other persons likely to be asked to receive them. The mere receipt of a notice to the effect that a note has been stolen does not preclude a person from saying that he took the note *bonâ fide* and for value. Thus, in the case of *Raphael* v. *Bank of England* (25 L. J., C. P., 33) it was shown that Raphael's principal, a Paris money-changer, had about April 1853 received notice of a robbery of Bank of England notes, and that he had placed the notice on a file. In June 1854 he cashed for a stranger a £500 note, one of the stolen notes. The jury found that when the money-changer took the note he had the means of knowing it had been stolen, if he had taken proper care of the notices actually delivered to him, but that he had actually no notice or knowledge to that effect at the time he took it. On that finding the Court held that Raphael was entitled to recover the amount of the note.

*Forged or Altered Notes.*—A forged note is a piece of waste paper, so far as value is concerned. A transferor, by delivery of a note warrants to his immediate transferee, being a holder of value, that the note is what it purports to be (Bills of Exchange Act 1882, s. 58 (3)). Therefore, if A delivers to B a forged note, B can recover from A what he may have paid him for the note. At common law a material alteration in a bank note, without the assent of the issuing bank, made the instrument void and worthless. Under this rule it was decided, in the case of *Suffell* v. *Bank of England* (L. R., 9 Q. B. D., 555) that a Bank of England note, the number of which had been altered so that it could not be identified as a stolen note, was materially altered and valueless. The Bills of Exchange Act 1882, s. 64, adopted the rule of the common law, but added a proviso that "where a bill (which includes promissory notes) has been materially altered, but the alteration is not apparent, and the bill is in the hands of a holder in due course, such holder may avail himself of the bill as if it had not been altered, and may enforce payment of it according to its original tenor." Thus, a country bank note for £5, altered so cleverly as to read for £50, could be enforced by a *bonâ fide* holder for value to the extent of £5. It has been held that Bank of England notes are not within this proviso (*Leeds Bank* v. *Walker*, L. R., 11 Q. B. D., 84). If this were not so, a mere alteration of the number of a Bank of England note, if not apparent, would not make it worthless. Various reasons for this decision were given, but perhaps the least forced is the fact that nothing in the Act is to affect the statutory privileges of the Bank of England.

# CHAPTER IV

## BANKS AND BANKING COMPANIES

*Composition of Banks.*—A bank may be composed of a single person, or of several persons in partnership, or of a company.

*Clergymen.*—By various Church Discipline Acts, clergymen are forbidden to trade, or to be managing partners or directors of companies, but as these Acts do not invalidate either the contracts made by clergymen, or make illegal the companies to which they may act as managers or directors, only their ecclesiastical superiors and not the general public are concerned with them.

*Registration of Partners.*—The 21st section of the Bank Charter Act applies to all bankers. It enacts that every banker shall, on the first day of January in each year, or within fifteen days thereafter, make a return to the Commissioners of Stamps and Taxes, at their head office in London, of his name, residence, and occupation; or, in the case of a company or partnership, of the name, residence, and occupation of every person composing or being a member of such company or partnership; and also the name of the firm under which each banker, company, or partnership carry on the business of banking, and of every place where such business is carried on. The penalty for non-compliance with this enactment, or for wilful misstatements, is £50. Banks making similar returns under the Companies Act 1862 are now exempt from making this return.

*Partnerships.*—As has been said in Chapter II, up to the year 1857 no ordinary partnership of more than six partners could be formed to carry on the business of banking. But, under the special provisions of various Acts of Parliament, a number greater than six could unite as a modified partnership or company. In that year the limit was raised to ten, at which figure it has since remained. The present law on this point is contained in the Companies Act 1862, s. 2, which enacts that no company, association, or partnership, consisting of more than ten persons, shall be formed after the commencement of the Act for the purpose of carrying on the business of banking, unless it be registered as a company under the Act, or is formed in pursuance of some other Act of Parliament, or of letters-patent. Every partnership is now governed by its partnership articles (if any), and the Partnership Act 1890. Banking partnerships, except as already mentioned, are in no way different from ordinary partnerships, and therefore nothing further will be said about them.

*Companies.*—The number of possible combinations of partnerships and companies formed under the Acts of 1826 and 1844, and modified under some later Act, is very large and embarrassing. As, however, a sketch of both these Acts has already been given, and a very large number of companies have registered themselves under the Companies Acts since the Act of 1879, it will be sufficient if we merely consider companies registered under the Companies Acts. These may be divided into two classes—companies formed before the Act of 1862 and since registered under it, and companies formed since the Act of 1862.

*Old Companies under the Act of* 1862.—Companies formed before the Act of 1862, and since registered under the Companies Acts, have, instead of memorandum and articles of association, their original deed of settlement or other similar document for the conditions and regulations of the company. Table A does not apply to such a company. The company may not alter any provision contained in any Act of Parliament relating to it, nor, without the sanction of the Board of Trade, may it alter any provision contained in any letters-patent relating to the company. There is a section dealing with debts and liabilities contracted before registration, and for these both members and past members continue liable, in the same way as if there had been no registration of the company. As to such liabilities, past members do not become exempt after having ceased for a year to be members. Such part of the deed of settlement, or other document, as would have been put into the memorandum of association, if the company had been formed under the Companies Acts, is unalterable. But now, under the Companies (Memorandum of Association) Act 1890, such a company may alter the form of its constitution by substituting a memorandum and articles of association for a deed of settlement, with or without an alteration of its objects, but subject in any case to confirmation by the Court (see p. 45). If the company desires to register as a limited company it must, by the Companies Act 1862, s. 188, give at least thirty days' previous notice to its customers.

*All Companies under Act of* 1862.—The general features of a company formed and registered under the Companies Acts are too well known to be dwelt on here, and the special features, other than those directly concerning banking companies, must be looked for on books on companies. The following sections, as directly affecting all companies coming under these Acts, must, however, be noticed. In the Act of 1862, s. 4 prescribes a limit of ten for partnerships formed after the commencement of the Act. S. 26 requires an annual list of members, with detailed accounts of the capital to be forwarded to the Registrar of Joint-Stock Companies; and if this section is complied with there need be no return under the Bank Charter Act. S. 44 is an important section applying to limited banking companies. Each such company must, on the first Monday in February and the first Monday in August in every year during which it carries on business, make a statement in the form marked D in the schedule to the Act (see Appendix, p. 295), or as near thereto as circumstances will admit; and a copy of such statement is to be put up in a conspicuous place in the registered office of the company, and in every branch office or place where the business of the company is carried on.

*Companies Act* 1879.—As has been already said, the Companies Act 1879 is the Act which has practically induced all the leading joint-stock banking companies of the country to register as limited companies. The 5th section of that Act enables an unlimited company, by the resolution passed by the members when assenting to registration as a limited company, to establish a reserve capital, which is only to be called up in the event of the company being wound up. This may be done by increasing the nominal amount of its shares and making the increase reserve capital, or by making part of its then uncalled capital reserve capital. By the same section a company already registered as limited may set aside as a reserve a portion of its uncalled capital. Companies formed after the coming into operation of the Act as limited companies can of course avail themselves of this section. S. 7 provides for a compulsory independent audit of every banking company registered after the passing of the Act as a limited company. The auditors are to be elected annually, and their remuneration fixed by the company in general meeting. Directors and officers of the company are ineligible as auditors. Every auditor is to have a list delivered to him of all books kept by the company, and is at all reasonable times to have access to the books and accounts of the company; and any auditor may, in relation to such books and accounts, examine the directors or any other officer of the company. The auditors are to make a report to the members on the accounts examined by them, and on every balance-sheet laid before the company in general meeting; every such report is to state whether, in their opinion, the balance-sheet referred to in the report is a full and fair balance-sheet properly drawn up, so as to exhibit a true and correct view of the state of the company's affairs, as shown by the company's books, and such report is to be read before the company in general meeting. The 8th section enacts that every balance-sheet submitted to the annual or other meeting of the members of every banking company, registered after the passing of the Act as a limited company, shall be signed by the auditors, and by the secretary or manager, and by the directors of the company, or three of such directors at the least. By s. 10 nothing in the constitution of a company is to prevent its registration under the Act.

So great now is the demand for publicity of accounts that the day of private banking firms seems drawing to a close. The crisis of the autumn of 1890 has largely contributed to this, and, while this chapter is being written, one private London bank, of two centuries' standing, announces its intention of adopting the Act of

1879 by registering as a limited company; another voluntarily begins to publish a balance-sheet; and the leading joint-stock banks are voluntarily preparing to issue monthly instead of six-monthly accounts.

*Purchase of Shares.*—A person becomes a member of a banking company by a purchase of shares and registration as a shareholder. A person ceases to be a member as soon as his name is rightfully removed from the register, but he is liable to be put on the list of contributories if the company goes into liquidation within a year of such removal. In order to prevent speculation in bank shares an Act was passed in the year 1879, generally known as Leeman's Act (Appendix, p. 275), which enacted that no contract for the purchase or sale of bank shares should be valid unless it contained the numbers distinguishing the shares. Thus it is not possible to sell shares of which one is not the owner.

# CHAPTER V

### POWERS OF A BANK AND ITS OFFICERS

IF a bank is formed by a partnership, it is possible for the partners to conduct the business in any way they think fit, and at any time, by agreement among themselves, to alter the nature or scope of the business. It is not so in the case of a company. The powers of a company are those powers and those only which are necessary for carrying out its objects, as expressed by its deed of settlement, or, in the case of a company formed under the Companies Act, by its memorandum of association. To take a very simple example: a banking company formed with the object of carrying on the business of banking in England only could not open branch banks in Canada. It is not usual, in the object clause of a memorandum of association, to do more than refer to the business of banking in general terms, or at anyrate not to enumerate exhaustively every act which a bank may from time to time find it expedient to perform. Under such a clause powers will be implied sufficient for carrying on the banking business as efficiently as if it were an ordinary partnership. Thus it has been said that, "where there are directors of a trading company, those directors necessarily have incidentally the power of doing that which is ordinarily and reasonably done in every such business, with a view of getting either better work from their servants, or with a view to attract customers to them." Under this principle it has been held that a banking company was acting within its powers in paying a half-yearly pension for five years for the benefit of the family of a deceased manager of the bank, although they had no express power to do such a thing (*Henderson* v. *Bank of Australasia*, L. R., 40 Ch. D., 170).

On the same principle it has been said that it is within the ordinary scope of banking business to borrow money on emergency, and therefore when banking business is an object of the company, no special power to borrow need be inserted. "The nature of a banker's business, especially if the bank be one both of issue and deposit, necessarily exposes him to sudden and immediate demands, which may be to the extent of a large proportion of his debts, while his profits are to be made in employing his own moneys and those intrusted to him in discounting bills, in loans, and other modes of investment. It is impossible that he should always have his assets in such a state as to be applicable immediately to the payment of all demands which may be made upon him; and if a partner has no power, under such circumstances, to borrow money for the partnership, either the assent of each individual member must be obtained, which may be often impracticable, or the concern must be ruined. We have no doubt at all, therefore, that in ordinary banking partnerships, such power exists, and that the directors, by the terms of their appointment, had all the general powers, and among the rest the power of borrowing, unless such power is excluded by other provisions of the deed. (Quoted from *Bank of Australasia* v. *Breillet*, 6 Moore, P. C., 152, at p. 104 in *Maclae* v. *Sutherland*, 3 E. & B., 1).

Part of the ordinary business of a bank is to lend

money or permit overdrafts upon security, and if a banking company has power to do this it has power to do all reasonable acts necessary for making its securities valid and effective. In the course of such acts the bank may acquire liabilities which it would be *ultra vires* for it to acquire for purposes other than the realisation of its security. Thus it may become a shareholder in another company, or liable on a building contract, or as a ship-owner, or in respect of matters of freight, or of any matters connected with a bill of lading which the bank holds as security. When bankers have thus acquired such liabilities, they cannot afterwards turn round and say that what they did was *ultra vires*.

But though a company will be allowed as full powers as a partnership, so far as relates to the carrying out of objects within the scope of its business, a company stands on an altogether different footing as regards an extension of the scope of its business. Until the passing of the Companies (Memorandum of Association) Act 1890, it was impossible for a company under the Companies Acts to alter its memorandum of association, which always contains the object clause of the company, except as regards its capital (see also p. 39). Fresh powers could only be obtained by reconstruction. Now it is possible to alter a memorandum within certain limits, if the sanction of the Court has been duly obtained. The sanction of the Court may be given if the alteration is required to enable the company—(*a*) to carry on its business more economically or more efficiently, (*b*) to attain its main purpose by new or improved means, (*c*) to enlarge or change the local area of its operations, (*d*) to carry on some business or businesses which, under existing circumstances, may conveniently or advantageously be combined with the business of the company, (*e*) to restrict or abandon any of the objects specified in the memorandum of association or deed of settlement. This Act will naturally tend to simplify the constitution of banking companies, and it may now be expected that a memorandum will contain the actual objects of the company rather than a farrago of odds and ends of powers which the promoters think it advisable to have ready against an emergency.

The directors of a company cannot have greater powers than the company itself has, and any ratification of an act of the directors, which would have been *ultra vires* of the company, is useless and of no effect. On the other hand, if the directors exceed their authority but keep within the powers of the company, the latter can ratify and adopt their act. It is usual for all the business powers of a banking company to be confided to the directors, and then the powers of the company and the powers of the directors are the same.

It has been held that the directors of a company, with extensive powers of carrying on a banking business, are not acting *ultra vires* in guaranteeing the payment of interest on the debentures of a limited company issued for the purpose of forming such company, provided that the establishment of the company was of importance to the bank (In re *West of England Bank*, L. R., 14 Ch. D., 317).

The directors of a banking company, being agents, are bound not to place themselves in a position where their interests and duties conflict. Any profit made out of an abuse of their position must be handed over to the company. In other words, no agent in the course of his agency, in the matter of his agency, can be allowed to make any profit without the knowledge and consent of his principal. Thus where new shares were allotted to a person, who found that he could not take them all up, and before his contract of purchase was complete, and while it was the duty of the directors to see that such contract was duly performed by him, applied to the directors to relieve him of some of them, and they severally took from him considerable numbers which they afterwards sold at a profit, it was held that each director must account to the bank for his profits. L.-J. Mellish said: "The main question is, how far a trustee or agent for sale is precluded from purchasing from his own purchaser the property which he is entrusted to sell. As long as the contract remains executory, and the trustee or agent has power either to enforce it or to rescind or alter it,—as long as it remains in that state he cannot repurchase the property from his own purchaser, except for the benefit of his principal" (*Parker* v. *M'Kenna*, L. R., 10 Ch. Ap., 96).

*Manager.*—The manager of a bank or a branch of it is the general agent of the company or the partners for carrying on the business of the bank. As to all acts within the ordinary scope of the banking business done by a manager the bank stands in the manager's shoes, whether the bank is suing or being sued.

Any restriction which, by agreement amongst the principals and their agent, is attempted to be imposed upon the authority which one possesses as general agent for the others, is operative only between the principals and the agent, and does not limit the authority as to third persons, who acquire rights by its exercise, unless they know that such restriction has been made.

Story on Agency expresses this rule thus: "The principal is liable to third persons in a civil suit for frauds, deceits, concealments, misrepresentations, torts, negligences, and other malfeasances or misfeasances, and omissions of duty, of his agent in the course of his employment, although the principal did not authorise, or justify, or participate in, or indeed know of such misconduct, or even if he forbade the acts, or disapproved of them."

When a manager proceeds to do an act outside the ordinary scope of banking business a different set of considerations comes into play. A customer dealing with the manager has no right to presume that the manager has any extraordinary authority. Accordingly, if a customer suffers damage through the wrongdoing or negligence of the manager in such a matter he can only recover damages against the bank on proof that the bank had expressly authorised the manager to do the act complained of, or had subsequently adopted such act for its own use and benefit. Illustrations of the practical effect of these principles are now given.

*Payment of Money.*—If money is paid to the manager of a bank as such, the customer can demand it of the bankers, although the money may never have come into the hands of the bankers. In the case of *Thompson* v. *Bell* (10 Ex., 10) Mrs. Thompson kept a deposit account at the Southampton branch of the National Provincial Bank of England. The manager of the bank advised her to purchase some houses for £595 on which the bank had an equitable mortgage. The manager received her deposit notes, gave a receipt for the £595 in his own name, and a fresh deposit note for the balance. He afterwards absconded with £595. Mrs. Thompson's husband sued the bank for a return of his money. The jury found that the manager intended to make Mrs. Thompson believe, and that she did believe, that the manager was acting in this transaction as agent for the bank. The Court held that the plaintiff could recover, on the ground that the money was still in the bank. "The manager of a bank is a person appointed to conduct the entire business irrespective of the partners; and in this case the manager undoubtedly received the money in the first instance from the plaintiff's wife, and gave her a deposit receipt. He then represents to her that some benefit would accrue by her investing that money in a different way. She listens to his suggestion and draws out the money, which she hands over to him, as manager of the bank, to be disposed of in the way suggested. That he does not do, therefore the money is still in the hands of the bank."

*Illusory Guarantee.*—In the case of *Barwick* v. *London Joint-Stock Bank* (L. R., 2 Ex., 259) the following transaction of a manager was held to be one for which the bank was responsible. Barwick had for some time supplied Davis with oats on credit, for carrying out a Government contract. This he did under some sort of a guarantee from the English Joint-Stock Bank. Barwick refused to supply further oats except on a better guarantee. Thereupon the bank manager gave a written guarantee to the effect that Davis's cheque on the bank, in favour of Barwick in payment for oats supplied, should be paid on receipt of the Government money, in priority to any other payment "except to this bank." Davis was then indebted to the bank to the amount of £12,000, but this fact was not known to Barwick, nor was it communicated to him by the manager. Barwick supplied oats to the value of £1227; the Government money, £2676, was received by Davis and paid into the bank; but Davis's cheque in favour of Barwick was dishonoured by the bank, who claimed to retain the £2676 in payment of Davis's debt to them. The Court held that there was evidence to go to the jury that the manager knew and intended that the guarantee should be unavailing, and fraudulently concealed from Barwick the fact that would make it so, and that for such fraud in their manager the bank would be liable.

*Representation of Solvency.*—It is usual for bankers to make and answer inquiries as to the solvency and responsibility of customers. It is not usual to answer inquiries made by private persons, and therefore an inquiry addressed by bank A to bank B is presumably liable to be communicated to some customer of bank A, for whom it may have been made. If therefore the manager of bank B makes a false answer to the inquiry of bank A, which is communicated to the customer of bank A, that customer may sue bank B for damages suffered through his acting on the false representation of the manager. In the case of *Swift* v. *Winterbotham* (L. R., 8 Q. B., 244) it appeared that Swift was asked to sell about £3000 worth of iron to Russell, and was referred to the Cheltenham branch of the Gloucestershire bank. Swift was a customer of a Sheffield bank, whose manager inquired, at Swift's request, of the manager of the Cheltenham branch as to Russell's monetary worth. The manager sent a reply which was false to his knowledge. Swift acted upon that and eventually lost his money through the insolvency of Russell. He therefore sued the Gloucestershire bank, and it was held that the bank was liable for the false representation of the manager.

*Fraud.*—Where the manager paid a private debt out of the bank funds, and took from the payee what the payee thought was a receipt but was really a cheque, the bank was not allowed to recover the amount of the cheque (*Foster* v. *Green*, 31 L. J., Ex., 168). So where the manager of a branch bank advances the bank's money, with knowledge that the borrower is obtaining the money for the sole purpose of misapplying it, the bank acquires no better title than the manager or the customer (*Collinson* v. *Lister*, 7 De G., M. & G., 634).

*Arrests and Prosecutions.*—It has been laid down that the arrest, and still less the prosecution of offenders, is not within the ordinary routine of banking business, and when the question of a manager's authority in such a case arises, it is essential to inquire carefully into his position and duties. These may, and in practice do, vary considerably. In the case of a chief or general manager, invested with general supervision and power of control, such an authority in certain cases affecting the property of the bank might be presumed from his position to belong to him, at least in the absence of directors. The same presumption might arise in the instance of a manager conducting the business of a branch bank at a distance from the head office and the board of directors. The necessary authority may be general, or it may be special and derived from the exigency of the particular occasion on which it is exercised. In the former case it is enough to show that the agent was acting in what he did on behalf of the principal; but in the latter case evidence must be given of a state of facts which shows that such exigency is present, or from which it might reasonably be supposed to be present (*Bank of New South Wales* v. *Owston*, L. R., 4 Ap. Ca., 270).

*Liability of Manager to Bank.*—A manager is not liable to his employers for the results of his acts, unless he exceeds the power and authority with which he is entrusted, or unless while acting within the scope of his authority he makes an abuse of his position to gain a private advantage at the expense of the bank.

A manager must not place his individual interest in

conflict with his duty to his employers. But when it is sought to charge him with a loss, it is not enough to show that he was indirectly interested in the transaction out of which the loss arose, it must be actually proved that he acted in bad faith.

## CHAPTER VI

### BRANCH BANKS

A BRANCH bank is in some respects treated as an independent bank, but in most respects it is treated as an integral part of the main business.

For purposes of bookkeeping and transmitting money from one branch to another a bank and its branches are treated as one (see p. 59).

The accounts of a customer who has a separate account at two branches of the same bank may be treated in the same way as two separate accounts of a customer at one branch (see p. 58).

A branch bank cannot continue to carry on business after notice that the main business has stopped; but there is no stoppage till such notice, for, till notice, there is no revocation of the authority to carry on business at such branch.

Where notice affects the liability of a bank it is not necessary that notice should be given to all the branches of a bank. It is enough to give notice at the head office, and such notice will then be good against all branches after a reasonable time has elapsed, to allow of a communication to be sent from the head office to the branches. In the case of *Willis* v. *Bank of England* (4 A. & E., 21) it appeared that one Norcliffe, on 12th March 1833, committed an act of bankruptcy, and absconded from Liverpool. He took with him two bank post bills of the Bank of England for £500 each. On 16th March an application was made to the bank in London to stop the bills. On 8th April a further application was made, and it was then stated that a fiat of bankruptcy against Norcliffe was expected by every post. On 12th April Norcliffe persuaded a friend, S, at Gloucester, who was known at the branch office of the Bank of England there, to get the bills changed for gold. S and the branch bank were both ignorant of the act of bankruptcy, and the bills were accordingly changed. Norcliffe's assignees in bankruptcy sued the bank for the amount of the bills, and it was held that they must succeed, as there was sufficient notice to the head office to prevent the payment being protected as a *bonâ fide* one before issue of the commission of bankruptcy, and that the notice to the head office operated as notice to the branch bank, a reasonable time having elapsed for transmitting it before the bills were received there.

*Exceptions.*—There are two purposes for which branch banks are considered distinct from the head office or other branches—first, for payment of cheques, and, secondly, for notices of dishonour.

A customer at one branch is not entitled to present a cheque elsewhere than at the branch where his account is. And a bank paying at one branch a cheque drawn on another branch is in the same position as if the cheque had been drawn on an entirely distinct bank. Any other rule than this would be unworkable, as the following example will show (*Woodland* v. *Fear*, 7 E. & B., 519). Fear held a cheque drawn by a customer of the Glastonbury branch of Stuckey's bank on the Glastonbury branch, and, being in the neighbourhood of Bridgewater, presented it at the Bridgewater branch of the same bank. As the officers there knew him they gave him cash for it. Had the cheque been presented at the same time at Glastonbury it would have been paid, but by the time the cheque in due course reached Glastonbury the customer had drawn out his balance, and the cheque was dishonoured. The bank sued Fear for a return of the money paid for the cheque; and it was held that it must succeed, as it was under no obligation to cash the cheque at Bridgewater, and did so on the credit of Fear, and not as the bankers of their Glastonbury customer.

The different branches of a bank may be separate indorsees of bills of exchange, and, on a bill being dishonoured, may each claim the usual time in which to give notice of dishonour. Thus where a bill of exchange was endorsed to the Portmadoc branch of the National Provincial Bank of England by a customer, and sent by them to the Pwllheli branch, and by them endorsed to the head establishment in London, on whose presentation it was dishonoured, it was held that each branch of the bank was to be considered as an independent indorsee, and entitled to the usual notice of dishonour; so that a notice of dishonour given by the Portmadoc branch to its customer in that course was good, although coming later than if sent direct from London (*Clode* v. *Bailey*, 12 M. & W., 51).

*Companies Act, s.* 44.—As has been said, on p. 40, the Companies Act 1862 requires a limited banking company to put up in a conspicuous part of the branch office, as well as of the head office, a copy of the statement of its capital, assets, and liabilities, required by the 44th section of that Act.

# CHAPTER VII

## BANKER AND CUSTOMER

*General Relation.*—The relation between a banker and his customer is the relation of a debtor to his creditor, or if the customer's account is overdrawn, that of a creditor to his debtor (*Foley* v. *Hill*, 2 H. of L. Ca., 28). There are some special features attaching to this relation, which will be considered when the effect of this primary principle has been investigated.

1. Money lodged by a customer with his banker becomes the money of the banker, and is absolutely at his disposal. It is no immediate concern of the customer that the banker should use the money paid in by his customer either as a prudent man of business, or, indeed, in the business at all. There is nothing fiduciary in the relationship, and it is not the duty of the banker, but only his interest, to use such money so as to secure a profit to himself.

So strict is this rule that even when money is paid into the bankers for a specific purpose, if the banker stops payment before taking any step towards applying it to the purpose, the customer cannot recover the money paid, but has merely a right of proof as a general creditor.

In the case of *Barned's Banking Company* (39 L. J., Ch., 635), it appeared that a bill of exchange for £185, drawn by Massey on Fox, was by the latter accepted, payable at the office of Prescott & Co., the correspondents in London of Barned's Banking Company. Massey, on the day before the bill became due, paid into the office of the company at Liverpool, with which neither Massey nor Fox kept an account, the proper amount to be remitted to Prescott & Co., in order to take up the bill on its becoming due. On the following day the bank stopped payment without having made the remittance to Prescott & Co. The bill was in consequence dishonoured, and subsequently paid by Massey. Massey claimed to be paid the whole amount in the winding-up of the bank. The Court held that the bank was not a trustee of the money, and that Massey was only a simple creditor entitled to a dividend.

If, however, the specific purpose has been partially carried out, the case is different. Thus in the case of *Farley* v. *Turner* (26 L. J., Ch., 710), it appeared that Farley was a customer of a bank, and had a sum of £942 standing to his account. He paid in a further sum of £707, with a written direction that £500 out of that sum should be forwarded to another bank to meet a bill about to become due. A sum of £500 was sent as directed, but before the bill became due the country bank ceased to carry on business. Farley claimed back this £500, and it was held that, as it had been specifically appropriated, it belonged to him, and not to the general creditors.

Where a banker allows his customer to accept bills payable at the bank, and the customer subsequently pays in money to meet them, such money is considered to be specifically appropriated for the payment of the bills.

2. In the absence of special agreement, the keeping of distinct accounts with different headings, for the same

customer, is purely a matter of account-keeping, and does not affect the rights of the parties as debtor and creditor. Thus, in the case of *Pedder* v. *The Mayor and Corporation of Preston* (31 L. J., C. P., 291), it appeared that the corporation of Preston, in addition to the ordinary functions of a municipal corporation, had functions under the Baths and Washhouses Act 1846, and others as a Local Board of Health, and kept at the plaintiffs' bank three separate accounts, corresponding to those three classes of transactions. At the time of the plaintiffs suspending payment, there was due from the defendants, on the account of the municipal affairs of the corporation, a large sum of money, and there was due from the plaintiffs to the defendants, in respect of the Local Board of Health account, a similar sum. It was held that the defendants might set off these claims one against the other, inasmuch as, though the accounts were separate, the defendants were debtors in the one and creditors in the other, and in the same right.

That the two accounts should be in the same right is a necessary as well as a sufficient condition, and thus two or more accounts may be combined, if they are respectively private and business accounts, or separate business accounts, but not if one is a private account and the other an account as executor, trustee, or public official.

The same rule applies to accounts kept by the same person at different branches of the same bank. In the case of *Garnett* v. *Mackewan* (L. R., 8 Ex., 10), it appeared that Garnett kept an account at the Leighton Buzzard branch of the London and County Bank, where the balance in his favour was £42, 18s. 10d. He also had an account at the Buckingham branch of the same bank, which he had overdrawn to the amount or £42, 15s. 11d. Garnett drew cheques on the Leighton Buzzard branch for £23, but, before the cheques were presented, the bank had transferred the account of the Buckingham branch to the Leighton Buzzard branch, and, on presentation of the cheques, refused to cash them. The customer thereupon brought an action against the bank, but, as he failed to show a special agreement to keep the accounts separate, the Court held that the bank had only done what they were entitled to do.

3. The debt of a banker to his customer, like any other simple contract-debt, is barred at the end of six years by the Statute of Limitations, unless it is taken out of the Statute by a part payment of principal, or the allowance of interest, or some other sufficient acknowledgment of the debt by the banker (*Pott* v. *Clegg*, 16 M. & W., 321).

4. If the balance of an account is claimed from a banker by two different persons, the banker must interplead; he cannot pay the money into Court under the Trustee Relief Acts, nor, unless there has been an absolute assignment of the debt in writing, can he avail himself of similar proceedings under the Judicature Act, s. 25, sub-s. 6.

5. The entries which the banker makes in books which he keeps for his own private purposes are not conclusive as to the state of the account between him and his customer until he has made a communication of those entries to his customer. In the case of *Prince* v. *The Oriental Bank Corporation* (L. R., 3 Ap. Ca., 325), it appeared that Prince paid into his account at the A branch of the Oriental Bank Corporation a promissory note which was payable at the B branch of the same bank. The note was passed on to the B branch, where the signatures of the makers were cancelled, and the note marked "paid." The amount of the note was transmitted by transfer drafts to the A branch, and corresponding entries made

in the books, and Prince was credited with the amount. Before this was communicated to Prince, it was discovered at the B branch that the maker's balance was insufficient to pay the note, and thereupon the note was at the A branch marked "cancelled in error," and was returned to Prince dishonoured. Prince brought an action against the bank for the amount of the note, but the Court held that the bank could not be charged with the receipt of the money.

### Special Features of the Relation

*Duty to Honour Customer's Cheques.*—It is a special feature of the relationship between debtor and creditor, created by the opening of a banking account, that the banker is under an obligation to honour the drafts of his customers to the extent of the customers' balance (*Foley* v. *Hill*, 2 H. of L. Ca., 28).

Provided that the balance is sufficient there is only one case in which a banker should not honour his customer's cheque, and that is when the customer is attempting to deal with that money so as to commit a breach of trust, and the banker, by honouring the cheque, would become a party to such breach.

In the latest case on the subject (*Gray* v. *Johnston* L. R., 3 E. & I., 1), the following rule was laid down by Lord Westbury: "Supposing that the banker becomes incidentally aware that the customer, being in a fiduciary or a representative capacity, meditates a breach of trust, and draws a cheque for that purpose, the banker, not being interested in the transaction, has no right to refuse payment of the cheque, for if he did so he would be making himself a party to an inquiry as between his customers and third persons. . . . But then it has been very well settled that if an executor or a trustee who is indebted to a banker, having the legal custody of the assets of a trust-estate, applies a portion of them in payment of his own debt to the banker, the banker has at once not only proof of the breach of trust, but participates in it for his own personal benefit." In the same case Earl Cairns expressed himself on the same point thus: "In order to hold a banker justified in refusing to pay a demand of his customer, the customer being an executor and drawing a cheque as an executor, there must, in the first place, be some misapplication, some breach of trust, intended by the executor, and there must, in the second place, be proof that the bank is privy to the intent to make this misapplication of the trust funds. . . . If it be shown that any personal benefit to the bankers themselves is designed or stipulated for, that circumstance, above all others, will most readily establish the fact that the banker is in privity with the breach of trust which is about to be committed."

There cannot even be a possible occasion for the application of this exceptional rule, unless the money is strictly trust money, and not merely money for which the customer must account to some third person. Thus, in the case of *Tassell* v. *Cooper* (9 C. B., 509), it appeared that Tassell had been farm-bailiff to Lord D. After Tassell had left Lord D.'s employment he received a cheque for £180 in payment for wheat belonging to Lord D., which he had sold on his account while acting as bailiff. This cheque Tassell paid into his bankers, who, in the usual way, received the money, and gave Tassell credit for it. Afterwards Lord D. went to the bank, informed them of the circumstances, claimed the money as his, and requested them not to honour Tassell's drafts. The bank agreed to do this upon receiving an indemnity from Lord D. Tassell finding his draft dishonoured brought an action against the bank, and the Court held that he was entitled to succeed, on the ground that, even assuming that the cheque had been improperly obtained by Tassell, still, as between him and his bankers, the amount was recoverable by him as money had and received by the bankers to his use.

If a banker wrongly refuses to honour his customer's cheque, the customer is entitled to nominal damages, even if he shows no actual damage as the result of the banker's refusal.

*Banker's Lien.*—The second special feature attaching to the relationship of banker and customer is the right of the banker, when the customer's account is overdrawn, to a lien on such of his customer's money securities as come into the banker's hands in the ordinary course of his business. This lien is part of the law merchant, and is to be judicially noticed, like the negotiability of bills of exchange (*Brandao* v. *Barnett*, 12 Cl. & Fin., 787). There is some doubt as to what are money securities within the rule, but negotiable instruments of all sorts are within it, so also share certificates, but apparently not a lease.

The rule is general, and will apply in all cases, unless the customer can prove an express contract, or circumstances that show an implied contract inconsistent with the existence of the lien. Thus it has been said that if bills of exchange were delivered to a banker merely for the purpose of being deposited in a box there could be no lien. In the case of *Brandao* v. *Barnett*, *supra*, it appeared that A kept an account with C, as his banker, and at C's banking house kept tin boxes, in which he deposited exchequer bills, and of which he kept the keys. On December 1, 1836, A took out of a tin box several exchequer bills, which he delivered to C, requesting C to get the interest due on them, and to get the exchequer bills exchanged for others. C did so. Before A came to take back the exchequer bills, acceptances of his beyond the amount of his cash credit account were presented at C's bank, and paid. A afterwards became bankrupt. It was held that C had not a lien on the exchequer bills in his hands for the balance due to him on A's account.

In a later case, In re *United Service Company* (L. R., 6 Ch. Ap., 212), it appeared that railway share certificates had been deposited with the company, who acted as bankers, for safe custody and the collection of dividends. The company was to receive a small commission. There it was said that the certificates came into the custody of the company in the ordinary course of its business as bankers, that they were deposited with the bank by a customer of the bank, and that such deposit was made under such circumstances as would have entitled the bank to a lien upon them for their general banking account.

A deposit of securities to cover an overdraft on one account, where the customer keeps several, is not inconsistent with the right of the banker to assert his lien on those securities for the general balance. Thus, in the case of In re *European Bank* (L. R., 8 Ch. Ap., 41), the Oriental Bank kept three accounts at the Agra Bank, namely, a loan, discount, and general account. In the course of usual transactions the Oriental Bank deposited three bills of exchange with the Agra Bank, accompanied by a letter stating that they proposed to draw upon them for £10,500, but that as their credit would not afford a margin to that extent they sent these bills as collateral security. The Oriental Bank became insolvent. The loan account was satisfied without recourse to the deposited bills, but the general balance was still against the Oriental Bank. The Agra Bank claimed to hold the bills for the balance of the general account, and the Court held that there was nothing in the terms of the contract under which they took the bills inconsistent with their right of lien.

If the banker has notice that the securities are not the property of his customer he cannot enforce his lien against the true owner (see p. 89, below). Nor has a banker a lien on securities which come into his hands by chance—as, for instance, by being accidentally left by a customer at the banking house (*Lucas* v. *Dorrein*, 7 Taunt., 278).

By the Bills of Exchange Act 1882, s. 27 (3), it is enacted that " where the holder of a bill has a lien on it arising either by contract or by implication of law, he is deemed to be a holder for value to the extent of the sum for which he has a lien."

*Customer's Right to Secrecy.*—The third special feature is that the banker must not disclose the state of his customer's account, except upon a reasonable and proper occasion. There is some doubt as to the exact foundation of this right to secrecy; if it is an implied term of the contract between banker and customer, then an unjustifiable disclosure is a ground of action for which nominal damages can be recovered, although the customer has suffered no actual loss or damage; if, however, and perhaps this is the better opinion, there is merely cast upon the banker a duty not to act to the prejudice of his customer, then special damage, such as actual loss of money or reputation, must be proved, otherwise the breach of duty is not actionable (*Hardy* v. *Veasey*, L. R., 3 Ex., 107).

The fact that the customer's account is overdrawn is not sufficient to warrant a disclosure of the state of the account, nor when a cheque is dishonoured is it

*Bankers' Charges.*—As long as the relation of banker and customer exists, the banker has the right to make charges for commission and interest. Sometimes customers make express bargains as to charges, and then the terms of the bargain must be observed until altered by a fresh agreement. Very often the customer merely acquiesces in the charges which the banker has thought fit to make, and then the Court will in general imply a promise by the customer to pay charges already acquiesced in, although such a promise may not reach to future charges. Thus it appeared in the case of *Williamson* v. *Williamson* (L. R., 7 Eq., 542) that a banking account which was largely overdrawn had been, for the half-year ending June 1867, charged with interest at 5 per cent., and with a gross sum of £500 for commission, in lieu of the charge of $\frac{1}{2}$ per cent. previously made. The pass-book balanced on this footing was sent to the customer, and the charges were explained to his agent. The customer died in December 1867 without having raised any objection to the charges, and the account was continued by his executors. It was held that the charge of £500 for commission had been acquiesced in, and was valid for June 1867; but that acquiescence could not be inferred for subsequent half-years, there being nothing in the entry for the particular half-year that amounted to a contract to the same effect in future. It has also been laid down that, when the accounts between banker and customer have been carried on for a series of years on a particular principle, the Court will assume that there is an agreement to that effect; but acquiescence in the principle does not amount to a settlement of account (*Morse* v. *Salt*, 32 L. J., Ch., 756). It is usual for the banker to add his charges on to the customer's debt, or to deduct them from his balance at fixed periods, and there is no objection to his charging in this way compound interest. If a customer becomes bankrupt or dies, the relationship of banker and customer ceases, and thereupon the banker ceases to be entitled to charge compound interest, and has merely the right to charge simple interest on the balance due to him at the time of the customer's bankruptcy or death (*Williamson* v. *Williamson,* supra).

# CHAPTER VIII

## BANKERS AND THIRD PERSONS

*Banker not Liable to Third Persons.*—We have seen that if a customer pays into his banking account money belonging to some third person, even when that fact is brought to his knowledge, the banker is not entitled to dishonour a cheque of his customer's, drawn for the purpose of drawing out that money. The correlative rule is equally good, and has been thus expressed: "If A pays money to B, who pays it to his banker to his own account without notice, A cannot recover that money from the banker." Thus, in the case of *Sims* v. *Bond* (5 B. & Ad., 393), it appeared that A was the managing owner of a vessel. He and the other part owners were as such the owners of two warrants of the East India Company for freight. These warrants were left in the hands of A the managing owner, who paid them into his banking account. The bankers received the money due on them and gave A credit for it. The other part owners sought to recover the money from the bankers, but it was held that they were not entitled so to do.

This rule also applies although the banker holds the money for the benefit of a third person, so long as notice of that fact has not been given to that third person. Thus in the case of *Moore* v. *Bushell*, (27 L. J., Ex., 3), it appeared that A accepted a bill of exchange payable at the correspondents of his bankers to one Moore. Just before the bill became due A paid its amount into his banking account for the purpose of taking up the bill, and the bankers promised to apply it to that purpose. The bankers entered the amount to the credit of their correspondents, but it did not appear that they had advised their correspondents to pay it. The drawer, the holder of the bill, sued A's bankers for the amount, but it was held that the action could not be supported, as, although the bankers were in fault, there was no privity between the parties.

*Except for Trust Moneys.*—This rule does not extend to anything in the nature of trust funds, and a third person may follow such funds even when mixed with other moneys in the banker's hands. A second rule is then as follows: "If money held by a person in a fiduciary character has been paid by him to his account at his bankers, the person for whom he held the money can follow it, and has a charge on the balance in the banker's hands" (see In re *Hallett's Estate*, L. R., 13 Ch. D., 696). If such money has been mixed with the customer's money, the whole will be treated as of the nature of trust property, except so far as the customer may be able to distinguish what is his own (*Frith* v. *Cartland*, 2 H. & M., 417). Thus in the case of *Hancock* v. *Smith* (L. R., 41 Ch. D., 456), it appeared that a stockbroker paid into his own banking account various sums belonging to his clients, and lodged in his hands for investment. He withdrew all his own money, and there was finally left a balance which was claimed by two of his clients, and no others, and was just sufficient to meet their claims. A judgment creditor of the stockbroker had, however, obtained a garnishee order on the balance. In the dispute that arose between the clients and the judgment creditor it was held that the money belonged to the clients.

For a further discussion of this subject the reader is referred to Chap. X on the "Appropriation of Payments." So far we have been discussing cases in which the banker has had no notice that the money paid into the customer's account has been impressed with a fiduciary character; as under such circumstances the banker cannot be called upon to pay twice, it is of little interest to him whom he eventually pays. But if a banker deals improperly with funds which he knows or ought to know bear a fiduciary character, he will be liable for any loss resulting therefrom to the real owners.

Notice of the nature of an account may be expressed, or may be implied from the heading of the account or other circumstances.

In the case of *Bodenham* v. *Hoskins* (21 L. J., Ch., 864), it appeared that Bodenham was the owner of an estate, and employed an agent to collect the rents. The agent paid the rents into a bank, to an account headed with the name of the estate to distinguish it from his private account. The bank allowed the agent to overdraw his private account, and then, in order to balance the account, allowed him to transfer the balance of the estate account to the private account. Bodenham brought a chancery suit against the bankers to obtain his rents, and on proof that the bank knew that the balance transferred was the produce of the rents of his estates a decree was made against the bankers for repayment.

Even where there is no actual transference of balance, and a customer has two accounts, one of which is a private account and the other in the nature of a trust account, a banker may incur a heavy loss if he allows his customer to overdraw the private account on the strength of a balance to his credit on the trust account. Thus, in the case of In re *Gross, ex p. Kingston* (L. R., 6 Ch. Ap., 632), it appeared that Gross, a county treasurer, kept two accounts at his bank, one headed "Police Account," and the other a private account. The bank treated the two accounts as practically one, and paid the interest on the total or net balance into his private account. Gross overdrew his private account, and absconded. The county magistrates brought a suit in equity to recover the balance of the police account, whereupon the bank attempted to set off the adverse balance on the private account. It was held that they were not entitled to do this.

## CHAPTER IX

### BANKERS' ACCOUNTS

*Pass Book.*—A banker, besides keeping the usual business books for his own convenience, gives to his customer a book now commonly called a pass-book, but once known as a passage book, in which the accounts between the parties are shown. The nature of this book, from a business point of view, was the subject of judicial inquiry in the year 1816, and the report[1] is still so applicable to modern banking business as to justify its reproduction here at length. "A book called a passage book is opened by the bankers and delivered by them to the customer, in which at the head of the first folio, *and there only*, the bankers by the name of their firm are described as the debtors, and the customer as the creditor, in the account; and on the debtor side are entered all sums paid or received by the bankers on account of the customer; and on the creditor side all sums paid by them to him, or on his account; and the said entries being summed up at the bottom of each page the amount of each, or the balance between them, is carried over to the next folio without further mention of the names

[1] This report is not a judgment of the Court, and the inferences drawn therein as to the effect of a customer's silence do not set forth the true legal consequence of such conduct.

of the parties, until, from the passage book being full, it becomes necessary to open and deliver out to the customer a new book of the same kind. For the purpose of having the passage book made up by the bankers from their own books of account, the customer returns it to them from time to time as he thinks fit; and the proper entries being made by them up to the day on which it is left for that purpose they deliver it again to the customer, who thereupon examines it, and if there appear any error or omission, brings it or sends it back to be rectified, or if not his silence is regarded as an admission that the entries are correct; but no other settlement, statement, or delivery of accounts, or any other transaction which can be regarded as the closing of an old, or the opening of a new account, or as varying, renewing, or confirming (in respect of the persons of the parties mutually dealing) the credit given on either side, takes place in the ordinary course of business, unless when the name or firm of one of the parties is altered, and a new account thereupon opened in the new name or firm. The course of business is the same between such bankers and their customers resident at a distance from the metropolis, except that, to avoid the inconvenience of sending in and returning the passage-book, accounts are, from time to time, made out by the bankers, and transmitted to the customer in the country when required by him, containing the same entries as are made in the passage books; but with the names of the parties, debtor and creditor, at the head and with the balance struck at the foot of each account; on receipt of which accounts, the customer, if there appears to be any error or omission, points out the same by letter to the bankers; but if not his silence after the receipt of the account, is in like manner regarded as an admission of the truth of the account, and no other adjustment, statement, or allowance thereof usually takes place"—*Devaynes* v. *Noble* (1 Mer., 530).

Entries in a banker's books are never evidence in his favour. Entries in the pass-book or other books of the banker are only *primâ facie* evidence against him (*Commercial Bank of Scotland* v. *Rhind*, 3 Macq., 643). It is open to the banker to show that the entries were made in mistake. Thus it appeared, in the case of *Hume* v. *Bolland* (1 C. & M., 130), that a partner in a bank had fraudulently sold stock entrusted to the bank by a customer. The dividends were, however, entered in the customer's account as having been received. The customer sued the bank for them, but it was held that it was open to the banker to prove that the dividends had never been received by them, and that on such proof they were not liable to pay the customer.

If the title of the banking firm is changed in the pass-book that is sufficient notice to the customer of a change in the firm; if the account is continued in the same way, except for the change of name, that is sufficient notice to the customer that the new firm has taken over the accounts and liabilities of the old firm (*Cavendish* v. *Greaves* 27 L. J., Ch., 314).

*Production of Accounts.*—It should be noticed that, in actions by or against the customers of a bank, it is often important to see the books of the customer's bankers, as they may afford very valuable evidence as to the business of a customer, and the payment to or by him of money. As, however, it was found very inconvenient for bankers that their actual business books should be taken away for production in Court, an Act was passed in the year 1876, called the Bankers' Books Evidence Act, which was subsequently replaced by an Act of the year 1879.

The latter Act enacts that a copy of any entry in a banking book shall (subject to certain provisos) be received in all legal proceedings as *primâ facie* evidence of such entry, and of the matters, transactions, and accounts therein recorded. Before the copy can be used it must be proved that the book was, at the time of the making of the entry, one of the ordinary books of the bank, and that the entry was made in the usual and ordinary course of business, and that the book is in the custody and control of the bank. Further, the correctness of the copy must be verified. Where the machinery of the Act is applicable a banker or officer of the bank is not to be compellable, in any legal proceeding to which the bank is not a party, to produce the books of the bank or to prove their contents, unless by order of a judge made for special cause. The Court or a judge may give parties to a legal proceeding leave to inspect and take copies of entries in a banker's books. A bank is entitled to three days' notice of any such order.

# CHAPTER X

## APPROPRIATION OF PAYMENTS

*Special Appropriation.* — It is competent for a customer to give any directions he may please as to the application of money paid by him into his banking account, and the banker by receiving it subject to such directions agrees that the money shall be applied as directed, and in no other way. Thus, if money is paid in by the customer with a particular object, as to take up a bill of exchange, the banker must apply it to that object, and, even if the customer's account is overdrawn, cannot keep it for himself. In default of special directions given by the customer, the banker may, within a reasonable time, appropriate the payment in; and, on communication of his appropriation to the customer, such appropriation becomes irrevocable. But when the payment of particular advances has been provided for in a particular way for several years, the banker cannot appropriate payments made by the customer to his general account in breach of the understanding between them. Thus it was held that where bankers had taken up bills for a customer on the security of consignments, and by a course of dealing with him had permitted him to draw on his account without reference to the advances on the consignments, they could not, by appropriating those advances to the debit side of the account, in the absence of express notice, treat it as overdrawn, and dishonour the customer's cheques before the consignments were realised (*Cumming* v. *Shand*, 5 H. & N., 95).

*Rule in Clayton's Case.*—It is, however, most usual for payments into and out of an account to be made without the customer giving any special direction, or the banker making a special appropriation, or *vice versâ*.

In such cases, the appropriation of the payment is governed by what is generally known as the rule in Clayton's case. This rule provides that a payment shall discharge the earliest debt, whether of the customer or the banker, then remaining unpaid. The practical effect of this most important rule will perhaps be best grasped from an example. A customer of a London private bank borrowed £2000 from the bank, and to secure repayment of that sum gave the bank nine promissory notes for £200 each, and one for £250. The bank also took a promise from a surety for repayment. The first note was payable about ten weeks after the loan, and the second a week later, and so on. The £2000 was placed to the customer's credit. On the first five due dates, the sums represented by the first five notes were debited by the bank to the customer in the current account, but the last five notes were not so debited. At the close of each of the first two due dates the balance was in the customer's favour, but afterwards the balances were considerably against the customer. After the last promissory note became due, enough was paid in to cover the total amount of the adverse balance as it stood when that note became due; but, as money was also constantly being withdrawn, the balance still stood against the customer. The bank sued the surety on the assumption that the promissory note had never been discharged, but the Court held that the customer's debts had been discharged in order of date under the rule in Clayton's case, so that the promissory notes had been paid (*Kinnaird* v. *Webster*, L. R., 10 Ch. D., 139).

A surety cannot, however, claim the benefit of this rule, if it was the intention of the parties that the security should be a continuing one to secure the customer's floating balance (see p. 130).

The rule has important effects if either the bankers or the customers are a firm of partners, whose constitution has changed without a discontinuance of the account. For instance, if there is a change in the banking firm, and an adverse balance against the customer, then subsequent payments by the customers to the new firm will be applied first to the extinction of the debt to the old firm. Meanwhile sums drawn out will be debts belonging to the new firm; and as soon as the old adverse balance has been wiped out by new payments in, the debt belonging to the old firm will have been extinguished, and the new firm will be creditors of the customers for the new adverse balance (see *Beal* v. *Caddick*, 26 L. J., Ex., 356). So where there has been a change in the customer's firm, as soon as the adverse balance has been wiped out by fresh payments in, the liability of the old firm to the bank will have been discharged, and the bank can only look to the new firm for the repayment of subsequent advances. If, however, the account of the old firm has been kept distinct, and accounts have been rendered to the customer on that footing, that is equivalent to an appropriation of the new payments to the credit of the new firm, and the liability of the old firm is not affected.

*Trust Money.*—It has been held that the rule in Clayton's case is not to be applied where a customer has mixed trust money with his own money. In such a case the customer must be taken to have drawn out his own money in preference to the trust money. Thus, if A has a balance of £400 at his bankers, and he then pays in £1000 out of a fund of which he is trustee, and afterwards pays in £1600 more of his own money, and draws out £1500, the draft of £1500 will not be taken to include the £1000 of trust money; but the £1500 remaining in the bank will be, as to £1000 thereof, trust money. If the trust moneys of several persons are thus mixed, and what is left is not sufficient to satisfy all, Clayton's case will apply as between the claimants. Thus, A has a balance of £400. To this he pays £300, of which he is trustee for B, £300 of which he is trustee for C, and £400 of which he is trustee for D. He afterwards pays in £600 of his own, and draws out £1500. Of the final balance of £500 B will be entitled to nothing, C to £100, and D to £400 (see In re *Hallett's Estates*, L. R., 13 Ch. D., 696.)

*Rights of Third Party.*—A banker may disable himself from appropriating a payment to his own debt by promising a third party that he will appropriate such payment of his customer for the benefit of the third party. In the case of *Kilsby* v. *Williams* (5 B. & Al., 815) it appeared that, on the payment in of a cheque by A for £250 drawn on B, another customer of the bank whose account was overdrawn, the bank wrote to say, that as the payments of B which were unappropriated only amounted to £237, they would hold the cheque, in the hope that more money would come in. More money came in, and the bankers refused to pay the cheque, and claimed to keep the moneys in reduction of the adverse balance due from B to them. It was held that A could sue the bankers for the £250 on the ground that they had arranged with him to appropriate it for his benefit.

## CHAPTER XI

### SPECIAL CUSTOMERS

*Married Women.*—Since the year 1882 marriage has ceased to vest the wife's property in her husband, either at the time of marriage or upon a subsequent acquisition of property by the wife, but her property may still be the subject of a settlement. A married woman is now capable of entering into and rendering herself liable in respect of and to the extent of her separate property on any contract, and of suing and being sued in contract in all respects as if she were a single woman. Her contracts are deemed to be entered into by her with respect to and to bind her separate property, unless the contrary is shown. A married woman is not liable unless she has separate property at the date of making the contract on which it is sought to make her liable; but if she had any separate property at such date, as to which she could reasonably be supposed to be contracting, the contract will bind her after acquired property. A married woman may have property settled upon her subject to a restraint against anticipation, and then she cannot contract so as to bind the future income of it, but only the income actually in her hands. The Courts have held that a woman cannot reasonably be supposed to contemplate binding by her contracts her clothes or personal ornaments, or a small balance of the income of property settled upon her, subject to restraint against anticipation. When a person has succeeded in getting judgment against a married woman, execution can only be levied upon her separate property. There is no personal remedy against the married woman, nor are proceedings in bankruptcy available, unless the married woman is carrying on a trade apart from her husband.

*Husband and Wife.*—If a married woman has no separate property she is, as far as contracts are concerned, in the same position as a married woman without settled property before any of the Married Women's Property Acts. The law as to the accounts of such persons has been thus expressed: "An ordinary banking account, supposing the husband to open it in the name of his wife, is, in fact, money lent with an obligation to repay it to the order of either the husband or wife. If the wife draws a cheque, which the bankers refuse to honour, the action brought upon that refusal can only be brought in the name of the husband" (*Lloyd* v. *Pughe*, L. R., 8 Ch. Ap., 88). Such banking accounts, as also banking accounts opened in the joint names of husband and wife, may be opened for one of two purposes—either for convenience, in which case the balance will pass, on the husband's death, to his personal representatives; or to secure an advancement for the wife, who will then be entitled to the balance on her husband's death. In both cases it is a question of intention, which may either be expressed or implied from conduct.

*Shareholders of the Bank.*—Where the bank is a company either under the Joint Stock Companies Acts, or under the Companies Act 1862, it is competent for a person who is a shareholder to be at the same time a customer, and as such may sue the banking company, or be sued by it. The Articles of Association, or that part of the deed of settlement which corresponds to Articles of Association, is a contract between the company and its shareholders, and it is usual to insert in the articles a provision giving the company a paramount lien on the shares of a shareholder for his debts to the company. The balance of an overdrawn account is a debt for which such lien attaches. After the company has received notice of the sale of the shares held by a customer, it cannot safely make fresh advances on their security (see p. 187).

*Corporations and Companies:* (a) *Power to Borrow.*—Corporations and companies differ from ordinary partnerships, inasmuch as their powers are limited. When such a body becomes a customer of a bank, the banker must be careful to assure himself of his customer's power to overdraw his account, or borrow in some other form. The rule is, that an express prohibition against borrowing must be obeyed, but that where there is not an express prohibition, in the case of a company or society constituted for special purposes, no borrowing can be permitted without express authority, unless it be properly incident to the course and conduct of the business for its proper purposes (In re *International Life Assurance Society,* L. R., 10 Eq., 312). Accordingly, where there are no express provisions, a sharp distinction is drawn between trading and non-trading associations. A trading association, although its objects may be more limited than in the case of a private partnership (see p. 43), has, for the purpose of carrying out its objects, exactly the same powers that a private firm would usually and reasonably avail itself of in carrying on the same business. Thus, if the nature of the business demands it, it may draw, accept, and indorse bills of exchange, or arrange for an overdraft with its bankers, and give security for such overdraft in any usual way, and this without express power to deal with bills or to borrow money. Thus, it has been held that a limited company, formed to carry on the manufacture of files, with express borrowing powers, limited to raising money by mortgage of its property, was not disabled from securing its overdraft at its bankers, which was a debt already incurred by a deposit of its title deeds. L.-J. Mellish said: "It would, in my opinion, be most undesirable to lay down a rule that no joint-stock company can raise money in this way. A mortgage by deposit is the kind of security most usually given by mercantile men to bankers, and such a rule would seriously cripple joint-stock companies in their business transactions" (In re *Patent File Co.*, L. R., 6 Ch. Ap., 83). In other words, a mercantile association is not within the scope of its business to be hampered because it is a company and not a partnership.

With regard to express powers, it is of course possible for a trading company to take them so as to be able to conduct its business in some unusual way; for instance, a railway company might take powers to draw, indorse, and accept bills of exchange, and then it would be perfectly legal for the company so to do. In the same way it is possible for non-trading associations to have express powers for such unusual purposes as borrowing or dealing with bills of exchange. But in both cases a banker should protect himself by inquiry as to the existence of such express powers.

A banker who allows a customer who has no power to borrow to overdraw his account, will not be allowed to avail himself of the rule in Clayton's case, and at the most will only be allowed to stand in the shoes of creditors who may have been rightly paid out of his advances. In the case of the *Blackburn Benefit Building Society* v. *Brooks* (L. R., 9 Ap. Ca., 857), it appeared that the Blackburn and District Benefit Building Society was allowed by its bankers (Messrs. Cunliffe, Brooks, & Co.), although it had no express power to borrow money, to make large overdrafts. The society carried on its business in the usual way, by promising advances to members, but these advances being promised before sufficient subscriptions came in, the company was obliged to overdraw. Ultimately certain deeds were declared by the officers of the society to be deposited with the bankers, as security for the balance of the account. It was admitted that part of the money was applied in payment of members withdrawing from the society, and the remainder in payment of salaries, legal expenses, and expenses of mortgaged property. The bankers claimed to retain the deeds until the overdraft was paid. It was held that the overdrafts were *ultra vires*, as not being properly incident to the course and conduct of the society's business for its proper purposes; that the bankers were not creditors of the society in respect of the overdrafts; but that they were entitled to hold the deeds as a security for repayment of so much only of the moneys advanced by them as was applied in payment of the debts and liabilities of the society properly payable, and had not been repaid to the bankers, excluding payments to withdrawing members; and lastly, that the burden of proving this lay on the bankers, and that in satisfying that burden the bankers could not have the benefit of the rule in Clayton's case.

(b) *Mode of Borrowing.*—If express power to borrow is given to a company incorporated under the Companies Acts, and in the articles of association regulations are inserted for the exercise of that power, and money is borrowed by the directors within the powers of the company but without conforming with the regulations, the company cannot say to third parties, on whom no duty is cast to see that the articles are carried out, that the borrowing is void: the company's only remedy is against the directors for a breach of duty. A banker is not an officer of the company, in the sense that there is any duty cast upon him to see that any security he may take from the company for an overdraft is given in compliance with the articles (In re *General Provident Assurance Co.* L. R., 14 Eq., 507).

(c) *Form of Instruments.*—The Companies Act 1862 has a section enacting that a promissory note or bill of exchange shall be deemed to have been made, accepted, or indorsed on behalf of any company under the Act, if made, accepted, or indorsed in the name of the company by any person acting under the authority of the company, or if made, accepted, or indorsed by or on behalf of or on account of the company by any person acting under the authority of the company. This section does not touch the power of the company to make, accept, or indorse such instruments.

*Trustee in Bankruptcy and Liquidator of Company.*— Both a trustee in bankruptcy and the liquidator of a company which is being wound up by order of the Court are now forbidden to pay official moneys into their own banking accounts. As a rule, such money must be paid into the Bank of England, but by special leave it may be paid into a local bank to a special account. All payments out have to be made by cheque payable to order, and every cheque is to have marked or written on the face of it the name of the estate, or the name of the company, as the case may be, and is to be signed by the trustee or liquidator, and be countersigned by at least one member of the committee of inspection, and by such other person, if any, in the case of a trustee, as the creditors or the committee of inspection may appoint, or, in the case of a liquidator, as the committee of inspection may appoint. (See the Bankruptcy Act 1883, ss. 74, 75, and General Rules 1886, rule 340, and the Companies Winding Up Act 1890, s. 11, and General Rules 1890, rule 81).

*Partners.*—The law of partnership is now statute law. The Partnership Act 1890, so far as is important for the present purpose, enacts (s. 5): " Every partner is an agent of the firm, and his other partners, for the purpose of the business of the partnership; and the acts of every partner, who does any act for carrying on in the usual way business of the kind carried on by the firm of which he is a member, bind the firm and his partners, unless the partner so acting has in fact no authority to act for the firm in the particular matter, and the person with whom he is dealing either knows that he has no authority, or does not know or believe him to be a partner;" and (s. 7) " where one partner pledges the credit of the firm for a purpose apparently not connected with the firm's ordinary course of business, the firm is not bound, unless he is in fact specially authorised by the other partners."

It is not in general carrying on business in the usual way, if one member of a partnership opens a banking account on behalf of the partnership in his own name, or in a name other than that of the firm. If such an account is overdrawn, the banker cannot recover the balance from the firm merely on proof that his customer was a member of the firm, and purported to be acting on its behalf; but he must show special circumstances relating to the particular partnership or trade, to show that the opening of such an account was within the ordinary course of the business. If the business of the partnership is such as ordinarily requires the use of bills of exchange, a partner has full authority to draw, accept, and indorse them, in the partnership name. He cannot bind the firm upon a bill, note, or cheque, except by using the partnership name. If a banker discounts for a customer bills drawn and indorsed in the partnership name, and obviously being used by the customer for his own private purposes, the banker is bound to ascertain the extent of his customer's authority, and if the dealing is not authorised he cannot recover upon the bills against the firm, except to the extent to which the firm may be indebted to the individual partner (*Darlington District Joint-Stock Bank, ex p.*, 34 L. J., Bk., 10). If a partnership account is kept at a bank, on which each partner has a right to draw cheques, and the individual partners have also private accounts at the same bank, it is not the duty of the bankers to inquire into the propriety of any transfer of funds which may be made from and to the different accounts (*Backhouse* v. *Charlton*, L. R., 8 Ch. D., 444). When there is a change in the constitution, or a transfer of business of the bank at which the partnership account is kept, it has been held that the acting member of the firm has implied authority to assent to the transfer of the account (*Beal* v. *Caddick*, 26 L. J., Ex., 356).

*Joint Accounts.*—Where money is paid into a bank on the joint account of persons not partners in trade, the bankers are not discharged by payment to one of those persons, without the authority of the others (*Innes* v. *Stephenson*, 1 M. & R., 145). And, in the same way, if bankers receive property for realisation on a joint account, they must hand the proceeds to all the persons from whom they received the property; if the bankers choose to pay the proceeds over to one only, and he misappropriates them, the bankers will be liable to make good the loss (*Magnus* v. *Queensland National Bank*, L. R., 37 Ch. D., 466). The most usual kinds of joint accounts are those of trustees, executors, administrators, and committees of various kinds.

*Trustees.*—For special points relative to trustees' accounts, the reader may refer to p. 68.

*Executors.*—An executor or administrator cannot, as a general rule, act until probate of the will or letters of administration has been taken out. A banker is not, however, bound to see that an executor or administrator has an absolutely good title. A *bonâ fide* payment made on the production of the probate or letters of administration is good, although the probate or letters are afterwards revoked. Nor is it the duty of the banker to see that such documents are sufficiently stamped.

An executor has no power to borrow money so as to bind the assets of the testator; he can only make himself personally liable (*Farhall v. Farhall*, L. R., 7 Ch. Ap., 123).

An executor has, however, power to give a lien on specific assets of the testator. It is therefore incumbent upon a banker who is asked to allow an overdraft by an executor to take as security assets of the testator, for, except by a lien on such assets, he will not be able to charge the testator's estate with such overdraft.

An executor may endorse bills and notes.

Co-executors being considered for many purposes as one person, one executor can bind another by certain acts, such as payment and release of a debt; but one cannot bind the others by contract (Williams *On Wills*, pp. 143, 144).

Where a balance belonging to a testator is transferred to a fresh account, in the name of the executors, that is to all intents and purposes a payment of the debt owed by the bank to the testator, and a loan of the balance by the executors to the bank. Cheques drawn upon such an account should be signed by all the executors, unless some express arrangement is made with the bank; for the honouring of such a cheque is no longer the payment of a debt due to the testator, for that has already been done once for all by the transfer to the new account.

If there is a sole executor who is also residuary legatee, the balance of the executorship account may, subject to the equities of other claimants, be treated as the executor's private money, and if such equities no longer exist, because all claims have been satisfied or provided for, so that the executor is alone beneficially interested in the balance of the account, it may be treated as his property in his individual account, as for instance by being set off against an overdraft on his private account (*Bailey* v. *Finch*, L. R., 7 Q. B., 34).

If a banker is privy to a breach of trust or misapplication of funds by an executor, and advances money on the security of the testator's assets he acquires no better title against the estate than the executor himself, and the security will be held invalid.

*Brokers and Agents.* — There has been considered already the case of a payment by a customer into his account of a third person's money; but there is still to be considered how far an agent can give a valid security over property belonging to his principal.

A banker cannot safely make advances on securities after he has notice that his customer is merely an agent, except to the extent of the agent's interest. Such notice may be an actual or an implied notice. In the case of *Locke* v. *Prescott* (32 Beav., 261), it appeared that bankers advanced to customers £300 to redeem some railway stock which had been transferred to another firm as a security for that sum. The stock was thereupon transferred in blank to the bankers. Subsequently the customers, in a letter to the bankers, stated that they had been requested by their principals to extend the term of the loan on the stock. The stock actually belonged to a third party. It was held that, after the receipt of this letter, the bankers had notice of the third party's right to the stock, and no subsequent advances made by the bankers to the customers could affect the stock, and they could not hold it as a security for the floating balance of the customer's account.

The doctrine of notice, so far as regards implied notice, has recently received considerable extension. The first case in which this happened was that of the *Earl of Sheffield* v. *The London Joint-Stock Bank* (L. R., 13 Ap. Ca., 333). In that case the information that the securities deposited were not the absolute property of the customer was held to be conveyed by the nature and extent of the customer's business. The action was brought by Lord Sheffield to redeem certain securities in the hands of three banks. It appeared that in order to raise a certain sum of money, on certain terms defined in writing, Lord Sheffield placed the securities in question at the disposal of one Easton, who procured the advance from Mozley, a money-dealer. Mozley divided the securities and deposited them in three lots, together with securities belonging to other customers of his, to cover his account with the several banks; Mozley eventually became insolvent. The banks knew that in most cases, if not in all, the securities which Mozley deposited with them were not his own absolute property; for Mozley's customers for the most part were persons on the Stock Exchange, and it was the usual practice for the banks on settling days to deliver out to Mozley the securities which he required to be released for the convenience of his customers, on an undertaking to re-deposit securities of equal value in the course of the day. The letters of deposit which Mozley gave the banks purported to charge, not merely Mozley's interest in the securities, but the securities themselves. The evidence for the bankers was, that such was the general banking practice in accounts with brokers. The Court, however, held that there was no such general custom proved as would bind a client dealing with a money-dealer, unless it was shown that the client had notice of the practice and dealt with the money-dealer on the footing of that practice. As such proof was not given in the case, the House of Lords held that, even though the banks had the legal title to the securities, they were not purchasers for value without notice, but ought to have inquired into the extent of Mozley's authority; and that, upon payment to the banks of the money advanced by Mozley to Easton, Lord Sheffield was entitled to the value of such of the securities as had been sold by the banks, and was entitled to redeem the remainder.

The effect of this decision is that a banker who takes securities from a customer whom he has reason to believe is only an agent, must inquire as to the extent of his authority; or, if the course of business makes that impracticable, the banker must trust to the personal character of his customers being such that they will not overpledge the securities given to them by their principals; for the banker will only have a charge upon the securities to the extent to which their customers are themselves interested in them.

Since this decision similar cases have been decided. In the case of *Simmons* v. *The London Joint-Stock Bank* (7 *Times* L. R., 160), the customer, one Delmar, was a stockbroker who pledged his customer's shares and bonds *en bloc* with other securities to cover his overdraft at his bankers. The true owner of the shares and bonds sued the bank for delivery up of his property.

In the Court of Appeal it was said: "The bank took it for granted that, if the bonds did not in fact belong to Delmar, he had been authorised by the real owner to raise money on the bonds, within the limit of their market value. This assumption and belief were based, not on inquiry and investigation, but on the bank's faith in the honesty of Delmar, and was in fact erroneous. But the bank did not believe that Delmar had been authorised by the real owner to deposit the bonds *en bloc*, together with other securities which belonged to other persons, and to raise a lump sum upon the whole. The bank were, indeed, honestly of opinion that Delmar might lawfully do so, but we think that they based this view upon a mistaken assumption that such deposit *en bloc*, without authority from the client, was recognised by the law. In other words, they knew that the bonds in question might probably belong to a third person; they did not know and did not believe that the owner had authorised their being deposited and pledged *en bloc*, but they honestly believed that such an authority from the owner was not necessary in law, if he had sanctioned (as the Bank assumed from their faith in Delmar's honesty to be the case) the pledging of the documents for any sum of money whatsoever. If this be the true view of the transaction, the bank never became *bonâ fide* holders for value without notice, since they never believed that Delmar was the true owner, and never, indeed, believed that any authority had been given by the true owner, which alone in law could justify what was being done. On the contrary, they chose to shut their eyes to this necessary part of the inquiry, under a misconception of the law. The case of *Earl Sheffield* v. *London Joint-Stock Bank* seems to show that under such circumstances the bank acquired no title to the bonds as against the true owner." In the case of *Baker* v. *Nottingham Banking Company* (7 *Times* L. R., 235), the learned judge at *nisi prius* distinguished the position of the bank, who were the holders of a security handed to them by a person known to be a stockbroker, and decided in favour of the bank.

It may be worth noting that the following arrangement has been held safe. A firm of bill-brokers sent bills to their banker under the terms of this guarantee :— "In consideration of your discounting for us any bills you may approve and think fit from time to time, we hereby guarantee the due payment of them as they respectively fall due." This arrangement was held to be equivalent to an indorsement on each bill by the brokers (*Bishop, ex p.*, L. R., 15 Ch. D., 400).

# CHAPTER XII

## BANKER AS BAILEE OF VALUABLES

A BANKER very often takes care of his customer's valuables, sometimes without extra charge, but sometimes for a reward. In such cases the banker is a bailee, and his liability is a matter of deduction from the general rules as to bailor and bailee.

Where the banker makes no extra charge, he is considered as a gratuitous bailee, as the profit, if any, he makes by keeping his customer's account is not treated as a consideration for acting as custodian. In such a case he is only liable for gross negligence, or, as it has been otherwise expressed, he must show the care of an ordinary prudent man in his own affairs (*Giblin* v. *MacMullen*, L. R., 2 P. C., 317).

If the banker receives a reward he must not show any negligence. If he is guilty of negligence he will be liable to his customer for such loss as is the natural result of such negligence. It has been held (In re *United Service Company*, L. R., 6 Ch. Ap., 212) that a banker who holds shares for his customer, and for a commission collects the dividends on them as they become due, is in the position of a bailee for hire. A banker is not an insurer, and is therefore not liable for accidental losses. It is a question of fact in each case whether negligence has been shown, and if so, whether slight or gross negligence. It is a question of law what damage is recoverable and what is too remote.

The deposit of securities for safe custody, or for collection of dividends, is a deposit made for a special purpose inconsistent with the existence of the banker's lien for an overdrawn account (see p. 62).

# CHAPTER XIII

### BANKER AS PAYER OF CHEQUES AND BILLS

*Payer of Cheques.*—It has already been said that it is part of the special duty of a banker to honour his customer's cheques to the amount of his balance. The converse of this is true, except so far as it has been modified by statute, namely, that the banker is bound not to pay away his customer's money, except upon his cheque or other order, and is liable to his customer for payments made to third persons, if not actually authorised by the customer.

*Customer's Signature.*—A banker is bound to know his customer's signature. If the signature of the drawer of a cheque is forged, the banker cannot charge the customer, whose name is forged, with the amount of the cheque.

*Payee's Endorsement.*—At common law a banker was bound to know the signature of his customer's payee. Till the year 1853 cheques payable to order, on demand, were not often used, as they required the same stamp as a bill of exchange. In that year the stamp upon all such cheques was reduced by 16 & 17 Vict., c. 59, to one penny, and as the effect of such reduction would be to bring cheques payable to order into common use, it was further enacted by the nineteenth section of that Act, that "any draft or order drawn upon a banker for a sum of money payable to order on demand which shall, when presented for payment, purport to be indorsed by the person to whom the same shall be drawn payable, shall be a sufficient authority to such banker to pay the amount of such draft or order to the bearer thereof; and it shall not be incumbent on such banker to prove that such indorsement, or any subsequent indorsement, was made by or under the direction or authority of the person to whom the said draft or order was or is made payable, either by the drawer or any indorser thereof."

In the case of *Charles* v. *Blackwell* (L. R., 2 C. P. D., 151), the question arose whether an indorsement of a cheque payable to order, and purporting to be by the agent of the person to whose order it was payable, was under the Statute a sufficient authority to the banker to pay the amount of such cheque, though the person who indorsed the cheque had no authority to indorse. It appeared that S. K., an agent of S. & Co., the plaintiffs, having authority to sell goods for them and to receive payment by cash or cheque, but not having authority to indorse cheques, received from the defendants, in payment for goods supplied, a cheque on their bankers, drawn payable to S. & Co., or order. S. K. indorsed it "S. & Co. per S. K. agent," received the money from the bankers, and misappropriated part of it. The bankers returned the cheque to the defendants, and the amount was allowed in account by the defendants. The Court held that the payment by the bankers was within the protection of the above Statute, and that the plaintiff could not maintain an action against the defendants, either for the price of the goods or for the cheque.

It should be noted that the Statute only protects the banker; *e.g.* Jones draws a cheque payable to Smith's order; Jones' clerk steals the cheque, forges Smith's indorsement, and (with the cheque) buys goods of Robinson, who has no knowledge of the forgery; Robinson pays the cheque into his bankers, where his account is overdrawn, and Robinson's bankers receive payment of the cheque from Jones' bankers; Jones' bankers may debit Jones with the payment, but Jones may sue either Robinson or Robinson's bankers for conversion of the cheque (see *Ogden* v. *Benas*, L. R., 9 C. P., 513).

*Material Alteration.*—When a cheque is materially altered (Bills of Exchange Act 1882, s. 64), it becomes void; there is a partial exception where the alteration is not apparent and the cheque is in the hands of a *bonâ fide* holder for value, in which case the holder may avail himself of the cheque as if it had not been altered, and may enforce payment of it according to its original tenor. Alterations of the date or the sum payable are material alterations. A banker cannot charge his customer with a payment made to the holder of a void instrument.

*Negligence.*—A customer may have so negligently conducted himself that he cannot be heard to say that a payment wrongly made by the banker was not a payment made on his account. This is called estoppel by negligence. Negligence, to amount to an estoppel, must be in the transaction itself, and be the proximate cause of leading the banker into mistake, and also must be the neglect of some duty which is owing to the banker or to the general public. As this rule is being constantly misunderstood, it will be further explained by a few illustrations.

1. In the case of *Bank of Ireland* v. *Evan's Charities* (3 H. L. Ca., 389), it appeared that a customer negligently lost his cheque-book, and so enabled some one to get hold of and forge a cheque. The customer's banker was not allowed to charge him with the payment of such a cheque, for there was no transaction in which the customer was

negligent, nor was the loss of the book the proximate cause of the bank paying the cheque. The proximate cause was the dishonesty of the forger.

2. In the case of *Arnold* v. *Cheque Bank* (L. R., 1 C. P. D., 578), it appeared that a cheque was sent through the post from abroad, but no separate letter of advice was sent. It was held that it was not competent for the banker, who had received payment of the cheque on a forged endorsement, to give evidence that it was an usual and almost invariable practice amongst merchants sending large remittances from abroad to send, besides the letter containing the remittance, a letter of advice by the same or the next mail, on the ground that the alleged negligence was collateral only to the transaction giving rise to the action.

3. So where the customer's confidential clerk had forged cheques, and the alleged negligence consisted in a failure to examine the pass-book and returned cheques, the examination of which would have led to the discovery of the earlier forgeries and so prevented the later forgeries, it was held that the customer was not estopped from recovering from his bankers the amount of the forged cheques honoured by them. (Unreported case.)

(4) The case which went furthest in the banker's favour was the case of *Young* v. *Grote* (4 Bing., 254). There a customer of a banker delivered to his wife certain printed cheques signed by himself, but with blanks for the sums, requesting his wife to fill the blanks up according to the exigency of his business. She caused one to be filled up with the words, fifty pounds two shillings, the fifty being commenced with a small letter, and placed in the middle of a line; and the figures 50, 2s. were also placed at a considerable distance from the printed £. In this state she delivered the cheque to her husband's clerk to receive the amount; whereupon he inserted, at

the beginning of the line in which the word fifty was written, the words "three hundred and," and the figure "3" between the £ and the 50. The bankers paid £350, 2s.; and it was held that the loss must fall on the customer. The true ground of decision has been thus set out: "In that case it was held to have been the fault of the drawer of the cheque, that he misled the banker on whom it was drawn by want of proper caution *in the mode of drawing the cheque*, which admitted of easy interpolation, and consequently that the drawer, having thus caused the banker to pay the forged cheque *by his own neglect in the mode of drawing the cheque itself*, could not complain of that payment" (*Arnold* v. *Cheque Bank*, supra).

*Operation of Cheque.*—A cheque does not operate as an assignment of the drawer's funds; nor is there any privity between the payee and the banker; and if the banker wrongly dishonours the cheque, the customer, and not the payee, is the person to sue the banker. It is possible for the payee and banker to make some special arrangement whereby privity is established between them, and then the payee can sue for breach of the contract so made.

*Property in Cheque.* — A cheque taken in payment remains the property of the payee only so long as it remains unpaid. When paid the banker is entitled to keep it as a voucher till his account with his customer is settled. After that the drawer is entitled to it as a voucher between him and the payee (*Charles* v. *Blackwell*, L. R., 2 C. P. D., pp. 162, 3).

*What is Payment.*—Payment by a banker is complete as soon as he has laid down the money on the bank counter, with the intention that the person to receive payment should take it up. In the case of *Chambers* v. *Miller* (32 L. J., C. P., 30), it appeared that a bank cashier paid a cheque, and while the recipient was counting the money discovered that the customer's account did not show sufficient assets. It was held that the cashier had no right to take back the money.

*Countermand of Payment.*—By the Bills of Exchange Act 1882, s. 75, it is enacted that the duty and authority of a banker to pay a cheque drawn on him by his customer are determined by—(1) countermand of payment; (2) notice of the customer's death.

If a customer tears up a cheque, that is a sufficient countermand of authority to pay it. Thus, where a cheque was presented which had been torn in pieces and pasted on a sheet of paper, and the banker paid it without inquiry, on proof that the customer had torn it up and thrown it away, the banker was held liable for the amount.

And, generally, if suspicious circumstances are brought to a banker's notice, he is put on inquiry (*Scholey* v. *Ramsbottom*, 2 Camp., 485).

*Banker as Payer of Bills.*—A banker is not bound to pay the bills which a customer accepts payable at his bankers (*Vagliano Brothers* v. *Bank of England*, 7 *Times* L. R., 333). But the acceptance of a bill by a customer payable at his banker's is tantamount to an order to the banker to pay the bill, if there are funds of the customer's in his hands; and, as a matter of practice, such order is always obeyed. The order is, however, an order to pay the bill to any person who, according to the law merchant, can give a valid discharge for it. If the bill is payable to order, it is an authority to pay the bill to any person who becomes holder by a genuine indorsement, and if the bill is originally payable to bearer, or if there is afterwards a genuine indorsement in blank, it is an authority to pay the bill to the person who seems to be the holder. A banker cannot debit his customer with payment made to a person who claims through a forged indorsement (*Robarts* v. *Tucker*, 16 Q. B., 60), for the statutory protection against forged indorsements only extends to cheques and bills payable to order on demand (Bills of Exchange Act 1882, s. 60). If there are circumstances amounting to a direction from the customer to the bankers to pay the bill without reference to the genuineness of the indorsement, or equivalent to an admission of its genuineness, inducing the banker to alter his position, then the customer will be precluded from showing that the indorsement was forged. These rules, no doubt, in practice bear hardly on bankers, as they have no greater opportunities of knowing the indorsements of payees of bills than those of payees of cheques; but, as was said by Baron Parke (*Roberts* v. *Tucker*, supra)—"If bankers wish to avoid the responsibility of deciding on the genuineness of indorsements, they may require their customers to domicile their bills at their own offices, and to honour them by giving a cheque upon the banker."

*Mode of Payment.*—Where a bill is left for payment, the presentment continues till the bill is called for, and if the bank receives sufficient funds from the customer, or on his behalf a reasonable time before the bill is called for, the bank must pay the bill.

A banker is not bound to pay a bill after banking hours (*Whitaker* v. *Bank of England*, 6 C. & P., 700).

A banker, if he pays bills, is bound to pay bills in the order of presentation to him.

*Payment through Correspondent.* —When a customer banks with a country bank, the customer sometimes accepts bills payable, not at his own bankers, but at the house of their London or other agents. In such a case, if the customer pays into his own bankers a sum of money under directions to transmit the same for the purpose of taking up the bill, then, upon the failure of such bankers, the right of the customer to recover the whole of the money depends upon whether the bank has or has not specifically appropriated and transmitted such money (see the cases set out at p. 56, supra).

*Material Alterations.*—The law as to material alterations is the same for bills as for cheques. The Bill of Exchange Act, s. 64, enacts—(1) Where a bill or acceptance is materially altered without the assent of all parties liable on the bill, the bill is avoided except as against a party who has himself made, authorised, or assented to the alteration, and subsequent indorsers. Provided that, where a bill has been materially altered, but the alteration is not apparent, and the bill is in the hands of a holder in due course, such holder may avail himself of the bill as if it had not been altered, and may enforce payment of it according to its original tenor. (2) In particular, the following alterations are material, namely, any alteration of the date, the sum payable, the time of payment, the place of payment, and, where a bill has been accepted generally, the addition of a place of payment without the acceptor's assent.

*Special Directions.*—If a customer's account is overdrawn and he has accepted bills payable at his banker, and has made no special arrangement with the banker, the customer is liable to have any money he pays in applied by the banker to the reduction of the adverse balance. It is usual, therefore, when a customer wishes a particular sum to be applied for taking up a particular bill to pay the sum into his account, with special directions to that end, and then the banker cannot apply the sum in any other way. Thus it appeared, in the case of *Hill* v. *Smith* (12 M. & W., 618), that A paid to a banking company a sum of £440, for the purpose of providing for three bills drawn by A upon the company's London bankers. A owed at that time more than £440 to the company, who, instead of applying the money according to his instructions, placed it to the credit of his account with them. The bill was refused acceptance; and, while it remained unpaid in the hands of the holder, A became bankrupt. It was held that when the company refused to perform its contract it ought to have returned the money to A, and accordingly A's assignees were entitled to recover from the company the whole amount of the bills.

Upon the same principles, so long as the bank remains willing to carry out its side of the special contract, the customer or his assignees cannot demand back the money paid in specially. Thus, where a sum had been carried to a special account as security against bills, not yet at maturity, drawn by the customer and discounted by the bankers, it was held that the assignees in bankruptcy of the customer could not recover that sum (*Chartered Bank of India* v. *Evans*, 21 L. T., 407).

In default of a special arrangement of the nature shown on p. 78, there is no privity between any of the parties to a bill, other than the acceptor, and the banker who has been furnished with funds for the payment of the bill. In the case of *Hill* v. *Royds* (L. R., 8 Eq., 290), it appeared that the acceptor of a bill paid the amount to his bankers in order to meet the bill. On the day it arrived at maturity the acceptor died, and the bankers dishonoured the bill, which was returned to the drawers and subsequently paid by them. The drawers then filed a bill in equity against the bankers to make good the amount. It was held that, though the bankers were wrong in not paying the bill, the drawers were not the right persons to institute such a suit, as there was no privity between them and the bankers.

The reader will have noted that a banker is in a much more favourable position in respect to a bill originally payable to bearer than in respect to a bill originally payable to order. In the former case the bank would be authorised to pay the amount to the person who was the holder, irrespective of his title. The Bill of Exchange Act 1882, s. 7, sub-s. 3, introduces a new rule which brings a class of bills payable to order within this more favourable rule. It enacts that, "where the payee is a fictitious or non-existing person the bill may be treated as payable to bearer." This section has recently received an important interpretation in the celebrated case of *Vagliano Brothers* v. *Bank of England* (7 *Times* L. R., 333). This case contains other points on the subject of bills of exchange, but here only a short summary of this side of the case is set out. Glyka, a clerk of Vagliano's, forged bills purporting to be drawn by one Vucina, and secured the genuine acceptances of Vagliano. The clerk selected for the name of payees the name of a firm of merchants at Constantinople, Petridi & Co., with whom Vucina had had business relations, and of whose existence Vagliano was aware. The bills were accepted payable at the Bank of England. The clerk stole the forged bills, forged indorsements of the payees, and received money for the bills across the counter at the Bank of England. One question raised was, "Were Petridi & Co. fictitious persons within the meaning of the above clause of the Bills of Exchange Act?" In the Court of Appeal, the Master of the Rolls alone answered this in the affirmative and the other five judges in the negative. The Master of the Rolls said, "The payee named on the face of the bill is, in my opinion, a fictitious payee. Petridi & Co. is not the real payee. If he were, he would be entitled to have possession of the bill and entitled to endorse it. He is the pretended payee. He who, in fact, drew the bill has pretended on the face of the bill that Petridi & Co. is the payee; but he intended that Petridi & Co. should not be the payee. He feigned that Petridi & Co. was the payee when he was not. To feign is an equivalent for to pretend. Then, using the adjective as applicable to the thing feigned, the payee in this case is a fictitious payee. The antithesis is between a real and a feigned or fictitious payee. That is the business meaning of fictitious." According to this reason, where the payee is an existing person, he is real or fictitious payee, according as the drawer intends or does not intend him to have possession of the bill. The five Lord-Justices held otherwise and said: " Whatever be the interpretation of the section, 'fictitious' it cannot mean what is contended for by the counsel for the bank. Petridi & Co. were old customers of Vucina, carrying on business at Constantinople, whose existence was known to the acceptor, and whose name was fraudulently introduced into the bill by Glyka, because it was the name of a real and known firm. . . . It was the very essence of his criminal device, that everybody who saw the draft should be led to think that a real firm—Petridi & Co. of Constantinople—were the persons to whom the money was to be paid. . . . According to the ordinary sense of the English language, the payees of these bills were not fictitious, but real persons from first to last, and to construe the sub-section otherwise would be to render it the source of needless disorder and confusion in business transactions. The instruments in question were not, therefore, payable to bearer." In the House of Lords, the Lord Chancellor disagreed with the reasoning of the Master of the Rolls, but held that the sub-section applied because " the real meaning of the sub-section is to imply the unreality of any person who is named upon the face of the instrument as the payee of the bill." Lord Selborne was not prepared to say that the majority of the judges in the Court of Appeal were wrong in their construction of the section given above, and disagreed with the results of Lord Herschell's reasoning. Lord Herschell supported the view that the case came within the sub-section, because if that did not apply there was no other section that did, and also on the same reasoning as that of the Master of the Rolls. Lord Bramwell took a strong view that the case was not within the sub-section, on the ground that Petridi & Co. could not be real or unreal according to the intent of the drawer, and on the further ground that the section is for the benefit of the holder, not for the benefit of the acceptor, and that, as the acceptor could not treat such a bill as payable to bearer, neither could the banker, his agent for payment.

It would seem then that a majority of the House of Lords considers that, since the Bills of Exchange Act, the rule laid down as to a bill originally drawn payable to order, viz. that the banker is only authorised to pay it to a person who has become holder by a genuine indorsement, no longer applies to cases where the person to whose order the bill is drawn was not intended by the drawer to be at any time in possession of the bill. It is well to bear in mind that the case was decided upon its own peculiar facts, and that in the future it may possibly be distinguished, and a return made to the general rule propounded by Lord Bramwell that "a banker cannot charge his customer with the amount of a bill paid to a person who had no right of action against the customer."

*Estoppel by Negligence.*—The law is here the same as in the case of cheques. A second point remains to be discussed that was raised in *Vagliano Brothers* v. *Bank of England*, viz., does the decision of that case alter the law as to estoppel by negligence. A careful consideration of the judgments will show that it does not. There is no doubt that Vagliano was negligent in not better supervising the forger Glyka. The Lord Chancellor is the only person who has held that the negligence of the customer was connected with the act of forgery. Lord Selborne thinks that the *primâ facie* obligation of a banker only to pay the person entitled to his customer's money is done away with if there is a representation made directly to the banker by the customer upon a material point, untrue in fact (though believed by the person who made it to be true), and on which the banker acted by paying money which he would not otherwise have paid. If the bank acted upon such a representation in good faith, and according to the ordinary course of business, and a loss had in consequence occurred which would not have happened if the representation had been true, the customer should bear the loss. Lord Selborne and Lord Macnaghten are careful to state that the case does not come within any of the previous cases. It must, therefore, be remembered that, when negligence is set up in subsequent cases, it cannot be said that the Vagliano case has overruled any of the past cases, nor can it be used as an authority on this point, except where the bill of exchange, and not merely its endorsement, is forged.

## CHAPTER XIV

### BANKER AS COLLECTOR OF CHEQUES AND BILLS

So far it has been assumed that the payments to the credit of a customer's account have been cash payments. As a matter of practice, in the case of private customers, many payments in will be of cheques, and in trade accounts of bills of exchange. The rule with regard to cheques has thus been laid down by the Court of Appeal, "when a customer pays a cheque to his bankers, with the intention that the amount of it shall be at once placed to his credit, and the bankers carry the amount to his credit accordingly, they become immediately holders of the cheque, for value, even though the customer's account is not overdrawn" (In re *Palmer*, L. R., 19 Ch. D., 409). The practice of bankers is not to sue on a dishonoured cheque, but to return it to the customer, unless the customer's account is overdrawn; but their right to sue is not dependent on the state of the account.

A banker to whom a customer hands a cheque to be placed to his credit receives it as the agent of the customer for the purpose of collection, and is bound to use due diligence in getting it paid. If the cheque was drawn by another customer of the same banker, the inference is still that the banker only receives it as agent to deal with it in the same way as if it had been a cheque drawn on any other banker. It is not the duty of the bankers, under such circumstances, immediately to tell the person presenting the cheque that they have not sufficient funds to honour it. The banker may take time to make inquiries, provided that he gives notice of dishonour within a reasonable time.

If the banker, as collector of a cheque for a customer, makes a special arrangement for the receipt of the money, he cannot afterwards assert his rights as banker of the drawer of the cheque (*Kilsby* v. *Williams*, 5 B. & Ald., 815, and p. 78, supra).

*What is Due Diligence?*—The next question is, What is due or reasonable diligence, when the collecting bank and the paying bank are not the same? In general the banker has the day after his receipt of a cheque, to present it for payment. If the two banks are not in the same town, the collecting banker is only bound to send it to his agent for presentment by the post of the day after that on which he has received it, and the agent has the following day to present it for payment. Thus, in the case of *Hare* v. *Henty* (30 L. J., C. P., 302), it appeared that a cheque upon a bank at Lewes was paid on a Friday morning into a bank at Worthing, by a customer of the Worthing bank, to the credit of his account with that bank. If the cheque had been presented at Lewes on Saturday it would have been paid. It was not presented there till Monday, when it was dishonoured. It was held that the customer had no cause of action against the Worthing bank for neglect of duty.

It is now the usual practice to send such cheques through the country clearing house in London; and, as long as that process does not consume more than the two days allowed, the customer cannot complain. Nor does the fact that presentment is in that way made through the post invalidate the presentment (*Bailey* v. *Bodenham*, 33 L. J., C. P., 282).

If the collecting bank, on receiving notice of dishonour, gives notice of dishonour to its customer, on or before the day following that on which the cheque was dishonoured, the bank is entitled, if they have credited the customer with the amount of the cheque, thereupon to debit him with such amount.

*Receipt of Money by Bank.*—It is a question of considerable importance to know when the collecting bank has received payment, so that its customer can charge it with the receipt of the money. If the collecting bank presents the cheque by an agent across the counter of the paying bank, payment is made to the bank as soon as the money has been laid down upon the counter by the cashier of the paying bank, with the intention that the agent of the collecting bank should take it up (see p. 99, supra). So where the agent is another bank, payment to the agent of the collecting bank (or even to a sub-agent) is payment to the principal, and the customer may charge the bank with the receipt of the money.

*Clearing House Customs.*—The usual mode in which cheques are passed through the country clearing house seems to be this. The collecting bank, A, forwards the cheque to its town agent, B. The town agent B sends the cheque to the clearing house, where it comes into the hands of the London bank C, printed on the cheque as the agent of the paying bank, D. This latter bank, C, does not at once give credit for the cheque, because it has no means of knowing the state of the drawer's account at its principals', D, but on the same day forwards it to its principals, D, the paying bank. If the cheque is honoured, the paying bank D at once instructs its London agents, C, to credit B with the amount. On the receipt of this advice by C, the day's accounts are made up on the footing that the amount of the cheque is payable by C to B. As soon as the day's accounts are settled by the necessary drafts, B has been paid, and whether A, the collecting bank, gets the money or no, the customer is entitled to the amount of the cheque as against his banker, A.

In London there is a special clearing house for London bankers, and in provincial towns there are also clearing houses on similar principles.

The following example is given to show what in practice has been held to be an irrevocable payment under the clearing house system. The bankers at Newcastle have accounts at the branch bank of the Bank of England; and it is the practice that each banker, having previously ascertained that the bills, cheques, etc., on the other banks will be paid, hands them to the Bank of England for collection; and they accordingly, at 2 P.M., present the bills, etc., to the drawees, and a cheque is drawn upon the Bank of England by the drawees for the aggregate amount, which is then placed to the debit of the drawee's account with the Bank of England. If that bank is itself the holder of that bill, it is presented earlier in the morning to ascertain whether it will be paid, and if so it is left with the drawee, and a credit note is given in exchange; and afterwards, upon the presenting of the cheques, this credit note is taken into account, and forms part of the sum for which the cheque on the Bank of England is given. The banks close to the public at 3 P.M., but the bankers' accounts with the Bank of England are kept open till 4; between 3 and 4 the bankers attend to correct mistakes and strike a final balance. It appeared in the case of *Pollard* v. *Bank of England* (L. R, 6 Q. B., 623), that a customer of the Bank of England had paid into his account a bill, which the bank discounted, accepted payable at L. & Co.'s, another Newcastle banker. When the bill became due it was treated in the ordinary course, and allowed for in the cheque given by L. & Co. to the Bank of England. After the closing of L. & Co.'s bank, on the same day, it was discovered that the acceptor's balance was not sufficient to pay the bill, and that the acceptor had stopped payment. Thereupon, at 3.30 P.M., L. & Co. requested the Bank of England to take back the bill. This it did, under protest. At this time the Bank of England had already placed the amount of the bill to the debit of L. & Co. It was decided that the customer was entitled to have credit for the bill with the Bank of England. For unless the giving the cheque by L. & Co. was provisional, and subject to ratification in going over the accounts later in the day, it became the duty of the bank at once to transfer the amount of the bill from the account of L. & Co. to that of the customer; and this, in effect, they did. Such a transaction might, no doubt, by arrangement between the bankers, be provisional only, and subject to be set aside; but it was for the bank to show that such an arrangement existed, in order to divest the transaction of what would otherwise be its necessary effect.

It should be carefully remembered that there is a distinction between rectifying a mistake and revoking an act. Thus, if several cheques are presented across the counter, and the cashier adds the amounts up wrong and gives £1 too much, the mistake may be corrected; and so, if he gave a bad coin, the recipient may exchange it for a good one. But the cashier cannot revoke the whole transaction, and claim back the whole of the money on the ground that he had made a mistake as to the customer's balance. So in the clearing house case we have just considered the bankers could rectify mistakes but they could not revoke payments except on an express agreement to that effect. But so long as there is no communication with the party to be paid, the banker is free to correct his mistakes, and if he cancels a cheque or a bill by mistake he can mark it "cancelled in error," and then on the return of the note or bill in that state the payee must treat it as uncancelled. The case of *Prince* v. *The Oriental Bank Corporation*, set out on p. 59, supra, is an instance of this.

The custom of the London clearing house on these points has been stated in a special verdict (*Warwick* v. *Rogers*, 5 Man. & G., 340) in the manner following. The clerks from the different banks using the clearing house assemble there daily at eleven o'clock of the forenoon, and remain or go backwards and forwards, as the case may be, until half-past five, when the clearing house is closed. Each banker has a separate drawer, into which drawer all bills, notes, and cheques then due, and which are payable at such bankers, are put by the other respective banker's clerks, holding the same, on arrival, at eleven o'clock, and so from time to time through the day. Up to four o'clock (but not later), bills, notes, and cheques, are put into the drawer as they arrive. Shortly after eleven o'clock the clearing clerk of each banker takes out of his drawer all the bills, notes, and cheques, which have been then put into it by other banker's clerks claiming payment, and takes or sends the same to his principal's bank, in order that the banker may examine them and determine as to the payment of them respectively; and the same course is pursued again at three o'clock in the afternoon, and from time to time afterwards during the remainder of the day until four o'clock. Each banker examines the bills and cheques so sent

S

or taken to him by their respective clerks, and the customer's accounts to which they refer; and such bills or cheques as are at the time intended to be paid are cancelled by drawing lines along and across the name of the party for whom such payment is intended to be made. Such of the bills and cheques as the bankers determine not to pay are returned by them to and deposited in the drawer at the clearing house of the bankers by whom the same were that morning brought to the clearing house. Sometimes this is done when the clerk returns at three o'clock to the clearing house, and sometimes the bankers (if they so please) retain them until three minutes before five o'clock, and then return and deposit them in the said drawer; and all bills not so returned and deposited by the last mentioned time are considered by the respective bankers as paid, the claims of the several bankers on each other being settled at five o'clock, and the final balance between them being then struck; though each banker's clerk makes up his account from time to time during the day, as may suit his convenience, until five o'clock, correcting it by the addition of such subsequent receipts and payments as may be necessary according to the items which afterwards come in. When a cancellation has occurred through error or mistake the same is indicated in writing on the bill note or cheque returned.

*Crossed Cheques.*—Some years ago the custom of crossing cheques grew up, and various Acts of Parliament were passed to decide what was the effect of different modes of crossing. The Crossed Cheques Acts of 1876 was, with a modification for the additional protection of bankers, incorporated in the Bills of Exchange Act, ss. 76 to 82. Those sections now contain the whole of the law upon the subject.

There are two sorts of crossing, general and special. A cheque is crossed generally when two parallel transverse lines are drawn across it, either with or without the words "and Company" between such lines, and either with or without the words "not negotiable." When there is added to a general crossing the name of a banker, the cheque is crossed specially, and to that banker.

An uncrossed cheque may be crossed generally or specially by the drawer or the holder.

A cheque crossed generally may be crossed specially by the holder. The holder may, in any case, add the words "not negotiable."

When a cheque is once crossed specially, such crossing becomes a material part of the cheque, and must not be altered or added to, except that the banker to whom it is crossed may again cross it specially to another banker for collection.

Where an uncrossed cheque, or a cheque crossed generally, is sent to a banker for collection, he may cross it specially to himself. This is a safeguard against the dishonesty of the banker's own servants.

If a cheque is crossed specially more than once, the banker on whom it is drawn must refuse payment of it unless the second crossing is made by a banker to another banker as his agent for collection. Where the banker on whom a cheque is drawn, which is crossed more than once, wrongfully pays it, he is liable to the true owner of the cheque for any loss he may sustain, owing to the cheque having been so paid.

The banker is liable to the true owner of a cheque in case of loss, if he pays a cheque crossed generally to any one but a banker, or a cheque crossed specially to any banker but the one to whom it is crossed, or to another banker as his agent for collection.

There is a proviso in the Act that if the crossing has been obliterated, and there is no apparent crossing or apparent alteration, the banker paying the cheque in good faith, and without negligence, is not to be responsible.

A banker paying in good faith and without negligence a crossed cheque in the proper manner, is in the same position as if payment of the cheque had been made to the true owner of it; and so also is the drawer of the cheque, provided that the cheque has come into the hands of the payee.

The effect of crossing a cheque as "not negotiable" is to render a person who afterwards takes the cheque incapable of having or giving a better title to the cheque than the person from whom he took it.

A collecting banker who receives payment in good faith, and without negligence on behalf of his customer, of a cheque crossed generally or specially to himself, to which cheque the customer has no title or a defective title, does not incur any liability to the true owner of the cheque by reason only of having received such payment.

*Collection of Bills.*—When a banker receives bills from his customer, he may receive them in one of two characters—as a factor, or as a purchaser. In the first case he holds them as collecting agent, in the second he becomes at once the debtor of his customer for their price.

Where the banker receives the bills merely for collection, the bills, even when endorsed to him, do not become his absolute property, and on the bankruptcy of the banker the customer may recover such as remain in specie in his hands. If, however, the banker, contrary to the faith of the understanding between himself and his customer, negotiates the bills, a person taking them *bonâ fide* and for value gets a good title, and the customer can only come in as a general creditor. The banker now, however,.

runs the risk of a criminal prosecution. The fact that the customer expects and is allowed to draw against the bills, whilst still remaining undue, does not make them the property of the banker, although the banker may have a lien to the extent of his advances. It follows, from what has been said, that if the bills were accidentally destroyed, without negligence on the part of the banker, the loss would fall on the customer.

*Short Bills.*—Bills remitted for collection are called "short" bills, and they are said to be entered "short," when they are treated in the banker's books as bills and not as cash. But a banker by entering a short bill as cash cannot alter the nature of the bills, for that depends on the intention of the parties; and the entries in the banker's book, not being admissible as evidence in his favour, cannot even be used to show the banker's intention. It is the duty of a banker to show due diligence in presenting bills given to him for collection.

*Banker and Correspondent.*—In the case of country banks, a banker is often employed by his customers to transmit bills for collection to a London or other agent. In such a case the London or other bank takes the bills, subject to the directions of the country bankers and not of their customer. Thus, in the case of *Johnson* v. *Robarts* (L. R., 10 Ch. Ap., 505), it appeared that the customers of country bankers paid in to the bankers a sum of money in bank notes, and also some bills of exchange, to be remitted to London in order to meet certain acceptances. The bankers sent to their London agents the bills and some bank notes, with a letter directing them to pay a certain sum of money, also giving them notice of the acceptances as payable at their bank, and giving directions as to other business. The country bankers stopped payment, owing a large balance to the London bankers. It was held that, as between the country customers and the London bankers, there was no appropriation of the bills and notes to meet the acceptances, and that the London bankers could retain the bills and notes without meeting the acceptances.

*Discounting Bills.*—To discount a bill is only another name for to purchase it. On discounting a bill the property passes to the banker, and the customer can at once sue for the price, or draw it from his account by cheques. It would be very unusual for a banker to discount a bill which his customer had not indorsed; and so if the discounted bill is dishonoured, the banker can claim its amount from the customer as indorsee.

A banker has full power to deal as he pleases with a discounted bill.

If it is a bill payable at his own bank, and the banker indorses and re-discounts it, the banker is in a double relation to the bill. Thus A draws a bill on his debtor B, payable to A's order. B accepts it payable at the X bank. A is a customer of the X bank, and gets the bank to discount the bill. The X bank indorses the bill to the Y bank. On presentation the X bank pays the bill, though B's account is overdrawn. This may be a payment by the bank as agents of B or as indorsees, and in the latter case, upon giving A due notice of dishonour, the bank may debit A with the amount of the bill as on a dishonoured bill. If there is no evidence to the contrary, the bank will be presumed to have paid as indorsee (*Pollard* v. *Ogden*, 3 E. & B., 459).

*Foreign Bills.*—It is very usual for a banker to refuse to discount foreign bills, except upon the security of the goods in payment of which the bills were drawn; this will be further gone into when the taking of security is considered.

*Marginal Notes.*—There is one arrangement which will be mentioned at once, and that is the practice of giving "marginal notes." When the whole of the price of bills is not paid or credited as cash, but a percentage kept back, which is to bear interest, but only to be payable when advice of the due payment of the bills has been received, and then is to be subject to any other claims of the bankers against the customer, such percentage retained is a margin, and the document expressing the arrangement is called a marginal note. An example is subjoined:—

CHARTERED BANK OF INDIA, AUSTRALIA, AND CHINA.

LONDON, 21*st February* 1873.

| | | |
|---|---:|---:|
| Bills Nos. 426, 427, for Rs.839, 13a. 0p., purchased at 1s. 11¾d., | £79 3 | 5 |
| Paid this day, | 59 3 | 5 |
| Leaving a margin of twenty pounds, | £20 0 | 0 |

to be accounted for to Messrs. Fastnedge & Co., on receipt of advice of the due payment of the above bills, and after providing for any deficiency or other liabilities of the said parties to the bank. Interest to be allowed at Bank of England minimum rates, but not to exceed 5 p. c. p. a.

J. H. SMYTHE, *Manager.*

Such a debt is only a contingent debt, and is not meant to be transferable (*Ex p. Kemp*, L. R., 9 Ch. Ap., 383).

# CHAPTER XV

## BANK INSTRUMENTS

This chapter will deal with those commercial instruments, other than bank notes, which are either exclusively or very usually issued by bankers, viz. bank post bills, letters of credit, and circular letters.

*Bank Post Bills.*—A bank post bill is a bill of exchange drawn and accepted by a bank, and not payable on demand. The only London bank which issues them is the Bank of England. The following is an example of one of their bills:—

No 1.                     LONDON, 1st *November* 1878.

At seven days' sight I promise to pay this my sole Bill of Exchange to A. B. or order, five hundred pounds sterling. Value received of Messrs. C. D. & Co.

             *Accepted*, 1st November 1878.
                           E. F.

             For the Governor and Company of the
                 Bank of England,
                         G. H.

The bank post bills of foreign banks are slightly different in form, and another example is given:—

         No. 445.—UNION BANK POST BILL.

CALCUTTA, 1st *July* 1847.—Company's rupees, 10,000.—At sixty days after sight of this our first Bill of Exchange, second and third of the same tenour and date not paid, we promise to pay on account of the proprietors of the Union Bank of Calcutta, to the order of Messrs. Cockerell, Larpent, & Co., the sum of Co.'s rups. 10,000, value received.

J. RENIER, } Directors.
W. P. GRANT,

These instruments are bills of exchange rather than promissory notes, and require acceptance. In 1855 it was said that the issue of such bills was an approved mode of doing business and was a most beneficial practice, and that such bills had been in use by the Bank of England for a century at the least.

*Letters of Credit.*—Letters of credit are of two kinds, according as they authorise the drawing of cheques or promise the acceptance of bills. In any case they are handed to the customer by the bank granting them, and are shown by the customer to the persons who are requested to give credit on the faith of them. The object of the first kind is generally the transmission of money, that of the second kind the guaranteeing of bills of exchange.

The nature of letters of credit for the transmission of money will be best gathered from an example. In the case of *Orr* v. *Union Bank of Scotland* (1 Macq., 513), it appeared that A, in Glasgow, wanted to pay B, in Liverpool, £460, 9s. A accordingly paid that sum into the Union Bank of Scotland, and obtained from them a letter of credit, addressed to the X bank at Liverpool, in these terms :—" Please to honour the drafts of B to the extent of £460, 9s., and charge the same to the account of our bank." This was posted to B, and the letter containing it was, in the absence of the heads of the business, opened by a clerk, who forged a cheque for the amount, presented the cheque and the letter, received the amount, and absconded. A sought to recover from the Union Bank the payment he had made to them. In the judgment the following rules were laid down:—

A letter of credit is an authority to make the payment indicated by it. Such a payment can only be proved by showing that there has been a draft by the person authorised to draw, and that such draft has been paid.

Payment of a forged draft is no payment as between the person paying and the person whose name is forged; but as through such a payment the person to whom the letter is addressed may get possession of it, the mere possession of the letter by such person is not a proof that a valid payment has been made.

As the person presenting the letter of credit is not necessarily the person entitled to make the draft, the bankers to whom the letter of credit is addressed are bound to do more than demand to see the letter of credit, they must see that the signature to the draft is genuine, or the loss will be their own.

When, for a sum paid down, a banker grants a letter of credit, he must show that it has been complied with, or pay back the money; and he cannot refuse to pay back the money on the ground that the letter of credit has not been returned to him.

A letter of credit is not a negotiable instrument, and the rules applicable to negotiable instruments do not apply to it.

On these grounds the Court held that A could recover from the Union Bank the amount he had paid to them. These rules contain, for practical purposes, the whole of the law on that class of letter of credit.

*Open and Documentary Credits.*—Letters of credit which promise the acceptance of bills of exchange often have blank forms of bills printed on the margin of the letter, and then they are called marginal letters.

A letter of credit may contain an absolute promise, on the part of the bank issuing it, to accept bills up to the limit indicated; or it may contain a promise conditional on the remittance of bills of lading or some other form of security. If the promise is absolute, the letter is generally called an open credit; if the promise is conditional on the remittance of bills of lading, it is generally called a documentary credit.

The object and nature of a documentary letter of credit have been thus stated (*Banner* v. *Johnston*, L. R., 5 E. & I., 157): "A, a merchant in Liverpool, wants to buy some cotton in Pernambuco. In the ordinary course of things he would write out to persons at Pernambuco, and request them to buy the cotton, and draw bills on himself for the price. But the parties may wish to take a different course. A may be a most respectable and solvent person, but, at the same time, it is thought desirable that there should be some name brought into the transaction for the purpose of using it in the Pernambuco market, some name perfectly well known there, whose credit is such that every person would accept it, provided only you can assure the merchant to whom you want to offer the bills drawn on that person that the bills will be accepted when they get home. How is that to be accomplished? There is a bank at Liverpool which has a great reputation, B's bank, and A knows that if he can get a letter from B's bank saying that these bankers will accept the bills when they come home, he can send that letter to his correspondents at Pernambuco, and they will be able to show it to any merchant to whom they might offer the bills to pay for the cotton, and the letter of credit so shown will be a certificate that the bills will be accepted when they come home, and so the bills will pass as current as if they were accepted bills. The letter of credit must contain besides the promise to accept, for the protection of the bankers, orders to those who are dealing with the cotton as to how they are to send home the shipping documents relating to the cotton. These orders are distinct from the promise, and are not for the protection of the bill holders." It follows from this, that if the bank, after accepting the bills, stops payment, and the goods are stopped before they come into the hands of the bank, the bill holders cannot come in as creditors for the whole of the amount of the bills, but can only claim for the surplus remaining after the goods consigned have been applied to satisfy the acceptances.

The object of letters of credit is then, shortly, to substitute the credit of a well-known bank for that of a private merchant, and this will not be effectively done (*a*) unless there is privity between the bill holder and the bank, and (*b*) unless the credit is given irrespective of the state of the accounts between the bank and its customer, the private merchant.

It has accordingly been held that where a letter of credit containing an offer to accept bills is intended, either expressly or as a matter of fair presumption, to be shown to third persons for the purpose of obtaining advances, then, upon such third person advancing money on the faith of the letter, the offer of the banker contained in the letter is turned into a contract between the banker and the person making the advance, and the latter is entitled to sue the banker if he does not accept the bills according to his promise (In re *Agra & Masterman's Bank*, L. R., 2 Ch. Ap., 391).

That bills negotiated under letters of credit will in general be payable irrespective of the state of accounts between the banker and the grantee of the letter is best shown by the same case. There it appeared that Agra & Masterman's bank addressed to D. T. & Co. a letter in these words: "No. 394. You are hereby authorised to draw upon this bank to the extent of £15,000, and such drafts I undertake duly to honour on presentation. This credit will remain in force twelve months from its date, and parties negotiating bills under it are requested to endorse particulars on the back hereof." D. T. & Co. drew bills under this letter to the amount of £6000, and endorsed them to the Asiatic Banking Corporation. The bank was afterwards ordered to be wound up, and as D. T. & Co. were indebted to the bank to an amount exceeding what was due on the bills, the bank claimed to set off their claim against D. T. & Co. against the claim of the Asiatic Banking Corporation, on the ground that the corporation being the equitable assignees of the benefit of a contract between the bank and D. T. & Co., must take subject to the same equities as their assignors—that is, subject to the state of account between the bank and D. T. & Co. Earl Cairns said: "The letter is a general invitation issued by the Agra & Masterman's Bank, through D. T. & Co., to all persons to whom the letter may be shown, to take bills drawn by D. T. & Co. on the Agra & Masterman's Bank with reference to the letter, and to alter their position by paying for such bills, with an assurance that, if they or any of them will do so, the Agra & Masterman's Bank will accept such bills on presentation. . . . Upon the offer in this letter being accepted and acted on by the Asiatic Banking Corporation, there was constituted a valid and binding legal contract against the Agra & Masterman's Bank in favour of the Asiatic Banking Corporation. . . . But, assuming the contract to have been at law a contract with D. T. & Co., and with no other, it is clear that the contract was in equity assignable. . . . Generally speaking, a chose in action assignable only in equity must be assigned subject to the equities existing between the original parties to the contract; but this is a rule which must yield when it appears from the nature or terms of the contract that it must have been intended to be assignable free from and unaffected by such equities. The essence of the letter is, that the person taking bills on the faith of it is to have the absolute benefit of the undertaking in the letter, and to have it in order to obtain the acceptance of the bills which are negotiable instruments payable according to their tenour, and without reference to any collateral or cross claims. Unless this is done, the letter is useless."

If the letter contains conditions or orders which are capable of performance before an advance is made, a person making an advance must see that they are performed, or the person giving the letter of credit will be entitled to refuse acceptance of the bills. In the case of the *Union Bank of Canada* v. *Cole* (47 L. J., C. P., 100), the letter was addressed to the grantee alone, and very long conditions were annexed, the general effect of which was as follows: " When goods have been shipped under the credit, you may draw bills against the shipping documents, and we will accept them. When the goods are not shipped, on giving us the security of the wheat in respect of which you wish to make disbursements, you may also draw bills, without attaching them to the shipping documents. But in that case we shall still have the security of the grain to be shipped; for, in the meantime, the property thus represented is to be held in trust for the givers of the credit as collateral security." The grantee drew a bill on the security of wheat coming to him in the course of business, but not otherwise defined, and not coming within the terms of the letter. The bill was then negotiated, and sent to England for acceptance. The acceptance was refused. The Court held that this refusal was justifiable, as either the directions and conditions showed that the letter was not intended to be shown to and acted on by third parties, or, if the letter was intended to be shown, there was no liability unless such of the conditions as could possibly have been fulfilled when the negotiation took place had then been fulfilled.

*Bankruptcy of Issuing Bank.*—When a bank has issued documentary letters of credit, the bankruptcy of the bank is no reason why the contract between the bank and the bill holder should not be carrred out, as it may be for the advantage of the bank to carry the contract through. In the case of banking companies in liquidation, the liquidator has in suitable cases received permission from the Court to accept and pay such bills. Thus, where the letter of credit authorised the drawing of bills on the deposit of bills of lading for the full amount of the bills of exchange, and before the bills were drawn the bank issuing the letter of credit failed, the grantee treated the failure as equivalent to a breach or repudiation of the contract; but it was held that that view was wrong, and that the grantee was not entitled to recover damages as upon a breach of the contract (*Tondeur, ex p.*, L. R., 5 Eq., 160).

*Circular Notes.*—Circular notes are modified forms of letters of credit, issued in return for money paid, and made payable by the correspondents of the grantors in various foreign towns. They are generally issued for the convenience of persons travelling abroad. A letter of indication is generally given with the notes; the letter is held by the grantee, but addressed to the different correspondents, and contains a space for the signature of the grantee. The correspondents can then require a signature before paying the notes, and have thus some security that they are paying the right person. If the notes are not used abroad, the grantee may return them to the bank and demand his money back. If the notes are lost or stolen, the bank need not refund except upon receiving an indemnity. As in the case of ordinary letters of credit, the rule holds good that a payment to a wrong person, *e.g.* through a forged signature, is not a good payment.

# CHAPTER XVI

## PERSONAL SECURITY

WHERE a bank determines to make advances to a customer on personal security, it may take such security either from the customer alone, or from the customer as principal and his friends as sureties. The security most usually given is a bond, a promissory note, or a guarantee. If a guarantee is taken, it should always be in writing, and signed by the person giving it. The subject may be considered in two parts—first, the relation of the banker to his customer, and then the relation of the banker to the surety, if any; but the former can be disposed of in a few lines.

The fact that the bank has taken personal security from the customer does not prevent the bank suing the customer for the balance of the account, unless the security is in the form of a bond to which the customer is alone a party. Thus, in the case of *Holmes* v. *Bell* (3 Man. & G., 213), it appeared that a banker took from his customer and a surety for him a bond conditioned in a penal sum of £10,000 for the payment of all sums already advanced, or thereafter to be advanced, to the customer. It was held that the banker might sue the customer, upon the simple relation existing between them as creditor and debtor, for the actual balance of £4091.

As a rule, the important question to the banker is whether or no he can sue the surety on the security.

*Statute of Limitations.*—Where the security taken is a promissory note payable on demand, if it is proved that the note was made as collateral security for the customer's banking account, it will remain in force (*i.e.* unbarred by the Statute of Limitations) for a period of six years, not from its date, but from the time when a balance was struck, and a demand made by the bank for payment. In the case of *Hartland* v. *Jukes* (1 H. & C., 667), it appeared that a note for £200, made by the customer and a surety, and dated 5th December 1855, was given to secure the customer's account. The balance against the customer on 31st December 1855 was £173, but no balance was then struck. A balance was struck on 30th June 1856, and every subsequent half-year, until the account was closed, in February 1861, with an adverse balance of £172. An action was not brought on the note until 28th March 1862, more than six years after the date of the note; and it was held that the bank could sue on the note, as six years had not elapsed since the first balance was struck.

A bond has this advantage over a promissory note, that the period for which it will remain in force is twenty instead of six years.

*Continuing Security.*—In the example just given, the note was expressly given as collateral security for the balance. When the promissory note is not payable on demand, but at a fixed date, *primâ facie* it is not intended to be a continuing security to meet the running balance from time to time due on an account, but to be given in consideration of an advance at the date of the note. If the payee asserts that the object of the note was to secure such a balance, the burden of proof lies on the payee. The question whether the note is a continuing security or not is one of the greatest practical importance, as, if the note is not intended to be a continuing security, it will be discharged *pro tanto* by every subsequent payment in to the customer's account, according to the rule in Clayton's case, and this although the adverse balance may not be materially diminished. For an example of this the reader is referred to the case of *Kinnaird* v. *Webster* (L. R., 10 Ch. D., 139), set out at p. 77, *supra*. Just as in the case of a promissory note, on proof that a bond was intended as a continuing security, the rule in Clayton's case will be excluded. Such a proof would be afforded if the bond was to secure the bank against advances which might *from time to time* be made to the customer; but it is not necessary to have an express stipulation if it can be inferred from the language and conduct of the parties, after execution of the bond, that they intended the bond to stand as a continuing security.

*Revocation.*—When the security is a continuing guarantee, either under seal or in writing, it is important to know when and how the surety can put an end to his liability. If the security takes the form of a promissory note, the question does not arise.

A continuing guarantee not under seal is revocable if it has not been acted on, and so far as it has not been acted on. Thus, in the case of *Offord* v. *Davies* (12 C. B. N. S., 748), it appeared that a guarantee was given for the due payment of all bills of exchange discounted for a certain firm to the extent of £600 during twelve months. Before any bills were discounted, the guarantor countermanded the guarantee. The Court considered two questions, namely, (*a*) whether the guarantee could be revoked before it was acted on; (*b*) whether, upon the guarantee being acted on for one bill, it could be revoked as to future bills,—and answered both in the affirmative. Each discount of a bill was held a separate transaction, creating a liability until the bill was met, and after that leaving the offer in the same position as if no discount had been made, that is to say, leaving it capable of revocation until again acted on.

The rule last given is based on the English doctrine of consideration, which does not apply to instruments under seal, such as a bond. Apparently, however, a bond given as a continuing security is revocable upon equitable principles, if the surety pays all that he owes under it at the time of his notice of revocation. Thus, it has been said (*Burgess* v. *Eve*, L. R., 13 Eq., 450), that if a man gives a guarantee that he will be answerable for money to be advanced to A. B., limited to a very large amount,—for example, £20,000,—and after the bank has advanced him £1000 only, the guarantor discovers that the person he has become security for is unworthy of credit, and of a totally different character from what was supposed when the guarantee was given, and that the money which the bank advanced to A. B. was utterly thrown away and wasted, he is entitled to give the bank notice of those facts, and to put an end to his liability by payment of the £1000 advanced. Such a rule does not seem to be a hardship upon the bank.

*Effect of Death.*—In the absence of a special stipulation, notice of the death of the guarantor is a revocation of the guarantee so far as regards advances made after such notice. Thus, in the case of *Coulthart* v. *Clemenson* (L. R., 5 Q. B. D., 42), it appeared that two guarantors jointly and severally guaranteed an overdrawn banking account, together with interest, commission, and other charges. It was stipulated that the guarantee was to be considered a continuing guarantee, and not to be withdrawn, but was to continue in full force until three months after notice to the manager of the bank of intention to discontinue or determine the same. About eight years afterwards, one of the guarantors died, the account being then largely overdrawn. The bank received notice of the death, but continued the account for another three years. Sufficient sums of money, after notice of the death, were paid into the account, and generally appropriated to the current account, to cover any balance which was in fact owing at the time of such notice. When the account was closed, there was an adverse balance of about £3000. The bank sued the executor of the deceased guarantor. The Court held that the bank could not succeed. The provision as to the three months' notice related only to the guarantor's life, and as there was no corresponding provision as to the notice to be given on his death, the guarantee could be legally determined at any time after the guarantor's death, by a proper notice to that effect. As to what constitutes a proper notice, it was said that it is not necessarily a special notice; and notice of the death of the testator, and of the existence of a will, is in general a constructive notice of the determination as to future advances of the guarantee. If the contracting parties desire that on the death of the guarantor a special notice shall be necessary to determine the guarantee, they can so provide in the guarantee itself.

*Discharge through Act of Bank.*—It often happens that just when a banker most wants to enforce his rights against the surety of a customer, the customer having gone as far as the banker can safely allow him, the banker loses his rights against the surety by making a new arrangement, which has in law the effect of discharging the surety, although such discharge is not contemplated either by the bank or the customer. A new agreement with the debtor, in variation of the original contract, is equivalent to a discharge of such original contract, and a substitution of the new contract in its place. It follows that if a third party has guaranteed as surety the due performance of the original contract, on the making of the new agreement he is discharged from liability, and there is nothing to affect him with any liability in respect of the substituted contract, unless, with full knowledge of all the circumstances, he consents to continue surety under it.

If, for instance, the creditor, by a new contract with the debtor, without the consent of the surety, enlarges the time of payment, the surety is discharged. The reason for this rule was thus expressed by Lord Eldon (*Samuell* v. *Howarth*, 3 Mer., 278): "The surety is held to be discharged for this reason, because the creditor, by so giving time to the principal, has put it out of the power of the surety to consider whether he will have recourse to his remedy against the principal or not, and because he, in fact, cannot have the same remedy against the principal as he would have had under the original contract." In another case, where there was a question as to a guaranteed overdraft from a bank, it was said (*Strong* v. *Foster*, 17 C. B., at p. 219): "What I understand by a giving of time in such a case is this—the surety has a right at any moment to go to the creditor and say, 'I have reason to suspect the principal debtor to be insolvent, therefore I call upon you to sue him, or to permit me to sue him.' If the creditor has voluntarily placed himself in such a position as to be compelled to say he cannot sue him, he thereby discharges the surety." Further, if the surety could be sued, as he in his turn would at once sue the principal debtor, the giving of time would have been rendered nugatory.

To produce a discharge of the surety by a giving of time two things are necessary—first, there must be a binding contract to give time, capable of being enforced; secondly, the contract must be with the principal debtor, and not merely with a third person. Thus, in the case of *Clarke* v. *Birley* (L. R., 41 Ch. D., 422), it appeared that the balance of the overdrawn account of a coal company with their bankers had been guaranteed by six sureties up to £25,000. Three of them afterwards, with a new surety, entered into a fresh agreement with the bank, whereby the guarantee was increased by another £8000. It was held that the new arrangement had not the effect of releasing the three sureties who were not parties to it.

It sometimes happens that the creditor may have dealt with the surety as a principal; then, if the creditor afterwards receives notice of the true relation between the surety and the debtor, any subsequent variation of the debt or contract guaranteed, without the consent of the surety, will discharge the surety from liability (*Leake*, 802–804). Thus it appeared, in the case of *Overend, Gurney, & Co.* v. *Oriental Financial Corporation* (L. R., 7 E. & I., 348), that H had brought to Overend's certain bills bearing the acceptances of the Financial Corporation. These bills had been accepted for the accommodation of H and his principals. The bills were renewed on a guarantee by H that the renewed bills should be met at maturity. The renewed bills were not paid, and Overend & Gurney gave, on 6th April 1866, notice of dishonour to all the parties whose names were on the bills. On 9th April the solicitor of the Financial Corporation gave full information to Overend's that H was the real principal on the bills, as the bills had been accepted merely for his accommodation. H afterwards gave, as collateral security, to Overend's bills to a much larger amount drawn on L. L., and Overend arranged with H not to sue on the old bills if the bills on L. L. should be paid. Nothing further was done for some months. These last bills were not paid, and then Overend's brought an action against the Financial Corporation to recover the amount of the bills originally accepted by the Financial Corporation. It was held that the action could not be sustained.

# CHAPTER XVII

## NEGOTIABILITY

A BANKER is constantly being offered by his customers an immense variety of instruments and documents as security for overdrafts. The object of this chapter is to discriminate generally between the various classes into which these documents may fall. To do this effectually, the reader must go back to some of the fundamental principles of English law. The first is that, except in the case of a sale in market overt, no person can acquire a title to a personal chattel from a person who is not an owner. The only exceptions to that rule arise by virtue of a statute, or by some custom of merchants prevailing in this country. The second principle is that the benefit of a contract is not assignable. Thus, if A owed B £100, payable in three months' time, at common law B could not sell the debt to C without A's concurrence. In equity this could be done, but C must give notice to A, and if A had any claim against B, he could enforce it against C, or, in other words, C took subject to equities. The Judicature Act has introduced a statutory assignment of the benefits of a contract, but the assignment has to be in writing, notice must be given to the debtor, and the assignee takes subject to equities. Negotiability is the name given to the exceptional qualities of a negotiable instrument, and a negotiable instrument may be defined as a written contract, the benefit of which will, by the law merchant, pass by indorsement and delivery, or by mere delivery, so that a person taking the instrument *bonâ fide* and for value gets a good title, can sue on it in his own name, and takes it free from any equities which could be enforced against the original holder.

*English Negotiable Instruments.*—The law merchant has made the following English instruments, but no others, negotiable, namely, bills of exchange, including exchequer bills and cheques; promissory notes, including bank notes.

Usage cannot add to that list or take away from it, much less can the isolated action of an individual.

*Foreign Negotiable Instruments.*—In the case of foreign instruments, such as Government bonds and scrip, debentures, and share certificates, containing words making them transferable by delivery, either with or without indorsement, the English Courts have decided, it is not apparent why, to treat such instruments as negotiable, subject only to proof in each particular case, that the instrument in question is, by custom, dealt with in England as a negotiable instrument.

The earliest example of a foreign instrument being held to be negotiable was the case of the King of Prussia's bonds, in which he declared himself and his successors bound to every person who should for the time being be the holders of the bonds for the payment of the principal and interest in a certain manner. It was proved that such bonds were negotiated like exchequer bills. The Court held the bonds to be instruments analogous to exchequer bills and other English instruments negotiable by the law merchant (*Gorgier* v. *Mieville*, 3 B. & C., 45).

The further general question arises, namely, What is

sufficient proof that a foreign instrument is by custom treated as negotiable? This is an important question now that the London market is continually seeing the birth of new instruments, such as corporation bonds of obscure South American towns.

In the case of *Simmons* v. *The London Joint - Stock Bank* (7 *Times*, L. R., 160), in which the subject-matter of the action was the right of the true owner to recover bonds of the Bank of Buenos Ayres, which were securities to bearer, issued with a Government guarantee, and circulated on the European markets, Lord Justice Bowen made the following remarks, though the case itself was decided on another point (see p. 90): "A contractual document may be such that, by virtue of its delivery, all the rights of the transferor are transferred to, and can be enforced by, the transferee against the original contracting party, but it may yet fall short of being a completely negotiable instrument, because the transferee acquires by mere delivery no better title than his transferor. An admission was made at the trial to the effect that these bonds were commonly transferred from hand to hand by delivery, and this must be taken to be true. But the admission was carefully limited, and still left uncovered the question whether they are negotiable instruments in the sense in which bills of exchange and promissory notes are negotiable, so that delivery by a person who has no title confers, nevertheless, a title on a *bonâ fide* holder for value without notice. We shall require either a more unqualified admission, or else more conclusive evidence, before we could accept the view that bonds like these had become part of the currency of this country, so as to have acquired the peculiar characteristics of a completely negotiable instrument." The test implied in those words, that a foreign instrument does not become negotiable unless custom puts it on a level with bills of exchange or bank notes, although well warranted by the early cases, is a stringent one. The Court would probably require evidence that a similar instrument having been lost by the true owner had been claimed by him, and that such claim had been successfully resisted by a *bonâ fide* holder, on the ground that there was a general usage amongst that part of the mercantile community which dealt in such instruments, to treat the instruments as completely negotiable.

The custom to treat a foreign instrument as negotiable must be an English custom, and the custom of the country of its issue is not sufficient. Thus, in the case of *Picker* v. *London and County Banking Company* (L. R., 18 Q. B. D., 515), a question arose as to the rights of a true owner against the *bonâ fide* holder of a Prussian bond without coupons for interest. The evidence showed that these bonds were treated as negotiable instruments in Berlin, but there was no evidence of similar usage in England. It was held that the bond was not negotiable.

*Negotiability by Estoppel.*—Neither usage nor the act of an individual person can make an instrument negotiable which does not fall within one or other of the two classes just dealt with. But a person (*a*) may issue an instrument drawn in such terms, or (*b*) may deal with an instrument so issued in such a way that he thereby represents that, so far as he is concerned, his rights arising upon that particular document shall be regulated on the footing that the instrument has one or all the qualities of negotiability. A person who has made such a representation is precluded, or estopped, when that representation has been acted on by another, from afterwards turning round and setting up claims inconsistent with his former conduct. There is no estoppel where there is no inconsistency. Negotiability by estoppel is a phrase that is becoming popular, but it is a misleading one, as it apparently expresses that an instrument can become negotiable by estoppel, whereas in fact only persons can be estopped, and the phrase merely expresses the fact that a particular person may be estopped from denying that a particular instrument is negotiable.

*Estoppel of the Issuer.*—There cannot be any estoppel unless the instrument contains words purporting to make it transferable by delivery, or by indorsement and delivery. The issuer of such a document will then be estopped from denying that a person who has become the holder of the instrument by delivery, or by indorsement and delivery, is entitled to sue on it, for that would be inconsistent with his representation.

If further words are inserted so that the instrument purports to be assignable free from equities, or if the mere presence of words making the document assignable by delivery, or by indorsement and delivery, is by a usage of trade equivalent to a representation that the instrument is assignable free from equities, the issuer of the instrument will be estopped from setting up as against a person who has become the holder of the instrument, claims which he has against the person to whom he delivered it, for that would be inconsistent with his representation. This does not impair the general rule that an assignee takes subject to equities, for we have already seen (p. 126) that the rule that a chose in action assignable only in equity must be assigned subject to the equities existing between the original parties to the contract, must yield when it appears, from the nature or terms of the contract, that it must have been intended to be assignable free from and unaffected by such equities.

How usage imports a representation into a document

was thus explained by Jessel, M.R.: The Merchant Banking Company had taken iron warrants originally issued by the Bessemer Phœnix Company to Smith & Co., to cover acceptances on behalf of a customer. The warrants were to the effect that so much iron was held by Bessemer, "deliverable, free on board, to Smith & Co., or their assigns, by endorsement hereon." By the usage of the iron trade, such warrants are considered to pass to holders for value free from any vendor's lien. The Merchant Company sought to enforce delivery of the iron without payment of the purchase money, which the original purchasers, Smith & Co., had never paid. It was held that the company could do so; and Jessel, M.R., said: "The form was invented about 1846, and the practice grew general about 1866, and I think, from that time till now, we must consider it, on the evidence, as an established custom, that any man who gives this warrant understands that it shall pass from hand to hand for value by indorsement, and that the indorsee is to have the goods free from any vendor's claim for purchase money. He is not to be asked whether he has a claim or not; if he chooses to issue it in this shape, he tells all the trade that they may safely deal on the faith of that warrant, and whether or not it becomes a negotiable instrument at common law, as distinct from equity, is, to my mind, utterly immaterial. That is the custom, and as the man who issues such a warrant knows that custom, it appears to me that the Phœnix Bessemer Company have issued these exactly as if they had said they were to be deliverable according to the custom of the iron trade, that is, to be deliverable, 'free from any vendor's lien,' to Messrs. Smith & Co., or their assigns, by indorsement. If those words had been inserted, as I think it will be desirable in future they should be inserted, can anybody doubt that the company, by issuing the warrant in that form, would be precluded in equity from afterwards alleging that they were unpaid vendors?" (*Merchant Banking Company* v. *Bessemer*, L. R., 5 Ch. Div., 205).

In the case of *Goodwin* v. *Robarts* (L. R., 1 Ap. Ca., 476), the subject matter of the action was some scrip, which stated on its face that on payment of certain instalments, " the bearer " would be entitled to receive a bond from the Russian Government. Such scrip was by the custom of the Stock Exchange treated as negotiable, and the instrument was therefore itself negotiable, but Earl Cairns rested his decision upon the further ground of estoppel, and said : " The scrip itself would be a representation to any one taking it . . . that if the scrip were taken in good faith, and for value, the person taking it would stand to all intents and purposes in the place of the previous holder ; . . . the plaintiff is in the position of a person who has made a representation on the face of his scrip that it would pass with a good title to any one on his taking it in good faith and for value." The term " bearer " is now so well known, and so constantly used to express the fact that the issuer is willing to have the instrument treated as negotiable so far as his rights are concerned, that the use of that word, apart from any trade custom or usage, is most probably sufficient to constitute a representation to that effect. Whether an instrument purporting to be payable to order would, apart from a trade usage as to the nature of the contract, be held to contain a similar representation, is a more difficult matter to decide, and one on which there is no satisfactory authority.

*Estoppel of Pastholder.*—It does not by any means follow that, because the issuer of an instrument would be estopped from denying that it might be treated as negotiable, subsequent holders would be so estopped. Such holder will only be estopped when he has so dealt with the instrument as to have become a party to the representations it contains. The kind of question which arises is this—A is the owner of an instrument transferable by delivery, and B becomes possessed of it in fraud of A, but manages to pass it on to his bankers, who take it *bonâ fide* and for value, under what circumstances is A precluded from asserting his title to the instrument against the bank? A will be so precluded or estopped when the instrument contains a sufficient representation that a person taking it *bonâ fide* and for value will get a good title (see preceding section), and A has so dealt with it that he has become a party to such representation, or, in other words, when that for A to assert his title to the instrument would be to do something inconsistent with his previous dealings with the instrument. Unluckily, what dealing is sufficient for this purpose is a question which is most uncertain. In the case of *Goodwin* v. *Robarts*, already referred to, the scrip was left by the plaintiff in his broker's hands, and the broker deposited it with his bankers to secure an overdraft. Earl Cairns decided that such dealing made the plaintiff a party to the representation on the face of the scrip, and estopped him from setting up his title as against the bankers. Lord Bramwell, in the recent case of *The Colonial Bank* v. *Cady* (L. R., 15 Ap. Ca., 282), said that he saw no ground for applying the doctrine of estoppel in *Goodwin* v. *Robarts*, as the plaintiff there was not making a claim inconsistent with anything he had theretofore said or done. When high legal authorities disagree, it would not befit the present writer to be dogmatic, and therefore it will be enough to say that, if and so far as Earl Cairns' decision lays down any rule as to the estoppel of holders, as distinguished from issuers, of

instruments not themselves negotiable, there seems a
general desire to distinguish that decision, and treat it as
either applicable only to its own special facts or as
actually wrong, so that the writer can only advise his
readers to wait for absolute certainty on this point until
it has been threshed out in fresh cases. A banker when
taking an instrument not itself negotiable, just as when
dealing with a customer known to be a broker, must for
the present depend upon the honesty of his customer.

## CHAPTER XVIII

### BILLS OF EXCHANGE.

*History.*—A bill of exchange was originally a means by which a trader in one country paid a debt in another country without the transmission of coin. If A in London owed money to C in Paris, but himself was owed an equal sum of money by B in Paris, A would order B to pay C, the debts would be cancelled, and the same effect would have been produced as if A had sent money to C, and B had sent money to A. A's written order to B, sent to C, and acceded to by B, was the first form of a bill of exchange. A was the drawer, B the drawee, who, upon consenting to the arrangement, becomes the acceptor, and C the payee. It was at one time of the essence of a bill that the drawer and acceptor should be traders in different countries; later, it was sufficient if they lived in different towns; now, by English law, it does not matter where the parties live, nor need bills be trade documents. The law as to bills had its origin in the custom of merchants known as the law merchant, and has recently been codified in the Bills of Exchange Act 1882. This chapter will give a summary of that statute.

*Definition.*—A bill of exchange is an unconditional order in writing, addressed by one person to another, signed by the person giving it, requiring the person to whom it is addressed to pay on demand, or at a fixed or determinable future time, a sum certain in money to or to the order of a specified person, or to bearer. The instrument must not order anything but the payment of money, and the order must not be to pay out of a particular fund, though the order, if in unqualified terms, may indicate the fund out of which the drawee is to reimburse himself or the account to be debited with the payment.

*Inland Bills.*—If the bill is, or on the face of it purports to be, drawn and payable within the British Islands, or drawn within the British Islands upon some person resident therein, it is an inland bill; otherwise, it is a foreign bill. Unless the contrary appear on the face of the bill, the holder may treat it as an inland bill.

*Dual Capacity.*—The drawer and payee may be the same person, or the drawee and payee may be the same person. Where the drawer and drawee are the same person (as in a bank post bill), or the drawee is a fictitious person, or a person not having capacity to contract, the holder may treat the instrument either as a bill or as a promissory note. The drawee must be named with reasonable certainty, and so must the payee, unless the bill is payable to bearer. The bill must not be addressed to two or more drawees alternatively or in succession. Where the payee is a fictitious or non-existing person, the bill may be treated as payable to bearer.

*Negotiable Bills.*—A bill is not negotiable if it contains words indicating an intention that it should not be transferable. A negotiable bill may be payable to bearer or to order. It is payable to bearer if expressed to be so, or if the last indorsement is in blank; otherwise, a bill is payable to order.

*Sum Payable.*—The sum payable is generally expressed

both in words and in figures; if there is a discrepancy, the words prevail.

*Time of Payment.*—A bill is payable on demand which is expressed to be payable on demand, or at sight, or on presentation, or in which no time for payment is expressed. An overdue bill, if accepted or indorsed, is, as regards such acceptor or indorser, payable on demand. For bills not payable on demand, three days of grace are allowed. If the last day of grace is a Sunday, Christmas Day, or Good Friday, the bill must be paid on the preceding business day; if a bank holiday, then on the succeeding business day.

*Acceptance.*—An acceptance is the signification by the drawee of his assent to the order of the drawer. It must be written on the bill and be signed by the drawee. The mere signature of the drawee is sufficient. The acceptance must not express that the drawee will perform his promise by any other means than the payment of money.

A bill may be accepted while incomplete, or when overdue, or after dishonour. An acceptance may be general or qualified. A general acceptance assents without qualification to the order of the drawer. A qualified acceptance in express terms varies the effect of the bill as drawn. An acceptance to pay at a particular place is not a qualified acceptance, unless it expressly states that the bill is to be paid there only, and not elsewhere.

*Inchoate Bill.*—A simple signature on a blank stamped paper delivered by the signer in order that it may be converted into a bill, operates as a *primâ facie* authority to fill it up as a complete bill for any amount the stamp will cover, using the signature for that of the drawer, or the acceptor, or an indorser. If a bill is wanting in any material particular, the person in possession of it has a *primâ facie* authority to fill up the omission in any way he thinks fit. A person who becomes a party prior to completion may refuse performance of his contract if the bill is not filled up within a reasonable time, or not strictly in accordance with the authority given, provided that the person suing on the bill is not a holder in due course, to whom the bill has been negotiated after completion.

*Delivery.*—Every contract on a bill is incomplete and revocable until delivery of the instrument in order to give effect thereto, except that a valid acceptance, of which notice has been given to or according to the directions of the person entitled to the bill, is irrevocable. If the bill be in the hands of a holder in due course, a valid delivery of the bill by all parties prior to him, so as to make them liable to him, is conclusively presumed. If the bill is no longer in the possession of a party who has signed it as drawer, acceptor, or indorser, a valid and unconditional delivery by each such party is presumed until the contrary is proved.

*Capacity to Contract.*—Any person who can contract may become liable on a bill, but a corporation can only become liable if it is a trading corporation, for whose business bills are necessary, or if it has express powers to draw, accept, or indorse bills.

The fact that the drawer or an indorser of a bill cannot be sued because of his incapacity to contract in that form, is no defence to the other parties when sued by the holder.

*Signature.*—There is no liability on a bill except upon signature, but a person who signs in a trade or assumed name is liable just as if he had signed in his own name, and the signature of the name of a firm is equivalent to the signature by the person so signing of the names of all persons liable as partners in that firm. A forged or unauthorised signature is wholly inoperative. An unauthorised signature can be afterwards ratified, but a forged signature cannot be ratified. A signature by procuration operates as notice that the agent has but a limited authority to sign, and the principal is only bound by such signature if the agent in so signing was acting within the actual limits of his authority. A signature indicating that the person signing signs for or on behalf of a principal, or in a representative character, does not make him personally liable; but for a signer to escape liability, it is not enough that there should be an addition of words describing him as an agent, or as filling a representative character.

*Consideration.*—Consideration may be (*a*) any consideration sufficient to support a simple contract, or (*b*) an antecedent debt or liability. If value has at any time been given for a bill, the holder is deemed to be a holder for value as regards the acceptor and all parties to the bill who became parties prior to such time. When the holder of a bill has a lien on it, he is a holder for value to the extent of his lien.

An accommodation party to a bill is a person who has in any way signed it without receiving value therefor, and for the purpose of lending his name to some other person. Such a party is liable to a holder for value, even if the holder took the bill knowing that the party was an accommodation party.

*Holder in Due Course.*—A holder in due course is one who has taken a complete and regular bill before it was overdue, or without notice of its previous dishonour, and in good faith and for value, and without notice of defect in the title of the person who negotiated it. The title of a person is defective when he obtained the bill, or its acceptance, by fraud, duress, or force or fear, or other unlawful means, or for an illegal consideration, or when he negotiates it in breach of faith, or under such circumstances as amount to a fraud. An innocent holder, whether for value or not (*e.g.* a banker who holds for collection), who derives his title to a bill through a holder in due course, has all the rights of that holder in due course as regards the acceptor and all parties to the bill prior to that holder.

*Presumptions of Value and Good Faith.*—Every party whose signature appears on a bill is *primâ facie* deemed to have become a party for value. Every holder of a bill is *primâ facie* deemed to be a holder in due course; but if, in an action in a bill, it is admitted or proved that the acceptance, issue, or subsequent negotiation of the bill is affected with fraud or illegality, the burden of proof is shifted, unless and until the holder proves that, subsequent to the alleged fraud or illegality, value has in good faith been given for the bill. This section has been held to mean that, when fraud is proved, the burden of proof is on the holder to prove, both that value has been given, and that it has been given in good faith and without notice of the fraud (*Tatam* v. *Hasler*, L. R., 23 Q. B. D., 345).

*Transference of Bills.*—A person becomes the holder of a bill payable to bearer, by delivery of the bill, of a bill payable to order, by indorsement of the holder followed by delivery. A transferee of a bill payable to order who takes for value, but without indorsement, gets such title as the transferor had, but no better title. He has the right to demand the indorsement of the transferor.

*Indorsement.*—An indorsement, to be effective, must be written on the bill, but need not be more than a simple signature. It must be an indorsement of the entire bill. If, in a bill payable to order, the payee or indorsee is wrongly designated, or his name is misspelt, he may indorse the bill as therein described, adding, if he think fit, his proper signature. Indorsements on a bill are taken to have been made in the order in which they appear on the bill, until the contrary is proved. An indorsement may be in blank, and then the bill becomes payable to bearer; or special, when a person is specified to whom or to whose order the bill is to be payable, and then the indorsee is practically in the position of a payee. The indorsement may also contain restrictive terms. The payer of a bill may pay an indorsee without regard to conditions attached to the indorsement.

When a bill has been indorsed in blank, any holder may convert the blank indorsement into a special indorsement, by writing above the indorser's signature a direction to pay the bill to or to the order of himself or some other person.

A restrictive indorsement is such as—" Pay D, only " or " Pay D for the account of X," or " Pay D, or order, for collection." Such an indorsement gives the indorsee the rights of the indorser, but gives him no power to transfer his rights as indorsee without express authority; and where such authority exists, subsequent indorsees take the bill with the same rights, and subject to the same liabilities, as the first indorsee under the restrictive indorsement.

*Overdue and Dishonoured Bills.*—A bill continues to be negotiable until restrictively indorsed or discharged by payment or otherwise. An overdue bill can only be negotiated subject to any defect of title affecting it at its maturity. A bill payable on demand (*e.g.* a cheque), is overdue when it appears from the face of the bill that it has been in circulation an unreasonable time. An indorsement not dated after maturity is *primâ facie* deemed to have been made before maturity. A dishonoured bill not overdue is, in the hands of a person taking with notice of the dishonour, subject to any defect of title attaching to it at the time of dishonour.

*Rights of Holder.*—The holder of a bill may sue on the bill in his own name. When his title is defective (*a*) he can give to a holder in due course a better title than he has himself got, and (*b*) payment to him in due course discharges the payer. If he is himself a holder in due course, he holds the bill free from any defect of title of prior parties, as well as from mere personal defences available to prior parties among themselves, and may enforce payment against all parties liable on the bill.

*Presentment for Acceptance.*—A bill payable after sight must be presented for acceptance in order to fix its maturity. A bill may expressly stipulate for presentment for acceptance; if that is so, or if the bill is drawn payable elsewhere than at the residence or place of business of the drawee, it must be presented for acceptance before presentation for payment; otherwise, the bill need not be presented for acceptance to render liable any party to the bill.

When a bill payable after sight is negotiated, the holder must either present it for acceptance or negotiate it within a reasonable time, and if he do not do so, the drawer and all indorsers prior to that holder are discharged.

*Mode of Presentment.*—The presentment must be by the holder or his agent to the drawee or his agent at a reasonable hour on a business day, and before the bill is overdue; if the drawee is dead, presentment may be made to his personal representatives; if bankrupt, to him or his trustee: where authorised by agreement or usage, a presentment through the Post-Office is sufficient.

*Presentment excused.*—Presentment is excused, and a bill may be treated as dishonoured by non-acceptance, if the drawee is dead or bankrupt, or is a fictitious person, or one incapable of contracting, or if, after the exercise of reasonable diligence, it cannot be affected; but not merely because the holder has reason to believe that the bill will be dishonoured.

*Non-acceptance.*— A bill duly presented and not accepted within the customary time must be treated as dishonoured by non-acceptance, or else the holder will lose his right of recourse against the drawer and indorsers. Such right of recourse immediately accrues, and no presentment for payment is necessary.

*Qualified Acceptance.*—The holder need not accept a qualified acceptance, and if that is all that he can get from the drawee, he may treat the bill as dishonoured by non-acceptance.

Where the holder takes a qualified acceptance, without authority from the drawer or an indorser, such drawer or indorser is discharged from liability, unless there is a subsequent assent to the qualified acceptance. Such assent is deemed to have been given if the drawer or indorser has received notice, and does not, within a reasonable time, express his dissent to the holder.

*Presentment for Payment*—(a) *When necessary.*—As a general rule, a bill must be presented for payment, otherwise the drawer and indorsers will be discharged. A bill presented at the proper place, where, after the exercise of reasonable diligence, no one authorised to pay or refuse payment can be found, need not be further presented; and presentment is dispensed with, where, after the exercise of reasonable diligence, it cannot be effected, or where the drawee is a fictitious person, or where presentment has been waived; and under certain circumstances in the case of an accommodation bill as to the accommodated parties.

The fact that the holder has reason to believe that the bill will, on presentment, be dishonoured, does not dispense with the necessity for presentment.

(b) *Time.* — Presentment of a bill not payable on demand must be made on the day it falls due, and of a bill payable on demand within a reasonable time after issue in order to make the drawer liable, or within a reasonable time after indorsement in order to make an indorser liable.

(c) *Mode.*—The bill must be presented by the holder or his authorised agent at the proper place to the payer, or his authorised agent at a reasonable hour on a business day.

(d) *Proper Place.*—The proper place is first the place of payment (if any) specified in the bill; secondly, the address of the acceptor (if any) appearing on the bill; thirdly, the acceptor's place of business, if known; fourthly, the acceptor's ordinary residence, if known; and as a last resource, wherever the acceptor can be found, or his last known place of business or residence.

(e) *Death of Acceptor.*—If the acceptor is dead and no place of payment is specified, presentment must be made to a personal representative, if such there be, and with the exercise of reasonable diligence he can be found.

(f) *By Post.*—If authorised by agreement or usage, a presentment through the Post-Office is sufficient.

(g) *Excusable Delay.*—Delay in making presentment is excused when the delay is caused by circumstances beyond the control of the holder, and not imputable to his default, misconduct, or negligence. When the cause of delay ceases to operate, presentment must be made with reasonable diligence.

*Dishonour by Non-Payment.*—This occurs when a bill is duly presented and payment is refused or cannot be obtained, or when presentment is excused and the bill is overdue and unpaid. Upon such dishonour a right of recourse against the drawers and indorsers accrues to the holder.

*Notice of Dishonour*—(a) *When necessary.*—When a bill has been dishonoured, either by non-acceptance or non-payment, as a general rule notice of dishonour must be given to the drawer and each indorser, and any drawer or indorser to whom such notice is not given is discharged. But if a bill is dishonoured by non-acceptance, the rights of a holder in due course, who has taken the bill after an omission to give notice, are not prejudiced by such omission. Due notice of dishonour for non-acceptance excuses notice for non-payment, unless in the meantime the bill has been accepted.

Notice is dispensed with when, after the exercise of reasonable diligence, it cannot be given to, or does not reach, the drawer or indorser sought to be charged; or if it has been waived; or under certain circumstances as to the accommodated parties in the case of an accommodation bill; or if the drawer or indorser is the person to whom the bill was presented for payment.

(b) *Successive Notices.*—Where a bill, when dishonoured, is in the hands of an agent, he may either himself give notice to the parties liable on the bill, or he may give notice to his principal. If he gives notice to his principal, he must do so within the same time as if he were the holder, and the principal, upon receipt of such notice, has himself the same time for giving notice as if the agent had been an independent holder.

Where a party to a bill receives due notice of dishonour, he has, after the receipt of such notice, the same period of time for giving notice to antecedent parties that the holder has after dishonour.

(c) *By Whom.*—The notice must be given by or on behalf of the holder, or by or on behalf of an indorser, who, at the time of giving it, is himself liable on the bill.

(d) *Effect.*—Where the notice is given by or on behalf of the holder, it enures for the benefit of all subsequent holders and all prior indorsers who have a right of recourse against the party to whom it is given; where given by or on behalf of an indorser, it enures for the benefit of the holder and all indorsers subsequent to the party to whom notice is given.

(e) *Mode.*—The notice may be, but need not be, in writing. It must identify the bill and intimate that it has been dishonoured by non-acceptance or non-payment. The return of a dishonoured bill is a sufficiently formal notice. A misdescription of the bill does not make the notice bad, unless it misleads the person to whom the notice is given. The notice may be given to the person entitled to notice, or to his special agent. If the drawer or indorser is dead, and the person giving notice knows that fact, the notice must be given to a personal representative, if such there be, and if with the exercise of reasonable diligence he can be found; if the drawer or indorser is bankrupt, notice may be given to such party himself or to his trustee.

(f) *Time.*—Notice may be given as soon as the bill is dishonoured, and must be given within a reasonable time. In general, a notice, if the persons to give and receive it reside in the same place, must be sent off in time to be received on the day after the dishonour of the bill, otherwise it must be sent off on the day after the dishonour of the bill, if there is a post at a convenient hour on that day; and if there is no such post, then by the next post thereafter. Where a notice is duly addressed and posted, the sender is deemed to have given due notice, notwithstanding any miscarriage by the Post-Office.

*Protest.*—In the case of the dishonour of a foreign bill, appearing on the face of it to be such, it must be protested, otherwise the drawer and indorsers will be discharged. The chief features of protesting are:

(a) *Mode.*—A protest must contain a copy of the bill, and must be signed by the notary making it, and must specify (1) the person at whose request the bill is protested, and (2) the place and date of protest, the cause or reason for protesting the bill, the demand made, and the answer given, if any, or the fact that the drawee or acceptor could not be found.

(b) *Time.*—When a bill is noted or protested, it must, in general, be noted on the day of its dishonour. When a bill has been duly noted, the protest may be subsequently extended as of the date of the noting. Where the acceptor of a bill becomes bankrupt or insolvent, or suspends payment before it matures, the holder may cause the bill to be protested for better security against the drawer and indorsers.

(c) *Place.*—A bill must be protested at the place where it is dishonoured, except that if presented and returned through the post dishonoured, it may be protested at the place of return, and on the day of its return if received during business hours; and if not so received, then not later than the next business day.

(d) *Lost Bill.*—Where a bill is lost or destroyed, or is wrongly detained from the person entitled to hold it, protest may be made on a copy or written particulars of it.

*Position of Acceptor.*—The acceptor is liable on a bill accepted generally without presentment for payment, and also on a bill with a qualified acceptance, unless it is expressly stipulated that he is to be discharged by the omission to present the bill on the day that it matures. He is not entitled to have the bill protested or to notice of dishonour. The payer may demand to see the bill before payment, and to have it delivered up upon payment.

*Funds in Drawee's Hands.*—A bill does not operate as an assignment of funds in the hands of the drawee available for its payment, and if the drawee does not duly accept he is not liable on the bill. In Scotland the bill does operate as such an assignment from the time when the bill is presented to the drawee.

*Effect of Acceptance.*—The acceptor by accepting a bill engages that he will pay it according to the tenor of his acceptance, and is precluded from denying to a holder in due course (*a*) the existence of the drawer, the genuineness of his signature, and his capacity and authority to draw the bill; (*b*) if the bill is drawn payable to drawer's order the then capacity of the drawer to indorse, if payable to a third person's order the existence of the payee and his then capacity to indorse, but not the genuineness or validity of the drawer's or payee's indorsement.

*Effect of Drawing.*—The drawer of a bill by drawing it (*a*) engages that on due presentment it shall be accepted and paid according to its tenor, that if it be dishonoured he will compensate the holder or any indorser who is compelled to pay it, provided that the requisite proceedings on dishonour be duly taken, and (*b*) is precluded from denying to a holder in due course the existence of the payee and his then capacity to indorse.

*Effect of Indorsing.*—The indorser of a bill by indorsing it makes a similar engagement as to the holder or a subsequent indorser, and is precluded from denying (*a*) to a holder in due course the genuineness and regularity in all respects of the drawer's signature and all previous indorsements, and (b) to subsequent indorsees that the bill was at the time of his indorsement a valid and subsisting bill, and that he had then a good title to it.

*Stranger.*—Where a person signs a bill otherwise than as drawer or acceptor, he incurs the liabilities of an indorser to a holder in due course.

*Measure of Damages.*—If a bill is dishonoured, the holder may recover from any party liable on the bill, and the drawer who has been compelled to pay the bill may recover from the acceptor, and an indorser who has been compelled to pay may recover from the acceptor, the drawer, or a prior indorser (1) the amount of the bill ; (2) interest from the time of presentment if the bill is payable on demand, otherwise interest from maturity ; (3) the expenses of noting or protest when necessary. In the case of a bill dishonoured abroad, the damages may be the amount of the re-exchange, with interest till the time of payment.

*Transfer by Delivery.*—The holder of a bill payable to bearer may negotiate it by delivery without indorsement; he does not become liable on the instrument, but he warrants to his immediate transferee for value that the bill is what it purports to be, that he has a right to transfer it, and that at the time of transfer he is not aware of any fact which renders it valueless.

*Discharge of Bill*—(a) *Payment.*—Payment in due course is payment made at or after the maturity of the bill to the holder of it in good faith, and without notice that his title to it is defective. Such payment discharges the bill when made by or on behalf of the drawee or acceptor, and in the case of an accommodation bill when made by the party accommodated.

In the case of a bill payable to or to the order of a third

person, payment by the drawer gives him the power to enforce payment of it against the acceptor, but not power to re-issue the bill.

Where a bill is paid by an indorser, or where a bill payable to drawer's order is paid by the drawer, the party paying it is remitted to his former rights as regards the acceptor or antecedent parties, and he may, if he thinks fit, strike out his own and subsequent indorsements, and again negotiate the bill.

A bill is also discharged by the acceptor becoming the holder of it in his own right at or after its maturity.

(*b*) *Waiver.*—A bill is discharged by the holder, at or after its maturity, absolutely renouncing his rights against the acceptor. The renunciation must be in writing, unless the bill is delivered up to the acceptor.

(*c*) *Cancellation.*—A bill is discharged by the intentional cancellation of the bill by the holder or his agent, if the cancellation is apparent. If such cancellation is of the signature of a party liable on the bill, such party is discharged, so is any indorser who would have had a right of recourse against him. An unintentional, mistaken, or unauthorised cancellation is inoperative.

(*d*) *Alteration.*—Where a bill or acceptance is materially altered without the assent of all parties liable on the bill, the bill is avoided except as against a party who has himself made, authorised, or assented to the alteration, and subsequent indorsers, provided when such alteration is not apparent, a holder in due course may enforce payment of the bill according to its original tenor. Among material alterations are—any alteration of the date, sum payable, time of payment, place of payment, and where a bill has been accepted generally, the addition of a place of payment without the acceptor's assent.

*Acceptance for Honour.*—Where a bill has been protested for dishonour by non-acceptance, or protested for better security, and is not overdue, any person, not being a person already liable on it, may with the consent of the holder intervene and accept the bill *supra* protest, for the honour of any party liable on it; but if the acceptance does not expressly state for whose honour it is made, it is deemed to be an acceptance for the honour of the drawer. Such an acceptance to be valid must be written on the bill, indicate that it is an acceptance for honour, and be signed by the acceptor for honour. An acceptor for honour engages to pay the bill on due presentment, if it is not paid by the drawee, provided it has been duly presented for payment, and protested for non-payment, and that he receive notice of these facts. An acceptor for honour is liable to the holder and all parties subsequent to the party for whose honour he has accepted.

When a bill is dishonoured by the acceptor for dishonour, it must be protested for non-payment by him.

*Payment for Honour.*—Where a bill has been protested for non-payment, any person may intervene and pay it *supra* protest for the honour of any party liable on it; such payment must be attested by a notarial act of honour founded on a declaration made by the payer for honour, or his agent in that behalf, declaring his intention to pay the bill for honour, and for whose honour he pays. Payment for honour discharges all parties subsequent to the party for whose honour it is paid, and the payer succeeds to both the rights and duties of the holder as regards the party for whose honour he pays and all parties liable to that party. The payer for honour on paying to the holder the amount of the bill and the notarial expenses incidental to its dishonour is entitled to receive both the bill itself and the protest. Where the holder of a bill refuses to receive payment *supra* protest, he loses his right of recourse against any party who would have been discharged by such payment.

*Lost Bill.*—If the holder loses a bill not overdue, he is entitled to another from the drawer upon giving a sufficient indemnity against other claims on the lost bill. In an action on a bill the Court or a judge may order that its loss shall not be set up, provided a satisfactory indemnity be given.

*Bills in a Set.*—Where a bill is drawn in a set, each part of the set being numbered, and containing a reference to the other parts, the whole of the parts constitute one bill, and subject to exceptions discharge of one part is a discharge of the whole. The acceptance must be written on one part only, and a drawee who accepts more than one part is liable to different holders in due course as on separate bills. So an acceptor who pays without the delivery to him of the part signed by him, and that part at maturity is outstanding in the hands of a holder in due course, is liable to the holder of it. So an indorser of parts to different persons is liable on every such part. Where two or more parts of a set are negotiated to different holders in due course, the holder whose title first accrues is as between such holders deemed the true owner of the bill, but without prejudice to the rights of a person who in due course accepts or pays the part first presented to him.

*Conflict of Laws.*—The validity of a bill as regards requisites in form is determined by the law of the place of issue, as regards requisites in form of acceptance, indorsement, or acceptance *supra* protest by the law of the place where such contract was made; but a bill issued out of the United Kingdom is not invalid merely because it is not stamped in accordance with the law of the place of issue, and if it conforms, as regards requisites in form, to the law of the United Kingdom it may, for the purpose of enforcing payment, be treated as valid between all persons who negotiate, hold, or become parties to it in the United Kingdom. The interpretation of the drawing, indorsement, acceptance, or acceptance *supra* protest is determined by the law of the place where such contract is made, but a foreign indorsement on an inland bill is to be interpreted as regards the payer according to the law of the United Kingdom. The duties of the holder as to presentment for acceptance or payment, and the necessity for or sufficiency of a protest or notice of dishonour are determined by the laws of the place where the act is done or the bill is dishonoured.

Where a bill is drawn out of but payable in the United Kingdom, and the sum payable is not expressed in English currency, the amount is, in the absence of express stipulation, to be calculated according to the rate of exchange for sight drafts at the place of payment on the day the bill is payable.

The date of a bill drawn in one country and payable in another is determined according to the law of the place where it is payable.

*Cheques.*—For this division, see Ch. XIII, at p. 95, and Ch. XIV, at p. 108.

*Promissory Notes.*—A promissory note is an unconditional promise in writing made by one person to another signed by the maker, engaging to pay, on demand or at a fixed or determinable future time, a sum certain in money, to or to the order of a specified person or bearer.

If the instrument is payable to the maker's order, it is not a note until it is indorsed by the maker.

A note may contain a pledge of collateral security with authority to sell and dispose of such security.

A note is incomplete until delivered to the payee or bearer.

Where there are two or more makers, they are liable according to the tenor of the note.

Where a note runs "I promise to pay," and is signed by two or more persons, it is deemed to be their joint and several note.

If an indorsed note payable on demand is not presented for payment within a reasonable time of the indorsement, the indorser is discharged.

Where a note payable on demand is negotiated, it is not deemed to be overdue, for the purpose of affecting the holder with defects of title of which he had no notice, by reason that it appears that a reasonable time for presenting it for payment has elapsed since its issue.

Presentment for payment is not necessary in order to render the maker liable, unless it is in the body of it made payable at a particular place, and then it must be presented at that place. Presentment is necessary in order to render an indorser liable.

The maker of a promissory note by making it engages that he will pay it according to its tenor, and is precluded from denying to a holder in due course the existence of the payee and his then capacity to indorse.

With the necessary modifications provisions as to bills apply to notes, and the maker of a note corresponds with the acceptor of a bill, the first indorser of a note with the drawer of an accepted bill payable to drawer's order. The provisions in connection with acceptance do not apply to notes, nor those as to bills in a set; and a dishonoured foreign note need not be protested.

*Good Faith.*—A thing is deemed to be done in good faith where it is in fact done honestly, whether it is done negligently or not.

*Signature.*—A person may sign by an authorised agent.

## CHAPTER XIX

### MISCELLANEOUS SECURITIES

*Exchequer Bills.*—An Exchequer bill is a kind of Government Bill of Exchange payable at a fixed future day, bearing interest from day to day from the date of its issue. It is usual for the buyer to pay the accrued interest. The following is an example of the form of an Exchequer bill issued in the year 1836:—

No. 8551, £1000.—By virtue of an Act, 6th and 7th Gulielm IV, Regis, for raising the sum of £14,007,950 by exchequer bills, for the service of the year 1836-7, this bill entitles ————, or order, to one thousand pounds, and interest after the rate of twopence halfpenny per centum per diem, payable out of the first aids or supplies to be granted in the next session of Parliament, and this bill is to be current and pass in any of the public revenues, aids, taxes, or supplies, or to account of His Majesty's exchequer at the Bank of England, after the 5th day of April 1837. Dated at the Exchequer this 19th day of December 1836. If the blank is not filled up, this bill will be paid to bearer. The cheques must not be cut off. J. NEWPORT.

If the blank is not filled up, the bill is transferable by delivery. If the blank is filled up, it will not be paid without the indorsement of the person whose name appears in the blank.

It has already been said (p. 138) that an Exchequer bill is by the law merchant a negotiable instrument.

Thus it appeared in the case of *Wookey v. Pole* (4 B. & Ald., 1) that an Exchequer bill, the blank in which was not filled up, had been placed for sale in the hands of A. A, instead of selling it, deposited it at his bankers, who made him advances to the amount of its value. A afterwards became bankrupt, and the banker kept it to satisfy the balance of the overdraft on A's account. It was held that the owner of the bill who had placed it in A's hands could not sue the banker for it.

*Dividend Warrants and Government Drafts.*—A dividend warrant is an order issued by the Bank of England to their cashiers, ordering them to pay to the owner of Government stock so much money by way of dividend. These warrants were, and still are, in some such form as the following, viz. :—

120th No. 28,729.        Reduced £3 per Cent. Annuities.
     28,237.

*To the Cashiers of the Bank of England.*

Pay to Joseph Ashby Partridge,
The sum of thirty-seven pounds ten shillings,
                         £37, 10s. 0d.,
for half a year's annuity, which became due the 15th day of April 1841, on the sum of £2500 interest or share in the capital or joint stock of reduced annuities at £3 per cent. per annum, consolidated by Acts of Parliament of the 25th and 26th of George II and the 5th and 21st of George III, and by other subsequent Acts, charged on the Sinking Fund.        J. GRETTON.

End. W. Hill.

I do hereby acknowledge to have received of the Bank of England the above-mentioned sum, in full payment for half a year's annuity, due as aforesaid, Witness my hand this 6th day of April 1841,
     *Witness*, G. ELLIS.           F. WAKEFIELD, *Attorney.*

It is a general rule for Government drafts to have a receipt attached to them, which the payee must fill up before demanding payment.

Where the warrant or draft is made out merely to the payee, and without words making it payable to the assignee of the payee, the instrument is not negotiable, and no usage of the mercantile world can now make it negotiable, nor can any estoppel arise to that effect, as there is no representation on its face that it is transferable by delivery. In the case of *Partridge* v. *Bank of England* (9 Q. B., 396), from which the above form of dividend warrant is taken, it was proved that one Wakefield had been authorised by Partridge to receive his dividends, that Wakefield in fraud of Partridge had given the warrant to his bankers for good consideration, and that the bankers had received credit for the warrant in their account with the Bank of England. Partridge sued the bank for the dividend due to him, and it was held that he could succeed. Partridge had never been paid, nor had he done anything which would preclude him from saying that he had been paid. It seems clear that the mere signing of the receipt is no ground of estoppel, as anybody taking the instrument after such signature takes it on the supposition that it has not been paid, and therefore the signature of the receipt cannot be a representation to any other effect than that the warrant has been in the hands of the person named in it; there is no representation that such person has parted with it or authorised any one to demand payment of it.

It is the custom of the Bank of England to pay such drafts or warrants, when duly signed, to any one who presents them; but they are not bound to do so, and they take upon themselves the risk of paying the wrong person.

On the same principle, a banker who collects for a customer the money due under such a warrant is liable, if the customer had no title, to an action by the true owner for the conversion of his warrant, in which action the damages will be the value of the warrant.

*Post-Office Orders.*— It is usual for customers to pay into their banking accounts post-office orders for the purposes of collection in the same way as cheques or bills. But it must be noted that such instruments are not negotiable (see p. 138), so that the banker gets no better title than the customer had. If, therefore, the banker collects what is due on them for a customer who is not entitled to the orders, he will be liable to account for their value to the true owner. Nor can the banker escape from this liability on the ground of any estoppel arising out of representations on the face of such instruments to which the owner may have become a party.

The Post-Office regulations with regard to post-office orders provide that, when presented for payment by a banker, they shall be payable without the signature by the payee of the receipt contained in the order, provided that the name of the banker presenting the order is written or stamped upon it. In the case of the *Fine Art Society* v. *Union Bank of London, Ltd.* (L. R., 17 Q. B. D., 705), it appeared that the plaintiffs banked with the defendants, and that it was the duty of the secretary to pay all moneys received by him on behalf of the plaintiffs into the defendant's bank to the credit of the plaintiffs. The secretary, without the knowledge of the plaintiffs, kept a private account at the defendants' bank. He paid into his private account post-office orders belonging to the plaintiffs, which the bank subsequently cashed. The plaintiffs sued the bank for the amount of the orders. It was argued on behalf of the bank that the plaintiffs were estopped from setting up their title because they entrusted to their secretary, for the purpose of their being paid into and cashed through a bank, instruments which in the hands of a banker become quasi-negotiable, instruments stating in their face that when presented by a banker they are payable without the signature of the payee. They thus gave the secretary the means of committing this fraud, and of inducing the bank to collect the orders and hand over the proceeds to him, and therefore should bear the loss. The Court held otherwise, and decided that the bankers must bear the loss.

*Iron Warrants.*—An iron warrant is a document issued by an ironmaster to a purchaser to enable the latter to sub-sell before delivery of the iron. It is obvious at once, from principles before referred to, that the sub-purchaser will not be able to claim delivery of the iron free from vendor's lien, unless there has been some representation on the part of the ironmaster that he will not insist on his lien as against a sub-purchaser who produces his iron warrant. In the case of *Merchant Banking Company* v. *Bessemer* (L. R., 5 Ch. D., 205), a case already dealt with at length on p. 143, the warrants were for iron "deliverable (f.o.b.) to Smith & Co., or their assigns, by indorsement thereon." The warrants came into the hands of the plaintiffs, who were bankers, as securities for bills accepted by the bankers on behalf of their customers, Smith & Co. Smith & Co. had not paid for the iron. It was proved that by the usage of the iron trade, any man who gave such a warrant understood that it would pass from hand to hand for value by indorsement, and that the indorsee was to have the goods free from any vendor's claim for purchase money. The Court held that the bankers were entitled to the iron free from the vendor's claim.

The question whether the bankers would have been entitled to hold such documents against a true owner rests on different considerations, namely, first, whether there was any representation either express or implied that a *bonâ fide* holder for value should get a good title irrespective of any defect in the title of a previous holder; and secondly, whether the conduct of the true owner had been such as to make him a party to such representations. These questions have never yet arisen in the case of these iron warrants. It has already been said that the latter question as to money securities has led to a divergence of opinions amongst the highest legal authorities.

It would give an incomplete view of the position of these documents if no reference was made to the case of *Dixon* v. *Bovill* (3 Macq., 1). This was a decision of the House of Lords in 1866, on the effect of an instrument given by an ironmaster to his vendee in these words, "I will deliver 1000 tons of iron when required, after Sept. 18th next, to the party lodging this document with me." No evidence of the practice or usage of the iron trade was given. The only point decided was that the instrument was not negotiable. If the case was reargued to-day, the plaintiff's case would be that as in the case last quoted, the ironmaster was estopped from setting up his vendor's lien. But it does not necessarily follow that the decision would be different now, unless evidence of trade usage was brought forward, for there were no words expressly making the contract assignable free from equities, and there was no evidence of a trade usage which could import by implication the required meaning into that phrase.

*Bills of Lading.*—(*Leake*, pp. 1195–1201, Smith's Leading Cases, vol. i., notes to *Lickbarrow* v. *Mason*.) A bill of lading is the document signed by the master of a ship upon the shipment of goods for carriage, acknowledging the receipt of the goods on board, and undertaking to deliver them to the consignee, "or to his order or assigns," upon payment of the freight therein stipulated for. By the custom of merchants, a bill of lading is taken to represent the goods shipped, and the indorsement and delivery of the bill of lading by the shipper or owner of the goods transfers the property to the indorsee, and subsequent transfers by the indorsee of the bill of lading are equivalent to a transfer of the property in the goods.

The consignor may stop goods *in transitu* before they get into the hands of the consignee, if the consignee has become insolvent; but if the consignee has assigned the bills of lading to a third person for a valuable consideration, the right of the consignor, as against such assignee, is divested.

Bills of lading are usually drawn in sets of three, one of which is given to the master of the ship, another forwarded to the consignee, and the last kept by the consignor as a protection against fraud on the part of the master of the ship.

A banker does not become a holder of a bill of lading until it has been indorsed by the consignee, and in practice he takes it as security either direct from a consignee who is a customer, or from some customer who has received it from the consignee.

The first question to be asked is, "When is a banker, who takes direct from the consignee, a holder for value?" Value in the case of a bill of lading is the same as in the case of bills of exchange and promissory notes, in that an antecedent debt or liability is a good consideration. Therefore a banker who takes a bill of lading to secure past advances is a transferee for value. This was established in the case of *Leask* v. *Scott* (L. R., 2 Q. B. D., 376). In that case it appeared that Geen & Co., the consignee of goods, were indebted to Leask. On a Saturday they applied to Leask for a further advance, which he agreed to make on being first covered. Geen & Co. promised to give him cover (not naming anything in particular), and Leask advanced them a further sum of £2000, being content with their promise. On the following Tuesday the bill of lading of the goods in question, consigned by Scott to Geen & Co., came to the possession of the latter, who, on the following day, Wednesday, deposited it with the plaintiff in fulfilment of their promise to cover him. Geen & Co. stopped payment before the goods arrived, and Scott sought to stop the goods *in transitu*. The question raised was this, was Leask a holder for value inasmuch as the advance of £2000 having been made before the transference of the bill of lading, was a past consideration, and, as such, in general, incapable of supporting a contract. The Court of Appeal held that the consideration was good, as it had a present operation by staying the hand of the creditor. They said that to hold otherwise would make commercial law a tissue of niceties; for instance, in the present case Leask might have said, "I cannot take this bill of lading safely as the consideration would be past, do it with the broker next door, and give me his cheque," an arrangement that would have been valid. A banker then will be safe in allowing his customer to overdraw on the faith of a similar vague promise, for the banker will take for value bills of lading subsequently handed over in pursuance of the promise; so, too, if a banker demands security for an account already overdrawn, bills of lading handed over in pursuance of such demand will be held for value. *A fortiori*, if a banker in return for the transference of bills of lading gives the customer some definite present benefit, such as a promise to forbear from pressing or suing for past advances or an actual advance, or the promise of future advances, the banker is a transferee for value.

A banker may fail to get a good title to a bill of

lading on the ground that his customer had no title, or was not authorised to transfer. A bill of lading is not negotiable in the sense that the transfer of it to a *bonâ fide* holder for value can pass to such transferee a better title to the property represented by it than the transferor himself had. The bill of lading only represents the goods, and the transfer of a bill of lading only gives a title to the goods when an actual transfer of the goods under the same circumstances would give a title. As has been said, the rule of the common law is that except by a sale in market overt no one can give a better title to goods than he himself possesses. It has been accordingly laid down that although the shipper may have indorsed in blank a bill of lading deliverable to his assigns, his right is not affected by an appropriation of it without his authority. If it be stolen from him, or transferred without his authority, a subsequent *bonâ fide* transferee for value cannot make title under it, as against the shipper of the goods (*Gurney* v. *Behrends*, 3 E. & B., 633). And the same principles apply in the case of subsequent owners, who have been wrongfully deprived of the bill of lading.

It is not unusual to make the indorsement and delivery of a bill of lading conditional upon the acceptance of bills of exchange for the price of the goods, or some similar condition. In such a case the indorsee cannot keep the bill of lading, while refusing to accept the bill of exchange; and if he do so, he will get no title to the goods, nor will he be able to give one to any transferee. So if it is a condition in the bill of lading that the goods are only to be delivered upon payment of a certain draft, every indorsee takes subject to that condition, and will have no title to the goods unless it be performed.

As bills of lading are very often drawn in parts, it is

possible that different parts may come through fraud into the hands of different *bonâ fide* holders for value. In such case it is always provided that one of the bills being accomplished, the other is to stand void. It has been decided "that the first person who for value gets the transfer of a bill of lading, though it be only one of a set of three bills, acquires the property; and all subsequent dealings with the other two bills must in law be subordinate to that first one, and for this reason, because the property is in the person who first gets a transfer of the bill of lading." But as regards the shipowner, or a Dock Company standing in the shoes of the shipowner, the law is that the shipowner is justified in delivering on production of one part, although there has been a prior indorsement for value to the holder of another part, provided the delivery be *bonâ fide*, and without notice or knowledge of such prior indorsement. In such a case the first indorsee has no remedy against the Dock Company or shipowner (*Glyn, Mills, Currie, & Co. v. East and West India Dock Co.*, L. R., 7 Ap. Ca., 591). In that decision it was suggested that any inconvenience caused by such a rule could be remedied by a practice to sign only one original bill, and to take two certified copies to fulfil the function of the second and third parts, or by a bank or other person refusing to advance money until all the parts were brought in; or thirdly, if a bank or other person had advanced money, by the lender being vigilant and on the alert, and taking care to be on the spot at the first arrival of the ship in dock.

According to the principle enunciated on p. 172, the contract contained in the bill of lading is not assignable at common law. But the Bill of Lading Act, 18 & 19 Vict. c. 111, provides—(1) that the rights of action and liabilities upon a bill of lading are to vest in and bind the consignee or indorsee *to whom the property in the goods shall pass;* and (2) that a bill of lading in the hands of a consignee or indorsee for value without notice shall be conclusive evidence of shipment against the master or other person signing the same.

A mere indorsement and delivery of a bill of lading, by way of pledge to secure a loan, does not pass the property in the goods within the meaning of the Bills of Lading Act, so as to make the indorsee liable in an action by the shipowner for the freight, or in similar actions. This was decided in *Sewell* v. *Burdick* (L. R., 10 Ap. Ca., 74). Lord Bramwell, in that case, said: "Consider what difficulties would be put on those who lend on such securities if an action for freight was maintainable. The banker who lent money on a bill of lading for goods which arrived in specie, but damaged by perils of the seas so as to be worthless, might lose the money lent and the freight. Another consequence would be that the transferee of the bill of lading, though only interested to the amount of the loan on it, would be the person to bring actions on the contract to carry."

But the indorsee, by claiming and obtaining delivery of the goods for the purpose of realising them, quite independently of the statute, is held to undertake a new contract to pay the freight and damage, and any other charges stipulated for in the bill of lading.

*Dock Warrants and Delivery Orders.*—A dock warrant is a receipt given by the owners of a dock to the effect that certain specified goods stand in their books in the name of a specified person, coupled with an order to deliver the goods to or to the order of the specified person. An indorsement of a dock warrant will pass the property in the goods. But, as in a case of a bill of lading, the warrant only represents the goods, and a person who, if in possession of the goods, could not give a title to them, does not by the indorsement and delivery of a dock warrant give the indorsee any title. Thus, in the case of *Johnson* v. *Credit Lyonnais* (L. R., 3 C. P. D., 32), it appeared that H, a merchant dealing in tobacco and a broker in that trade, had fifty hogsheads of tobacco lying in bond in his name in the K dock. The warrants for them had been issued to him. Johnson bought the tobacco from H, and paid for it, but he left the dock warrants in the possession of H, and took no steps to have any change made in the books of the Dock Company as to the ownership of the tobacco. H, being the ostensible owner of the tobacco, fraudulently obtained advances by a pledge of the tobacco. It was held that the case did not come within the existing Factors' Acts (they have since been amended to cover this case), and by the rules of the common law H could not pass a better title to the tobacco than he himself had; nor was the conduct of Johnson in leaving the indicia of title in H's hands, thus enabling him to obtain advances on the security of the goods, such as to disentitle Johnson to recover the value of the tobacco from the pledgee.

The statutory authority on dock warrants is now the Factors' Act 1889.

The rightful possession of a dock warrant is equivalent to the rightful possession of the goods mentioned in the warrant. A delivery order by itself is merely a means towards obtaining either a dock warrant or actual possession. The indorsement of a delivery order does not pass the property in the goods. Thus, in the case of the *Imperial Bank* v. *London and St. Katharine's Dock Company* (L. R., 5 Ch. D., 195), it appeared that according to the usage of the London Dry Goods Market, a broker who contracts for the sale of goods without disclosing his principals is personally liable in default of his principal. On March 3rd, certain goods belonging to C, lying at the dock in the custody of the Dock Company, were bought by D, as broker for buyers and sellers, of C for B & Co., without disclosing the names of his principals, B & Co., and D indorsed to B & Co., the delivery order he had obtained from the seller on the representation that the goods were wanted for immediate shipment. B & Co., however, pledged their interest in the goods to the bank, and indorsed the delivery order to them. On March 18th, the prompt day, a clerk from the bank lodged the delivery order at the London office of the Dock Company, with this memorandum, "Hold within to our order, and have warrants made out as soon as possible." He was told that the warrants would be ready with the goods on March 20th. Three hours later, a messenger from the London office reached the warrant office at the Dock House with a notice that the order had been lodged. Meanwhile B & Co. had stopped payment, and D being so informed, and having no notice of the title of the bank, on the same day paid C for the goods, and through a clerk, who reached the Dock House before the messenger had arrived, obtained at the warrant office a warrant for the goods in the name of C. C then indorsed the same to D, and gave him a second delivery order. The first delivery order was returned to the bank by the Dock Company, who refused to act upon it. The bank claimed the goods. It was held that D was the surety, and B & Co. the principal debtors; that the unpaid vendor's lien had passed to D, and that the title to the goods was in D and not in the bank. In the course of his judgment, Jessel, M.R., said: "What was the position of the bank? They had a modified ownership in the goods, but they were not the actual owners. They were pledgees of the goods. They were armed with the delivery order, and they had a right to require one of three things from the Dock Company. They might go to the Dock Company and say, 'Here is our delivery order; deliver us the goods standing in the name of C,' who had given a delivery order. Of course, if nothing had intervened, that is, if there had been no stop, and nothing to prevent the Dock Company delivering the goods, they would have delivered the goods; they would have been carted away, and there would have been an end of it. Or they might say to the Dock Company, 'We do not want you to deliver the goods; we want you to hold them for us, and be our bailees (that is, instead of making actual delivery), and so to make a constructive delivery to us by entering them in our name in your books, by which we should become owners to the same extent as if they had been delivered to us, and you to be our warehousemen or bailees of the goods for us.' Or they might have superadded to this second proposal a third thing, and might have said, 'Besides entering our names in your book, give us a dock warrant, which will show our title to the goods, and enable us to confer a title, by indorsement, on the buyer of the goods.' What is the effect of bringing the delivery order to the office? It seems to me that it does not transfer the property in the goods. . . . There is no delivery of constructive possession until the delivery order gets down to the docks, and is recognised by an entry in the dock books."

# CHAPTER XX

## THE FACTORS' ACTS

A FACTOR is an agent entrusted with goods for the purpose of selling them for his principal. Originally, a factor did not, as a matter of mercantile usage, deal with the goods entrusted to him otherwise than by selling them. Later it became a usual and accustomed course for factors entrusted with goods for sale to make advances to their principals either in money or by the acceptance of bills against their consignments, or to keep themselves in funds by repledging the documents of title with bankers or other money dealers. The Courts of law, however, continued to hold that a pledge was out of the scope of an authority to sell, and that therefore a pledge by a factor, not being an act within the limits of his ostensible authority, did not bind his principal (see *Fuentes* v. *Montis*, L. R., 3 C. P., at pp. 277, 278).

To remedy this difference between law and mercantile usage, the law was altered by two Acts of the year 1823. Those Acts gave rise to several difficult questions, and in the year 1842 a further Act was passed. In 1877 it was found advisable to make special enactments as to revocation of agency, and as to unauthorised dealings of vendors and vendees with documents of title in their possession. In the year 1889 all these Acts were consolidated and amended by the Factors' Act 1889. A summary of this Act is now given.

*Definition of Mercantile Agent.*—A mercantile agent means one who has, in the customary course of his business as such agent, authority either to sell goods, or to consign goods for the purpose of sale, or to buy goods, or to raise money on the security of goods.

*Definition of Document of Title.*—Documents of title include any bill of lading, dock warrant, warehouse keeper's certificate, and warrant or order for the delivery of goods, and any other document used in the ordinary course of business as proof of the possession or control of goods, or authorising or purporting to authorise, either by indorsement or by delivery, the possessor of the document to transfer or receive goods thereby represented.

*Definition of Pledge.*—A pledge includes any contract pledging, or giving a lien or security on goods, whether in consideration of an original advance, or of any further or continuing advance, or of any pecuniary liability.

*Validity of Dispositions of Goods by Agent.*—The first case of the disposition of goods dealt with is the disposition of them by a mercantile agent who is, with the consent of the owner (which consent is presumed in the absence of evidence to the contrary), in possession of goods or documents of title to goods. Any sale, pledge, or other disposition of the goods by such agent, in the ordinary course of his business, is as valid as if the agent had express authority to make the same, provided that the person taking under the disposition acts in good faith, and has no notice at the time of the disposition of an actual absence of authority in the agent to make the disposition.

The second case dealt with is where the agent has been in possession with the consent of the owner, and the consent has been determined. Any disposition by such agent, which would have been valid if the consent had continued, is still to be valid, provided that the person taking under the disposition has no notice at the time of it of such determination.

A mercantile agent often, as the result of holding goods or documents of title, obtains further documents. For instance, as holder of a bill of lading he may get a dock warrant. In such cases, if he was in possession of the first goods or documents of title with the consent of the owner, he is also deemed to hold derivative documents with the consent of the owner.

*Pledges of Documents.*—A pledge of the documents of title to goods is deemed a pledge of the goods.

*Pledge for Antecedent Debt.*—It should be very carefully noted that under the Act where a pledge of goods is taken as security for past advances or liabilities, the pledgee acquires no further right to the goods than could have been enforced by the pledgor at the time of the pledge.

*Consideration.*—The consideration necessary to support a sale, pledge, or other disposition of goods may be a payment in cash, the delivery or transfer of other goods, or of a document of title to goods, or of a negotiable security; but in all cases, except that of a cash payment, the pledgee acquires no right or interest in the substituted goods in excess of the value of the goods, documents, or security when so delivered or transferred in exchange.

*Consignor apparent Owner.*—Where the consignor appears as owner, and the consignee has no notice to the contrary, the consignee, in respect of advances made to or for the use of such consignor, has the same lien on the goods as if the consignor were the owner of the goods, and may transfer any such lien to another person.

*Dispositions by Seller in Possession.*—Where a person, having sold goods, continues or is in possession of the goods, or of documents of title to the goods, the delivery or transfer by that person, or by a mercantile agent acting for him, of the goods or documents of title under any sale, pledge, or other disposition, or any agreement for a sale, pledge, or other disposition, to any person receiving the same in good faith and without notice of the previous sale, has the same effect as if the person making the delivery or transfer were expressly authorised by the owner of the goods to make the same.

*Dispositions by Buyer in Possession.*—When a person, having bought or agreed to buy goods, obtains, with the consent of the seller, possession of the goods or the documents of title to the goods, the delivery or transfer by that person, or by a mercantile agent acting for him, of the goods or documents of title, under any sale, pledge, or other disposition, or under an agreement for a sale, pledge, or disposition of them, to any person receiving the same in good faith and without notice of any lien or other right of the original seller in respect of the goods, has the same effect as if the person making the delivery or transfer were a mercantile agent in possession of the goods or documents of title with the consent of the owner.

*Vendor's Lien.*—Where a document of title to goods has been lawfully transferred to a person as a buyer or owner of the goods, and that person transfers the document to a person who takes it in good faith and for valuable consideration, the last-mentioned transfer shall have the same effect for defeating any vendor's lien or right of stoppage *in transitu*, as the transfer of a bill of lading has for defeating the right of stoppage *in transitu* (see p. 172).

*Rights of Owner.*—The owner may redeem the goods, and may recover from any person with whom the goods have been pledged any balance of money remaining in his hands as the produce of the sale of the goods after deducting the amount of his lien.

# CHAPTER XXI

## SECURITY FOR FLOATING BALANCES

*Bank Mortgages.*—The usual form in which a bank takes a legal mortgage from a customer is in the form of a mortgage for past and future advances not exceeding a fixed sum. Such a mortgage is a valid security for the floating balance, provided that the mortgagor has not given a subsequent mortgage of which the bank has notice. It was for a long time supposed that within the fixed limit the bank obtained priority notwithstanding notice of the subsequent mortgage, but in the year 1865 the House of Lords laid down the rule that a first mortgagee for present and future advances is not, as against a second mortgagee, entitled to priority in respect of advances made by him after notice of the second mortgage (*Hopkinson* v. *Rolt*, 9 H. L. C., 514). The following is taken from the judgment of Lord Westbury in that case: "Although the mortgagor has parted with the legal interest in the hereditaments mortgaged, he remains the equitable owner of all his interest not transferred beneficially to the mortgagee, and he may still deal with his property in any way consistent with the rights of the mortgagee. How is the first mortgagee injured by the second mortgage being executed, although the first mortgagee having notice of the mortgage, the second mortgagee should be preferred to him as to subsequent advances? The first mortgagee is secure as to past advances, and he is not obliged to make any further advances. He has only to hold his hand when asked for a further loan. Knowing the extent of the second mortgage, he may calculate that the hereditaments mortgaged are an ample security to the mortgagees; and if he doubts this, he closes his account with the mortgagor and looks out for a better security. The benefit of the first mortgage is only lessened by the amount of any interest which the mortgagor afterwards conveys to another, consistent with the rights of the first mortgagee. Thus far the mortgagor is entitled to do what he likes with his own. The consequence certainly is that, after executing such a mortgage as we are considering, the mortgagor by executing another such mortgage, and giving notice of it to the first mortgagee, may at any time give a preference to the second mortgagee as to subsequent advances, and as to such advances reduce the first mortgagee to the rank of puisne incumbrancer. But the first mortgagee will have no reason to complain, knowing that this is his true position, if he chooses voluntarily to make further advances to the mortgagor. The second mortgagee cannot be charged with any fraud upon the first mortgagee in making the advances with notice of the first mortgage; for, by the hypothesis, each has notice of the security of the other, and the first mortgagee is left in full possession of his option to make or refuse further advances, as he may deem it prudent. The hardship upon bankers from this view of the subject at once vanishes, when we consider that the security of the first mortgage is not impaired without notice of a second; and that when this notice comes, the bankers have only to consider (as they do as often as they discount a bill of exchange) what is the credit of their customer, and whether the proposed transaction is likely to lead to profit or to loss."

*Compound Interest.*—If a banker, instead of taking a mortgage for the balance of the customer's running account, takes a mortgage for a fixed sum, say the amount of the balance at a given date, he must not afterwards mix the banking and mortgage accounts. It is usual as between banker and customer to strike balances, after adding interest and charges, each half year (or at other convenient periods), and this is, of course, equivalent to charging compound interest with half-yearly rests. But a mortgagor is not entitled, except by express agreement, to charge compound interest. Therefore, when the mortgage is for a fixed sum, and there is no special agreement, the fixed sum and the simple interest on it must not be introduced into the banking account, but must constitute a separate account; and as to such an account the relation of the parties is no longer that of banker and customer, but that of mortgagor and mortgagee (*Morse* v. *Sall*, 32 L. J., Ch., 756).

*Sale by Owner of Mortgaged Premises.*—The principle of *Hopkinson* v. *Rolt* applies equally to legal and equitable mortgages, and to subsequent interests acquired either by mortgage or sale. In the case of the *London and County Banking Company* v. *Radcliffe* (L. R., 6 Ap. Ca., 722), the facts were as follows: The owner of land had deposited his title-deeds with a bank as security for all sums then or thereafter to become due on the general balance of his account with the bank. Subsequently the landowner contracted, with the knowledge of the bank, to sell the land to a purchaser who had notice of the terms of deposit. The vendor afterwards paid into his own account at the bank sums which in the whole exceeded the debt due to the bank on his balance at the time of the contract of sale, so that, on the principle of Clayton's case, that debt was discharged. The bank, without giving notice to the purchaser, continued the account, and made fresh advances to the vendor, so that on the general balance there was always a debt to the bank. The purchaser, who never had notice of the fresh advances, paid the purchase money by instalments to the vendor. The bank sought to enforce their equitable charge for the amount of the current balance. The House of Lords held, affirming the decision of the Court of Appeal, that on the principle of *Hopkinson* v. *Rolt*, the bank had no charge on the land as against the purchaser for the fresh advances; and also that the bank had no charge upon the purchase money. Lord Blackburn, in further discussing the effect of a pledge by an unpaid vendor of his lien on the land with notice of such pledge given to the purchaser, said: "A purchaser of land, with notice that the title-deeds have been deposited with the bank as security for the general balance on the vendor's present and future account, is not bound to inquire whether the bank has, after notice of the purchase, made fresh advances. The burden lies on the bank advancing on the security of the unpaid vendor's lien to give the purchaser notice that it has so done, or intends so to do."

*Advances on Security of Shares in Limited Companies.*—Sometimes a bank is in the position of a second incumbrancer, and then it gets the benefit of the principle of *Hopkinson* v. *Rolt*. Thus, that principle has been held to apply to advances by a bank on the security of shares in a limited company on which the company has a lien for debts due to it from the shareholder. For instance, in the case of the *Bradford Banking Company Limited* v. *Briggs* (L. R., 12 Ap. Ca., 29), it appeared that by the articles of association of the defendant company, the company had "a first and permanent lien and charge, available at law and in equity, upon every share for all debts due from the holder thereof." A shareholder deposited his share certificates with the plaintiffs as security for the balance due and to become due on his current account, and the plaintiffs gave the defendants notice of the deposit. The certificates stated that the shares were held subject to the articles of association. It was held by the House of Lords that the defendants could not, in respect of moneys which became due from the shareholder to the company after notice of the deposit with the bank, claim priority over advances by the bank made after such notice, but that the principle of *Hopkinson* v. *Rolt* applied. The House of Lords further held that the notice to the company of the deposit with the bank was not a notice of a trust within the meaning of the Companies Act 1862, s. 30, and that the bank, by giving notice of the deposit, did not seek to affect the company with notice of a trust, but only to affect the company in their capacity as traders, with notice of the interest of the bank.

## CHAPTER XXII

### SHARES AND DEBENTURES

*Shares.*—Shares may be taken as security for an overdraft of the customer, so that the banker becomes the legal or equitable holder of them.

A banker does not become the legal owner of shares taken as security until he has completed his title by becoming the registered owner of them; but once registered, he is, as between the company and himself, the sole owner of the shares, and he will be liable as a contributory. If the bank is a partnership, one partner in the firm has authority to take a transfer of shares as security for a loan. Even if the loan is paid off, and the shares re-transferred, the bank is, for one year from the date of such re-transfer, liable, as a past member, to be made a contributory.

If the registration of the shares has never been completed through the default of the company, the liquidator cannot obtain a rectification of the register, so as to place the bank on the list of contributories.

A deposit of the share certificates is enough to give a bank which advances money on them a good equitable title.

Shares have been held to be choses in action, and therefore do not come within the order and disposition clause of the Bankruptcy Act.

The usual way of giving security upon shares is for the mortgagor to execute a blank transfer, which he deposits with the bank or other mortgagee along with the share certificates. The blank transfer is given, and probably effectually given to enable the banker to turn his equitable interest into a legal interest by filling up the blank transfer with his own name, and thus getting a registration of the shares in his own name.

A banker or other mortgagee cannot give a better title than he has himself got, and therefore, if the mortgagee fills up the blanks with the name of a purchaser from him, such purchaser will take no greater interest in the shares than the mortgagee had, unless the real owner is precluded or estopped from making a claim for the shares. Notice that a person holds certificates of shares and a blank transfer is sufficient notice that such person may not be the owner of the shares, and a person having such notice is put upon inquiry, and in default cannot raise any question of estoppel as against the true owner.

The essence of a transfer is that the person entitled to the shares should have agreed to the transfer of them, and therefore, if a transfer is forged, the transferee, though registered, has no title to the shares.

One or two recent examples of the application of these principles are now given. In the case of *France* v. *Clark* (L. R., 26 Ch. D., 257), the facts were as follows: France was the registered owner of ten fully paid-up shares in the Anglo-Egyptian Banking Company. France, in February 1881, deposited the certificates, together with a transfer of the shares executed by himself, in which the date, the name of the transferee, and the consideration were left in blank, with Clark as security for a loan of £150. Clark deposited the certificates and the blank transfer with Quihampton as security for £250 lent by him to Clark. In April,

Clark died insolvent. In June, Quihampton filled up the blanks in the transfer, and was registered as owner of the shares. It was disputed whether the registration did or did not take place before the company received notice of France's right of redemption. The question of law was this, Could Quihampton hold the shares as security for the £250 he had advanced, or only for the £150 which his immediate predecessor in title, Clark, had advanced? It was decided that he could only hold the shares as security for £150. Lord Selborne said as to a person who takes a blank transfer, "that he must necessarily have had notice that the documents required to be other than they were when he received them, in order to pass any other or larger right or interest, as against the person whose name was subscribed to them, than the person from whom he received them might then actually and *bonâ fide* be entitled to transfer or create; and if he makes no inquiry, he must at the most take that right (whatever it may happen to be), and nothing more." As to the authority given with a blank transfer, Lord Selborne said: "It was said that when a man, in a transaction for value, does what France did, and delivers a blank form of transfer to a creditor by way of security, together with the certificates of shares, his meaning must necessarily be that the creditor may complete his security by obtaining registration of the shares, either in his own or (possibly) in some other name; and that he therefore entrusts him with the requisite authority for that purpose. Granting this, what follows? Only that the creditor to whom such an authority is given may execute it or not, for the purpose of giving effect to the contract in his own favour, as he pleases; but not that, if he does not execute it, he can delegate the like authority to a stranger for purposes foreign to, and possibly (as in this case) in fraud of, the contract." As to any estoppel which might arise from the fact that France had by the blank transfer and certificate enabled Clark to represent himself as the true owner of the shares, Lord Selborne said: "Apart from the fact that the documents themselves showed that Clark was not the owner, and therefore could not be the ground of a representation to that effect, there was no evidence of any mercantile usage to the effect that blank transfers, accompanied by certificates of shares registered in the names of transferors, pass from hand to hand like negotiable instruments. A plea of such mercantile usage had been originally put upon the defence, and subsequently abandoned."

In the case of the *Société Générale de Paris* v. *Walker* (L. R., 11 Ap Ca., 20), there was a conflict between two equitable titles. J. M. Walker had given J. S. Walker certificates for a hundred shares in the Tramways Union Limited, together with a blank transfer, as a security for a debt. J. M. Walker subsequently gave another blank transfer of the same shares to the plaintiffs as security for another debt, and in that transaction alleged that the certificates had been lost or mislaid. The articles of association of the company were, as to transfer, in the common form. The plaintiffs filled up the blank transfer, but as the company was not promised a sufficient indemnity against the consequences of registering without the production of the certificate, the transfer was never registered. The plaintiffs, therefore, never got a legal title, nor was their equitable title so good as J. S. Walker's. The latter was first in point of time, and was in possession of the certificates, which on their face stated that there should be no change of the registered title without the production of the certificates. Nothing more could be necessary, on any reasonable or intelligible principle, to perfect their equitable title, which they were under no obligation to convert into a legal title by registration.

It may be noted in connection with this case, that in the case of shares of companies under the Companies Acts, as no notice of trusts can be entered on the register, and it is generally provided in the articles that the company will not be bound by trusts, it is not, as a rule, necessary to give notice of an equitable assignment in order to keep priority over subsequent equitable assignees.

In the case of the *Colonial Bank* v. *Whinney* (L. R., 11 Ap. Ca., 426), there had been an equitable mortgage to the bank by deposit and blank transfer of certain shares in a Scotch company. The mortgagor became bankrupt, and his trustee in bankruptcy claimed the whole interest in the shares on the ground that they were still in the reputed ownership of the registered owner. Such shares were only transferable by deed. As to the blank transfer, Lord Blackburn said: "It was inoperative as a transfer, but was evidence that the deposit of the certificates was intended to be as a security." As to the reputed ownership, he referred to the usual note on the certificate itself as to production, and to the custom of the Stock Exchange, and said: "It was clear that any one who was about to give credit to the bankrupts as being the owners of the entire interest in those shares ought to know that he had no legitimate ground for believing that they were such owners of the whole interest, unless the certificates were produced or accounted for, and that therefore in this case the bankrupts were not the reputed owners of the interest of the Colonial Bank in the shares." Lastly, the House of Lords held that shares are "things in action," within the meaning of the proviso in the reputed ownership clause of the Bankruptcy Act 1883.

Two cases have been before the Court in which questions arose as to the legal nature of certificates with blank transfers on the back. In both cases, the certificates were issued by the New York Central Railroad Company to a registered shareholder. Each certificate is for ten shares, and on the back there is a blank form of transfer, and a blank form of power of attorney to execute a surrender and cancellation of the certificate. The mode of transfer is as follows: The transfer and power of attorney are signed by the registered shareholder. When this blank transfer reaches the hand of some holder who desires to be registered, his name is filled in by himself or on his behalf, and the certificate is left with the company; it is then cancelled, the transferee is registered, and a new certificate in his name is issued.

In the first case, that of the *Colonial Bank* v. *Hepworth* (L. R., 36 Ch. D., 36), Hepworth, the purchaser of the shares, left them in the hands of his broker. The broker deposited them with the Colonial Bank as security for an overdraft. The broker got them back from the bank under a promise to substitute the new certificates. These new certificates, were made out not in the name of the bank, but in Hepworth's name. It was held by Chitty (J.), that the title of Hepworth was superior to that of the bank. The only estoppel that Chitty (J.) recognised as between holders other than the transferor who had signed the blank transfer was as follows: "Where the transfers are duly signed by the registered holders of the shares, each prior holder confers upon the *bonâ fide* holder for value of the certificates, for the time being, an authority to fill in the name of the transferee, and is estopped from denying such authority."

In the second case, which went to the House of Lords (*Colonial Bank* v. *Cady*, L. R., 15 Ap. Ca., 267), the facts were these. The registered owner died, and his executors obtained probate of the bill. The executors, in order that the shares might be registered in their own names, signed as executors the transfers on the back of each certificate, without filling up the blanks, and sent the certificates to their broker, who fraudulently deposited the certificates with the Colonial Bank, which took them *bona fide* and without notice as security for advances. The bank retained the certificates, and took no steps to obtain registration. By the law of New York, a delivery of signed transfers by the registered owner of shares would estop him from setting up his title against a purchaser for value, and Lord Herschell said that the English law was the same. But neither on the New York nor on the London Stock Exchange are transfers so signed by executors treated as being in order or received as sufficient security for advances, unless duly authenticated. The executors brought an action against the bank to establish their title to the certificates, and it was held that they were so entitled, on the ground that the conduct of the executors in delivering the transfers was consistent either with an intention to sell or pledge the shares, or to have themselves registered as the owners, and therefore did not estop them from setting up their title as against the bank, for the bank ought to have inquired as to the broker's authority. Lord Herschell said: " In the case of a transfer signed by the registered owner, he must, presumably, have signed it with the intention at some time or other of effecting a transfer. No other reasonable construction can be put on his act. And if he entrusts it in that condition to a third party, I think those dealing with such third party have a right to assume that he has authority to complete a transfer. But when the indorsement is signed by executors who are the registered owners, there can be no such presumption. They may well have signed it merely to complete their title without the intention of ever parting with the shares."

A foreign share certificate cannot have the qualities of a negotiable instrument attached to it by the custom of English bankers and dealers in public securities, if, on the face of the instrument, it appears to be intended that the only parties who can really become the owners are the parties to whom it is granted, or persons to whom it is transferable on the register. (See p. 138, and *London and County Banking Co.* v. *London and River Plate Bank*, L. R., 20 Q. B. D., 232.)

The law as to forged transfers has recently received an illustration in the case of *Barton* v. *North Staffordshire Railway Co.* (L. R., 38 Ch. Div., 458). There one of two executors and trustees forged the signature of his co-trustee to a transfer of railway stock standing in their joint names, and appropriated the proceeds. Afterwards a new trustee was appointed in the place of the forger, and it was held that the trustees were entitled to treat the transfers as nullities, and that the company must be ordered to register them as owners of the stock. It was also held that the cause of action was the refusal by the company, when the forgeries were made known to them, to treat the trustees as owners of the stock, and that therefore time under the Statute of Limitations did not begin to run against the trustees until such refusal.

*Debentures.*—In dealing with shares, the most usual question involved is the decision of the ownership of shares to which there are different claimants. In the case of debentures, the point to be decided is generally this, What right has the holder against the company issuing the same? A debenture being a chose in action not assignable at common law, is *primâ facie* assignable subject to equities. Therefore, if the debentures were originally issued in fraud of the company, even a *bonâ fide* purchaser for value will not stand in any better position than the first obligee. In the same way, if the company has a set-off against the person to whom the debentures were originally issued, that set-off is available against subsequent holders. Thus, in the case of In re *South Blackpool Hotel Company* (L. R., 8 Eq., 225), it appeared that by the articles of association £1700 was to be paid to the promoter, he indemnifying the directors against all costs, charges, and expenses incurred previously to the allotment of the shares. Seventeen debentures of £100 each were issued to the promoter, but he did not pay all the costs, charges, and expenses as agreed. Such costs, charges, and expenses were, to the amount of about £208, proved in the winding up of the company. It was held that the company was entitled to set-off one-seventeenth part of the sum so proved against the amount due on each debenture.

Though it may be to the advantage in the winding up of a company to set off equities, the knowledge that, possibly, equities attach to the debentures does not tend to make them readily marketable. Accordingly, it is not unusual to put words on the face of the bonds to show either that there are no equities, or that the company does not intend to enforce equities. If there is a sufficient representation to that effect, the company cannot afterwards turn round and seek to set up an equity. In general, a representation on the face of the debenture that it is payable to bearer, is a representation not only that the debenture may be transferred by delivery without a deed of transfer, but also that the transferee will take free from equities. So also it has been said "the authorities go to this, that where there is a distinct promise held out by a company, informing all the world that they will pay to the order of the person named, it is not competent for that company afterwards to set up equities of their own, and say that because the person who makes the order is indebted to them they will not pay" (*General Estates Co.* ex p. *City Bank*, L. R., 3 Ch. Ap., 758, at p. 762).

The only case which is opposed to the view that holds such representations sufficient to exclude the right to set up equities was a case (In re *Natal Investment Co.*, L. R., 3 Ch. Ap., 355), in which Earl Cairns held that a promise to pay to "C., or to his executors, administrators, or transferees," was equivalent to the usual promise in a money bond to pay to C or his executors, administrators, or assigns, and therefore made no representation as to equities, while the addition of the further words "or to the holder for the time being" only dealt with the mode of transfer. And though, perhaps, there is no logical distinction between the words "bearer" and "holder for the time being," the word bearer is so much more commonly used than the longer phrase both in connection with instruments actually negotiable and also those which the issuers intend to represent as negotiable that it would be very difficult now to convince a Court that the use of the word "bearer" was only intended to imply a mode of transfer by delivery, and not a transfer free from equities. As has been recently said by the present Lord Chancellor, "Undoubtedly a document may by usage become so well understood in a particular sense that a person may well be estopped from denying that when he issues it to the world it must bear the sense which usage has attached to it" (*Colonial Bank* v. *Cady*, L. R., 15 Ap. Ca., at p. 274).

The company may in like manner, by subsequent conduct, debar themselves from setting up equities, as, for instance, by receiving notice of assignment without taking objection thereto, or by registering the transferee.

As between the true owner of a bond and a subsequent *bonâ fide* holder for value there is no estoppel, unless the true owner has done something which amounts to an adoption of the representation made by the company on the face of the document. The mere acceptance of a debenture bond cannot be the ground of such an adoption, nor, in spite of what Earl Cairns said in *Goodwin* v. *Robarts* (L. R., 1 Ap. Ca., 476), is it by any means certain that leaving the bonds with a broker is a sufficient adoption (see p. 144). In *Crouch* v. *Credit Foncier of England Limited* (L. R., 8 Q. B., 374), bonds payable to bearer were stolen from M, and afterwards came into the hands of C, a *bonâ fide* holder, for value. Apparently it would now be held that C could sue the company, who would be estopped from denying C's title, while M could sue C to recover the bonds or their value, for M had not been party to any representation contained on the face of the debenture.

The issue of debentures is a form of borrowing, and we have already discussed at p. 81 the position of companies as borrowers in general. If a company has no power to borrow either express, or implied from the nature of its business, it cannot issue valid debentures.

Again, if a company is authorised to borrow to a limited amount and on defined terms, it cannot borrow to a larger amount or on other terms. Therefore, when the limit of the borrowing powers has been reached, subsequent debentures will be void.

As to any formalities required to be observed in the issue of debentures, the following distinction has been drawn, *Fountaine* v. *Carmarthen Railway Co.* (L. R., 5 Eq., 316, at p. 322) :—" Where directors are the special agents of the company, and do not possess the power of affixing the corporate seal, except under certain prescribed rules, a person who deals with the directors is taken to have notice of the rules. In the case of a registered joint-stock company, all the world, of course, have notice of the general Act of Parliament, and of the special deed which has been registered pursuant to the provisions of the Act; and if there be anything to be done which can only be done by the directors under certain limited powers, the person who deals with the directors must see that these limited powers are not being exceeded. If, on the other hand, the directors have power and authority to bind the company,—but certain preliminaries are required to be gone through on the part of the company before that power can be duly exercised,—then the person contracting with the directors is not bound to see that all these preliminaries have been observed. He is entitled to presume that the directors are acting lawfully in what they do." In a case In re *Romford Canal Company* (L. R., 24 Ch. D., 85), where a question arose upon debentures issued by a company, pursuant to a resolution passed at a meeting at which an insufficient number of shareholders were present, to a person who had notice of the irregularity, but who afterwards transferred them to *bonâ fide* holders for value without notice, the following general rules were laid down by Mr. Justice Kay: " Where a company has power to issue legally transferable securities, an irregularity in the issue cannot be set up against even the original holder if he has a right to presume *omnia rite acta*. If such securities be legally transferable, such an irregularity, and *à fortiori* any equity against the original holder, cannot be asserted by the company against a *bonâ fide* transferee for value without notice. Nor can such an equity be set up against an equitable transferee, whether the securities were transferable at law or not, if by the original conduct of the company in issuing the securities, or by their subsequent dealing with the transferee, he has a superior equity. If the original conduct of the company in issuing debentures was such that the public were justified in treating it as a representation that they were legally transferable, there would be an equity on the part of any person who had agreed for value to take a transfer of these debentures to restrain the company from pleading their invalidity, although that might be a defence at law to an action by the transferor."

The bankers of a company are not in the position of officers of the company, who are bound to see that all required formalities are complied with (In re *General Provident Assurance Company* ex p. *National Bank*, L. R., 14 Eq., 507).

# CHAPTER XXIII

## CRIMINAL LAW

BANKERS and other mercantile persons usually trusted with securities are subject to the following special enactments (24 & 25 Vict., c. 96, ss. 75 and 76) :—

S. 75. "Whosoever having been trusted, either solely or jointly, with any other person, as a banker, merchant, broker, attorney, or other agent, with any money or security for the payment of money, with any direction in writing to apply, pay, or deliver such money or security, or any part thereof respectively, or the proceeds or any part of the proceeds of such security, for any purpose, or to any person specified in such direction, shall, in violation of good faith, and contrary to the terms of such direction, in anywise convert to his own use or benefit, or the use or benefit of any person other than the person by whom he shall have been so intrusted, such money, security, or proceeds, or any part thereof respectively; and whosoever having been intrusted, either solely or jointly, with any other person, as a banker, merchant, broker, attorney, or other agent, with any chattel or valuable security, or any power of attorney for the sale or transfer of any share or interest in any public stock or fund, whether of the United Kingdom, or any part thereof, or of any foreign state, or in any stock or fund of any body corporate, company, or society, for safe custody, or for any special purpose, without any authority to sell, negotiate, transfer, or pledge, shall, in violation of good faith, and contrary to the object or purpose for which such chattel, security, or power of attorney shall have been intrusted to him, sell, negotiate, transfer, pledge, or in any manner convert to his own use or benefit, or the use or benefit of any person other than the person by whom he shall have been so intrusted, such chattel or security, or the proceeds of the same, or any part thereof, or the share or interest in the stock or fund to which such power of attorney shall relate, or any part thereof, shall be guilty of a misdemeanour, and being convicted thereof, shall be liable, at the discretion of the Court, to be kept in penal servitude for any term not exceeding seven years and not less than three years, or to be imprisoned for any term not exceeding two years, with or without hard labour, and with or without solitary confinement; but nothing in this section contained relating to agents shall affect any trustee in or under any instrument whatsoever, or any mortgagee of any property, real or personal, in respect of any act done by such trustee or mortgagee in relation to the property comprised in or affected by any such trust or mortgage; nor shall restrain any banker, merchant, broker, attorney, or other agent from receiving any money which shall be or become actually due and payable upon or by virtue of any valuable security, according to the tenor and effect thereof, in such manner as he might have done if this Act had not been passed; nor from selling, transferring, or otherwise disposing of any securities or effects in his possession upon which he shall have any lien, claim, or demand entitling him by law so to do, unless such sale, transfer, or other disposal shall extend to a greater number or part of such securities or effects than shall be requisite for satisfying such lien, claim, or demand."

S. 76. "Whosoever, being a banker, merchant, broker, attorney, or agent, and being intrusted, either solely or jointly with any other person, with the property of any other person for safe custody, shall, with intent to defraud, sell, negotiate, transfer, pledge, or in any manner convert or appropriate the same, or any part thereof, to or for his own use or benefit, or the use or benefit of any person other than the person by whom he was so intrusted, shall be guilty of a misdemeanour, and being convicted thereof, shall be liable, at the discretion of the Court, to any of the punishments which the Court may award as hereinbefore last mentioned."

Officers of the Bank of England or Ireland are subject to the following special provision (24 & 25 Vict., c. 96, s. 73):—

"Whosoever, being an officer or servant of the governor and company of the Bank of England, or of the Bank of Ireland, and being intrusted with any bond, deed, note, bill, dividend warrant, or warrant for payment of any annuity or interest, or money, or with any security, money, or other effects of or belonging to the said governor and company, or having any bond, deed, note, bill, dividend warrant, or warrant for payment of any annuity or interest, or money, or any security, money or other effects of any other person, body politic or corporate, lodged or deposited with the said governor and company, or with him as an officer or servant of the said governor and company, shall secrete, embezzle, or run away with any such bond, deed, note, bill, dividend or other warrant, security, money or other effects as aforesaid, or any part thereof, shall be guilty of felony, and being convicted thereof, shall be liable, at the discretion of the Court, to be kept in penal servitude for life, or for any term not less than five years, or to be imprisoned for any term not exceeding two years, with or without hard labour, and with or without solitary confinement."

# CHAPTER XXIV

## SCOTCH LAW

*History.*—There has never been a bank in Scotland which corresponds with the Bank of England. The earliest chartered Scotch bank was the Bank of Scotland established in 1695, but given no monopoly. In 1727 the Royal Bank of Scotland was established, and in 1746 the British Linen Company. The distinctive features of the Scotch banking system are its £1 notes, and the cash credit system.

*Bank Notes.*—The issue of notes is regulated by 8 & 9 Vict., c. 38 (1845). Roughly speaking, the principle of the Act is an application to all banks alike in Scotland of a combination of the separate regulations applied by the Bank Charter Act respectively to country banks and the Bank of England. Banks issuing notes on the 6th of May 1844 are to be allowed to continue their average issue as in England, and also a further issue up to the amount of gold and silver coin held by such banker at the head office or principal place of issue of such banker. Bank of England notes are not a legal tender in Scotland, though there is nothing to prevent their circulation. Bank notes can only be issued for one or more pounds without the addition of fractional parts of a pound.

*Formation of Banks.*—As Scottish banking legislation

has closely followed the course of English legislation, and the Companies Acts 1862 to 1890 apply to both countries, it is unnecessary to add anything further here on this subject.

*Bank Agents.*—Branch establishments are usually worked through a special class of managers called bank agents. The powers of these agents vary according to the regulations of the particular bank for which they act; but in ordinary cases they are authorised to discount bills and do other usual business, either on their own responsibility or at least under a responsibility for a certain proportion of the discounts. It is not usual to delegate to a bank agent the power of granting cash credits. Caution or security to a large amount is required from bank agents; on the failure of the agent, apparently the money found in the desks, drawers, or boxes used for carrying on the business of the bank is the specific property of the bank, and may be reclaimed by it, although the identical notes issued by the bank may have been replaced by others. A clause empowering the bank summarily to terminate the agency, and to seize and carry off the whole notes, cash, obligations, and effects belonging to the bank, is usually inserted in the bond of caution taken by the bank from the agent.

*Cash Credits.*—A cash credit is an arrangement by which advances are made up to a fixed limit to a customer on the security of a bond. Their peculiarity is that the customer opens the account with the object of obtaining a cash credit. The credit and loan are secured by a bond for such amount of debt, not exceeding a certain limited sum, as shall ultimately arise on a balance of the deposits and drafts. A ready mode of ascertaining the balance due is provided by the stipulation that a certificate of the amount due on the account, extracted from the bank books and signed by the cashier or other principal officer, shall be sufficient to constitute and ascertain the debt due under the bond. The bond being the ground of charge, summary diligence may proceed at once upon the certificate so made up, without registration of the account.

Heritable property could not at one time be given for future debts; and now if the customer is anxious to avail himself of property of that description, he must comply with the requirements of 19 & 20 Vict., c. 91, s. 7.

*Banker's Lien.*—In Scotland, a banker's lien extends to debts not yet due, provided the debtor be either bankrupt or *vergens ad inopiam*.

*Bills of Exchange and Cheques.*—By the Bills of Exchange Act 1882, s. 53, (2), it is enacted that "in Scotland, where the drawee of a bill has in his hands funds available for the payment thereof, the bill operates as an assignment of the sum for which it is drawn in favour of the holder from the time when the bill is presented to the drawee."

# CHAPTER XXV

### IRISH BANKS

IRISH law is now practically the same as English law. Two differences are, however, worthy of notice.

*Bank Notes.*—Up to the year 1845 the history of the Bank of Ireland was very similar to that of the Bank of England, the Bank possessing a limited monopoly within a radius of fifty miles of Dublin. By an Act of the year 1845 (8 & 9 Vict., c. 37), the note issue of the country was regulated by an Act almost identical with the Act for Scotland already mentioned. The Bank of Ireland takes its place on a level with other Irish banks, which, if issuing notes on 6th May 1844, are allowed to continue their average issue together with a further issue to an amount not exceeding their respective reserves of gold and silver.

Bank of England notes are not a legal tender in Ireland, but their circulation is not prohibited.

*The Bankers' Acts.*—There are certain statutes of the old Irish Parliament known as the Bankers' Acts still unrepealed. The most important is 33 Geo. II, c. 14 (Ir.), called "an Act for providing a more effectual remedy for the security and payment of debts due by bankers." This statute provides for the registration of certain conveyances made by bankers, and for the validity of settlements made by them, and other matters. The Act itself is printed in the notes to *Copland* v. *Davies* (5 L. R., E. & I., 358), and that case should be referred to for fuller information on the subject.

# APPENDIX

## BANKING PARTNERSHIPS ACT

### 7 Geo. IV, cap. 46

*An Act for the better regulating Copartnerships of certain Bankers in England, and for amending so much of an Act of the thirty-ninth and fortieth years of the reign of His late Majesty King George the Third, intituled " An Act for establishing an Agreement with the Governor and Company of the Bank of England, for advancing the Sum of Three Millions towards the Supply for the Service of the Year One thousand eight hundred," as relates to the same.*

[26th May 1826]

WHEREAS an Act was passed in the thirty-ninth and fortieth years of the reign of His late Majesty King George the Third, intituled " An Act for establishing an agreement with the governor and company of the Bank of England, for advancing the sum of three millions towards the supply for the service of the year one thousand eight hundred": and whereas it was, to prevent doubts as to the privilege of the said governor and company, enacted and declared in the said recited Act, that no other bank should be erected, established, or allowed by Parliament; and that it should not be lawful for any body, politic or corporate, whatsoever, erected or to be erected, or for any other persons united or to be united in covenants or partnership, exceeding the number of six persons, in that part of Great Britain called England, to borrow, owe, or

*39 & 40 G. 3, c. 28.*

take up any sum or sums of money on their bills or notes payable on demand, or at any less time than six months from the borrowing thereof, during the continuance of the said privilege to the said governor and company, who were thereby declared to be and remain a corporation, with the privilege of exclusive banking, as before recited; but subject nevertheless to redemption on the terms and conditions in the said Act specified: and whereas the governor and company of the Bank of England have consented to relinquish so much of their exclusive privilege as prohibits any body, politic or corporate, or any number of persons exceeding six, in England, acting in copartnership, from borrowing, owing or taking up any sum or sums of money on their bills or notes payable on demand, or at any less time than six months from the borrowing thereof; provided that such body, politic or corporate, or persons united in covenants or partnerships, exceeding the number of six persons in each copartnership, shall have the whole of their banking establishments and carry on their business as bankers at any place or places in England exceeding the distance of sixty-five miles from London, and that all the individuals composing such corporations or copartnerships, carrying on such business, shall be liable to and responsible for the due payment of all bills and notes issued by such corporations or copartnerships respectively: be it therefore enacted by the King's most Excellent Majesty, by and with the advice and consent of the Lords, spiritual and temporal, and the Commons, in this present Parliament assembled, and by the authority of the same, that from and after the passing of this Act it shall and may be lawful for any bodies, politic or corporate, erected for the purpose of banking, or for any number of persons united in covenants or co-partnership, although such persons so united or carrying on business together shall consist of more than six in number, to carry on the trade or business of bankers in England, in like manner as copartnerships of bankers consisting of not more than six persons in number may lawfully do; and for such bodies, politic or corporate, or such persons so united as aforesaid, to make and issue their bills or notes at any place or places in England,

*Copartnerships of more than six in number may carry on business as bankers in England, 65 miles from London, provided they have no establishment as bankers in London, and that every member*

exceeding the distance of sixty-five miles from London, payable on demand or otherwise at some place or places specified upon such bills or notes, exceeding the distance of sixty-five miles from London, and not elsewhere, and to borrow, owe, or take up any sum or sums of money on their bills or notes so made and issued at any such place or places as aforesaid: provided always, that such corporations or persons carrying on such trade or business of bankers in copartnership shall not have any house of business or establishment as bankers in London, or at any place or places not exceeding the distance of sixty-five miles from London; and that every member of any such corporation or copartnership shall be liable to and responsible for the due payment of all bills and notes which shall be issued, and for all sums of money which shall be borrowed, owed, or taken up by the corporation or copartnership of which such person shall be a member, such person being a member at the period of the date of the bills or notes, or becoming or being a member before or at the time of the bills or notes being payable, or being such member at the time of the borrowing, owing, or taking up of any sum or sums of money upon any bills or notes by the corporation or copartnership, or while any sum of money on any bills or notes is owing or unpaid, or at the time the same became due from the corporation or copartnership; any agreement, covenant, or contract to the contrary notwithstanding. *shall be liable for the payment of all bills, etc.*

II. Provided always, and be it further enacted, that nothing in this Act contained shall extend or be construed to extend to enable or authorise any such corporation, or copartnership exceeding the number of six persons, so carrying on the trade or business of bankers as aforesaid, either by any member of or person belonging to any such corporation or copartnership, or by any agent or agents, or any other person or persons on behalf of any such corporation or copartnership, to issue or re-issue in London, or at any place or places not exceeding the distance of sixty-five miles from London, any bill or note of such corporation or copartnership, which shall be payable to bearer on demand, or any bank post bill; nor to draw upon any *This Act not to authorise copartnerships to issue, within the limits mentioned, any bills payable on demand; nor to draw bills upon any partner, etc. so resident, for less than £50;*

partner or agent, or other person or persons who may be resident in London, or at any place or places not exceeding the distance of sixty-five miles from London, any bill of exchange which shall be payable on demand, or which shall be for a less amount than fifty pounds: provided also, that it shall be lawful, notwithstanding anything herein or in the said recited Act contained, for any such corporation or copartnership to draw any bill of exchange for any sum of money amounting to the sum of fifty pounds or upwards, payable either in London or elsewhere, at any period after date or after sight.

<small>nor to borrow money, or take up or issue bills of exchange, contrary to the provisions of the recited Act, except as herein provided.</small>

III. Provided also, and be it further enacted, that nothing in this Act contained shall extend or be construed to extend, to enable, or authorise any such corporation, or copartnership exceeding the number of six persons, so carrying on the trade or business of bankers in England as aforesaid, or any member, agent or agents of any such corporation or copartnership, to borrow, owe, or take up in London, or at any place or places not exceeding the distance of sixty-five miles from London, any sum or sums of money on any bill or promissory note of any such corporation or copartnership payable on demand, or at any less time than six months from the borrowing thereof, nor to make or issue any bill or bills of exchange or promissory note or notes of such corporation or copartnership contrary to the provisions of the said recited Act of the thirty-ninth and fortieth year of King George the Third, save as provided by this Act in that behalf: provided also, that nothing herein contained shall extend, or be construed to extend, to prevent any such corporation or copartnership, by any agent or person authorised by them, from discounting in London, or elsewhere, any bill or bills of exchange not drawn by or upon such corporation or copartnership, or by or upon any person on their behalf.

<small>Such copartnerships shall, before issuing any notes, etc., deliver at the stamp office in</small>

IV. And be it further enacted, that before any such corporation or copartnership exceeding the number of six persons, in England, shall begin to issue any bills or notes, or borrow, owe, or take up any money, on their bills or notes, an account or return shall be made out according to the form contained in the schedule marked (A) to this Act annexed, wherein shall be set forth the true names, title, or firm of such intended or existing corporation or copartnership, and also the names and places of abode of all the members of such corporation or of all the partners concerned or engaged in such copartnership, as the same respectively shall appear on the books of such corporation or copartnership, and the name or firm of every bank or banks established or to be established by such corporation or copartnership, and also the names and places of abode of two or more persons, being members of such corporation or copartnership, and being resident in England, who shall have been appointed public officers of such corporation or copartnership, together with the title of office or other description of every such public officer respectively, in the name of any one of whom such corporation shall sue and be sued as hereinafter provided, and also the name of every town or place where any of the bills or notes of such corporation or copartnership shall be issued by any such corporation, or by their agent or agents; and every such amount or return shall be delivered to the commissioners of stamps, at the stamp office in London, who shall cause the same to be filed and kept in the said stamp office, and an entry and registry thereof to be made in a book or books to be there kept for that purpose by some person or persons to be appointed by the said commissioners in that behalf, and which book or books any person or persons shall from time to time have liberty to search and inspect on payment of the sum of one shilling for every search. *London an account containing the name of the firm, etc.*

V. And be it further enacted, that such account or return shall be made out by the Secretary or other person, being one of the public officers appointed as aforesaid, and shall be verified by the oath of such secretary or other public officer, taken before any justice of the peace, and which oath any justice of the peace is hereby authorised and empowered to administer; and that such account or return shall, between the twenty-eighth day of February and the twenty-fifth day of March in every year, after such corporation or copartnership shall be formed, be in like manner delivered by such secretary or other public *Account to be verified by secretary.*

officer as aforesaid, to the commissioners of stamps, to be filed and kept in the manner and for the purposes as hereinbefore mentioned.

*Certified copies of returns to be evidence of the appointment of the public officers, etc.*

VI. And be it further enacted, that a copy of any such account or return so filed or kept and registered at the stamp office, as by this Act is directed, and which copy shall be certified to be a true copy under the hand or hands of one or more of the commissioners of stamps for the time being, upon proof made that such certificate has been signed with the handwriting of the person or persons making the same, and whom it shall not be necessary to prove to be a commissioner or commissioners, shall in all proceedings, civil or criminal, and in all cases whatsoever, be received in evidence as proof of the appointment and authority of the public officers named in such account or return, and also of the fact that all persons named therein as members of such corporation copartnership were members thereof at the date of such account or return.

*Commissioners of stamps to give certified copies of affidavits, on payment of 10s.*

VII. And be it further enacted, that the said commissioners of stamps for the time being shall and they are hereby required, upon application made to them by any person or persons requiring a copy certified according to this Act, of any such account or return as aforesaid, in order that the same may be produced in evidence or for any other purpose, to deliver to the person or persons so applying for the same such certified copy, he, she, or they paying for the same the sum of ten shillings and no more.

*Account of new officers or members in the course of any year to be made.*

VIII. Provided also, and be it further enacted, that the secretary or other officer of every such corporation or copartnership shall, and he is hereby required, from time to time, as often as occasion shall render it necessary, make out upon oath, in manner hereinbefore directed, and cause to be delivered to the commissioners of stamps as aforesaid, a further account or return according to the form contained in the schedule marked (B) to this Act annexed, of the name or names of any person or persons who shall have been nominated or appointed a new or additional public officer or public officers of such corporation or copartnership, and also of the name or names of any person or persons who shall have ceased to be members of such corporation or copartnership, and also of the name or names of any person or persons who shall have become a member or members of such corporation or copartnership, either in addition to or in the place or stead of any former member or members thereof, and of the name or names of any new or additional town or towns, place or places, where such bills or notes are or are intended to be issued, and where the same are to be made payable; and such further accounts or returns shall from time to time be filed and kept, and entered and registered at the stamp office in London, in like manner as is hereinbefore required with respect to the original or annual account or return hereinbefore directed to be made.

IX. And be it further enacted, that all actions and suits, and also all petitions to found any commission of bankruptcy against any person or persons, who may be at any time indebted to any such copartnership carrying on business under the provisions of this Act, and all proceedings at law or in equity under any commission of bankruptcy, and all other proceedings at law or in equity to be commenced or instituted for or on behalf of any such copartnership against any person or persons, bodies politic or corporate, or others, whether members of such copartnership or otherwise, for recovering any debts or enforcing any claims or demands due to such copartnership, or for any other matter relating to the concerns of such copartnership, shall and lawfully may, from and after the passing of this Act, be commenced or instituted or prosecuted in the name of any one of the public officers nominated as aforesaid for the time being of such copartnership, as the nominal plaintiff or petitioner for and on behalf of such copartnership; and that all actions or suits, and proceedings at law or in equity, to be commenced or instituted by any person or persons, bodies politic or corporate, or others, whether members of such copartnership or otherwise, against such copartnership, shall and lawfully may be commenced, instituted, and prosecuted against any one or more of the public officers, nominated as aforesaid for the time being

<small>Copartnerships shall sue and be sued in the name of their public officers.</small>

of such copartnership, as the nominal defendant for and on behalf of such copartnership; and that all indictments, informations, and prosecutions by or on behalf of such copartnership, for any stealing or embezzlement of any money, goods, effects, bills, notes, securities, or other property of or belonging to such copartnership, or for any fraud, forgery, crime, or offence committed against or with intent to injure or defraud such copartnership, shall and lawfully may be had, preferred, and carried on in the name of any one of the public officers nominated as aforesaid for the time being of such copartnership; and that in all indictments and informations to be had or preferred by or on behalf of such copartnership against any person or persons whomsoever, notwithstanding such person or persons may happen to be a member or members of such copartnership, it shall be lawful and sufficient to state the money, goods, effects, bills, notes, securities, or other property of such copartnership, to be the money, goods, effects, bills, notes, securities, or other property of any one of the public officers nominated as aforesaid for the time being of such copartnership; and that any forgery, fraud, crime, or other offence committed against or with intent to injure or defraud any such copartnership, shall and lawfully may in such indictment or indictments, notwithstanding as aforesaid, be laid or stated to have been committed against or with intent to injure or defraud any one of the public officers nominated as aforesaid for the time being of such copartnership; and any offender or offenders may thereupon be lawfully convicted for any such forgery, fraud, crime, or offence: and that in all other allegations, indictments, informations, or other proceedings of any kind whatsoever, in which it otherwise might or would have been necessary to state the names of the persons composing such copartnership, it shall and may be lawful and sufficient to state the name of any one of the public officers nominated as aforesaid for the time being of such copartnership; and the death, resignation, removal, or any act of such public officer, shall not abate or prejudice any such action, suit, indictment, information, prosecution, or other proceeding commenced against or by or on behalf of such copartnership, but the same may be continued, prosecuted, and carried on in the name of any other of the public officers of such copartnership for the time being.

X. And be it further enacted, that no person or persons, or body or bodies politic or corporate, having or claiming to have any demand upon or against any such corporation or copartnership, shall bring more than one action or suit, in case the merits shall have been tried in such action or suit, in respect of such demand; and the proceedings in any action or suit, by or against any one of the public officers nominated as aforesaid for the time being of any such copartnership, may be pleaded in bar of any other action or actions, suit or suits, for the same demand, by or against any other of the public officers of such copartnership.

*Not more than one action for the recovery of one demand.*

XI. And be it further enacted, that all and every decree or decrees, order or orders, made or pronounced in any suit or proceeding in any Court of equity against any public officer of any such copartnership carrying on business under the provisions of this Act, shall have the like effect and operation upon and against the property and funds of such copartnership, and upon and against the persons and property of every or any member or members thereof, as if every or any such members of such copartnership were parties members before the Court to and in any such suit or proceeding; and that it shall and may be lawful for any Court in which such order or decree shall have been made, to cause such order and decree to be enforced against every or any member of such copartnership, in like manner as if every member of such copartnership were parties before such Court to and in such suit or proceeding, and although all such members are not before the Court.

*Decrees of a Court of Equity against the public officer to take effect against the copartnership.*

XII. And be it further enacted, that all and every judgment and judgments, decree or decrees, which shall at any time after the passing of this Act be had or recovered or entered up as aforesaid, in any action, suit, or proceedings in law or equity against any public officer of any such copartnership, shall have the like effect and operation upon and against the property of such copartner-

*Judgments against such public officer shall operate against the copartnership.*

ship, and upon and against the property of every such member thereof as aforesaid, as if such judgment or judgments had been recovered or obtained against such copartnership; and that the bankruptcy, insolvency, or stopping payment of any such public officer for the time being of such copartnership, in his individual character or capacity, shall not be nor be construed to be the bankruptcy, insolvency, or stopping payment of such copartnership; and that such copartnership and every member thereof, and the capital stock and effects of such copartnership and the effects of every member of such copartnership, shall in all cases, notwithstanding the bankruptcy, insolvency, or stopping payment of any such public officer, be attached and attachable, and be in all respects liable to the lawful claims and demands of the creditor and creditors of such copartnership, or of any member or members thereof, as if no such bankruptcy, insolvency, or stopping payment of such public officer of such copartnership had happened or taken place.

**Execution upon judgment may be issued against any member of the copartnership.**

XIII. And be it further enacted, that execution upon any judgment in any action obtained against any public officer for the time being of any such corporation or copartnership carrying on the business of banking under the provisions of this Act, whether as plaintiff or defendant, may be issued against any member or members for the time being of such corporation or copartnership; and that in case any such execution against any member or members for the time being of any such corporation or copartnership shall be ineffectual for obtaining payment and satisfaction of the amount of such judgment, it shall be lawful for the party or parties so having obtained judgment against such public officer for the time being, to issue execution against any person or persons who was or were a member or members of such corporation or copartnership at the time when the contract or contracts or engagement or engagements in which such judgment may have been obtained was or were entered into, or became a member at any time before such contracts or engagements were executed, or was a member at the time of the judgment obtained: provided always, that no such execution as last mentioned shall be issued without leave first granted, on motion in open court, by the court in which such judgment shall have been obtained, and when motion shall be made on notice to the person or persons sought to be charged, nor after the expiration of three years next after any such person or persons shall have ceased to be a member or members of such corporation or copartnership.

XIV. Provided always, and be it further enacted, that every such public officer in whose name any such suit or action shall have been commenced, prosecuted, or defended, and every person or persons against whom execution upon any judgment obtained or entered up as aforesaid in any such action shall be issued as aforesaid, shall always be reimbursed and fully indemnified for all loss, damages, costs, and charges, without deduction, which any such officer or person may have incurred by reason of such execution, out of the funds of such copartnership, or in failure thereof, by contribution from the other members of such copartnership, as in the ordinary cases of copartnership. *Officer &c. in such cases indemnified.*

XV. And to prevent any doubts that might arise whether the said governor and company, under and by virtue of their charter, and the several Acts of Parliament which have been made and passed in relation to the affairs of the said governor and company, can lawfully carry on the trade or business of banking, otherwise than under the immediate order, management, and direction of the court of directors of the said governor and company: be it therefore enacted, that it shall and may be lawful for the said governor and company to authorise and empower any committee or committees, agent or agents, to carry on the trade and business of banking, for and on behalf of the said governor and company, at any place or places in that part of the United Kingdom called England, and for that purpose to invest such committee or committees, agent or agents, with such powers of management and superintendence, and such authority to appoint cashiers and other officers and servants as may be necessary or convenient for carrying on such trade and business as aforesaid; and for the same purpose to issue to such *Governor and company of the Bank of England may empower agents to carry on banking business at any place in England.*

committee or committees, agent or agents, cashier or
cashiers, or other officer or officers, servant or servants,
cash, bills of exchange, bank post bills, bank notes,
promissory notes, and other securities for payment of
money: Provided always, that all such acts of the said
governor and company shall be done and exercised in such
manner as may be appointed by any bye-laws, constitutions,
orders, rules, and directions from time to time hereafter
to be made by the general court of the said governor and
company in that behalf, such bye-laws not being repugnant to the laws of that part of the United Kingdom
called England; and in all cases where such bye-laws,
constitutions, orders, rules, or directions of the said general
court shall be wanting, in such manner as the governor,
deputy governor, and directors, or the major part of them
assembled, whereof the said governor or deputy governor
is always to be one, shall or may direct, such directions
not being repugnant to the laws of that part of the United
Kingdom called England; anything in the said charter
or Acts of Parliament, or other law, usage, matter, or
thing to the contrary thereof notwithstanding: provided
always, that in any place where the trade and business of
banking shall be carried on for and on behalf of the said
governor and company of the Bank of England, any promissory note issued on their account in such place shall
be made payable in coin in such place as well as in London.

*Copartner-
ships may
issue un-
stamped
notes, on
giving bond.*
XVI. And be it further enacted, that if any corporation
or copartnership carrying on the trade or business of
bankers under the authority of this Act shall be desirous
of issuing and re-issuing notes in the nature of bank
notes, payable to the bearer on demand, without the same
being stamped as by law is required, it shall be lawful for
them so to do on giving security by bond to His Majesty,
his heirs and successors, in which bond two of the
directors, members, or partners of such corporation or
copartnership, shall be the obligors, together with the
cashier or cashiers, or accountant or accountants employed
by such corporation or copartnership, as the said commissioners of stamps shall require; and such bonds shall be
taken in such reasonable sums as the duties may amount

unto during the period of one year, with condition to
deliver to the said commissioners of stamps, within fourteen
days after the fifth day of January, the fifth day of April,
the fifth day of July, and the tenth day of October in
every year, whilst the present stamp duties shall remain
in force, a just and true account, verified upon the oaths or
affirmations of two directors, members, or partners of such
corporation or copartnership, and of the said cashier or
cashiers, accountant or accountants, or such of them as the
said commissioners of stamps shall require, such oaths or
affirmations to be taken before any justice of the peace,
and which oaths or affirmations any justice of the peace is
hereby authorised and empowered to administer, of the
amount or value of all their promissory notes in circulation
on some given day in every week, for the space of one
quarter of a year prior to the quarter day immediately
preceding the delivery of such account, together with
the average amount or value thereof according to such
account; and also to pay or cause to be paid into the hands
of the receivers-general of stamp duties in Great Britain,
as a composition for the duties which would otherwise
have been payable for such promissory notes issued within
the space of one year, the sum of seven shillings for every
one hundred pounds, and also for the fractional part of one
hundred pounds of the said average amount or value of
such notes in circulation, according to the true intent or
meaning of this Act; and on due performance thereof
such bond shall be void; and it shall be lawful for the
said commissioners to fix the time or times of making
such payment, and to specify the same in the condition
to every such bond; and every such bond may be required
to be renewed from time to time, at the discretion of the
said commissioners or the major part of them, and as
often as the same shall be forfeited, or the party or parties
to the same, or any of them, shall die, become bankrupt
or insolvent, or reside in parts beyond the seas.

XVII. Provided always, and be it further enacted, that no such corporation or copartnership shall be obliged to take out more than four licences for the issuing of any promissory notes for money payable to the bearer on

*No corporation compelled to*

*take out more than four licences.* demand, allowed by law to be re-issued in all for any number of towns or places in England; and in case any such corporation or copartnership shall issue such promissory notes as aforesaid, by themselves or their agents, at more than four different towns or places in England, then, after taking out three distinct licences for three of such towns or places, such corporation or copartnership shall be entitled to have all the rest of such towns or places included in a fourth licence.

*Penalty on copartnership neglecting to send returns, £500.*

XVIII. And be it further enacted, that if any such corporation or copartnership exceeding the number of six persons in England, shall begin to issue any bills or notes, or to borrow, owe, or take up any money on their bills or notes, without having caused such account or return as aforesaid to be made out and delivered in the manner and form directed by this Act, or shall neglect or omit to cause such account or return to be renewed yearly and every year, between the days or times hereinbefore appointed for that purpose, such corporation or copartnership so offending shall, for each and every week they shall so neglect to make such account and return, forfeit the sum of five hundred pounds; and if any secretary or other officer of such corporation or copartnership shall

*Penalties for making false returns.* make out or sign any false account or return, or any account or return which shall not truly set forth all the several particulars by this Act required to be contained or inserted in such account or return, the corporation or copartnership to which such secretary or other officer so offending shall belong shall for every such offence forfeit the sum of five hundred pounds, and the said secretary or other officer so offending shall also for every such offence

*False oath perjury.* forfeit the sum of one hundred pounds; and if any such secretary or other officer making out or signing any such account or return as aforesaid, shall knowingly and wilfully make a false oath of or concerning any of the matters to be therein specified and set forth, every such secretary or other officer so offending, and being thereof lawfully convicted, shall be subject and liable to such pains and penalties as by any law now in force persons convicted of wilful and corrupt perjury are subject and liable to.

XIX. And be it further enacted, that if any such corporation or copartnership exceeding the number of six persons, so carrying on the trade or business of bankers as aforesaid, shall, either by any member of or person belonging to any such corporation or copartnership, or by any agent or agents, or any other person or persons on behalf of any such corporation or copartnership, issue or re-issue in London, or at any place or places not exceeding the distance of sixty-five miles from London, any bill or note of such corporation or copartnership which shall be payable on demand; or shall draw upon any partner or agent, or other person or persons who may be resident in London, or at any place or places not the exceeding distance of sixty-five miles from London, any bill of exchange which shall be payable on demand, or which shall be for a less amount than fifty pounds; or if any such corporation or copartnership exceeding the number of six persons, so carrying on the trade or business of bankers in England as aforesaid, or any member, agent or agents of any such corporation or copartnership, shall borrow, owe, or take up in London, or at any place or places not exceeding the distance of sixty-five miles from London, any sum or sums of money on any bill or promissory note of any such corporation or copartnership payable on demand, or at any less time than six months from the borrowing thereof, or shall make or issue any bill or bills of exchange or promissory note or notes of such corporation or copartnership contrary to the provisions of the said recited Act of the thirty-ninth and fortieth years of King George the Third, save as provided by this Act, such corporation or copartnership so offending, or on whose account or behalf any such offence as aforesaid shall be committed, shall for every such offence forfeit the sum of fifty pounds. *Penalty on copartnership for issuing bills payable on demand; or drawing bills of exchange payable on demand, or for less than £50; or borrowing money on bills, except as herein provided.*

XX. Provided also, and be it further enacted, that nothing in this Act contained shall extend or be construed to extend to prejudice, alter, or affect any of the rights, powers, or privileges of the said governor and company of the Bank of England; except as the said exclusive privilege of the said governor and company is by this Act specially altered and varied. *Not to affect the rights of Bank of England except as herein specially altered.*

*Penalties how recovered.*

XXI. And be it further enacted, that all pecuniary penalties and forfeitures imposed by this Act shall and may be sued for and recovered in His Majesty's Court of Exchequer at Westminster, in the same manner as penalties incurred under any Act or Acts relating to stamp duties may be sued for and recovered in such Courts.

*Act may be altered.*

XXII. And be it further enacted, that this Act may be altered, amended, or repealed by any Act or Acts to be passed in this present session of Parliament.

---

### SCHEDULES REFERRED TO BY THIS ACT

#### SCHEDULE (A)

RETURN or ACCOUNT to be entered at the Stamp Office in London, in pursuance of an Act passed in the seventh year of the reign of King George the Fourth, intituled [*here insert the title of this Act*], viz. :

Firm or name of the banking corporation or copartnership, viz. [*set forth the firm or name*].

Names and places of abode of all the partners concerned or engaged in such corporation or copartnership, viz. [*set forth all the names and places of abode*].

Names and places of the bank or banks established by such corporation or copartnership, viz. [*set forth all the names and places*].

Names and descriptions of the public officers of the said banking corporation or copartnership, viz. [*set forth all the names and descriptions*].

Names of the several towns and places where the bills or notes of the said banking corporation or copartnership are to be issued by the said corporation or copartnership, or their agent or agents, viz. [*set forth the names of all the towns and places*].

A. B. of          secretary [*or other officer, describing the office*] of the above corporation or copartnership, maketh oath and saith, that the above doth contain the name, style, and firm of the above corporation or copartnership, and the names and places of the abode of the several members thereof, and of the banks established by the said corporation or copartnership, and the names, titles, and descriptions of the public officers of the said corporation or copartnership, and the names of the towns and places where the notes of the said corporation or copartnership are to be issued, as the same respectively appear in the books of the said corporation or copartnership, and to the best of the information, knowledge, and belief of the deponent.

Sworn before me, the          day of
   at           in the county of
           C. D. Justice of the Peace in and
                for the said county.

---

### SCHEDULE (B)

RETURN or ACCOUNT to be entered at the Stamp Office in London, on behalf of [*name the corporation or copartnership*] in pursuance of an Act passed in the seventh year of the reign of King George the Fourth, intituled [*insert the title of this Act*], viz:

Names of any and every new or additional public officer of the said corporation or copartnership; viz.

A. B. in the room of C. D. deceased or removed [*as the case may be*] [ *set forth every name*].

Names of any and every person who may have ceased to be a member of such corporation or copartnership; viz. [*set forth every name*].

Names of any and every person who may have become a new member of such corporation or copartnership [*set forth every name*].

Names of any additional towns or places where bills or notes are to be issued, and where the same are to be made payable.

A. B. of          secretary [*or other officer*] of the above-named corporation or copartnership, maketh oath and saith, that the above doth contain the name and place of abode of any and every person who hath become

or been appointed a public officer of the above corporation or copartnership, and also the name and place of abode of any and every person who hath ceased to be a member of the said corporation and copartnership, and of any and every person who hath become a member of the said copartnership since the registry of the said corporation or copartnership on the              day of
last, as the same respectively appear on the books of the said corporation or copartnership, and to the best of the information, knowledge, and belief of the deponent.

    Sworn before me, the              day of
       at              in the county of

            C.D. Justice of the Peace in and
            for the said county.

## BANK NOTES (LICENCE, Etc.) ACT

### 9 GEO. IV., CAP. 23

*An Act to enable Bankers in England to issue certain unstamped Promissory Notes and Bills of Exchange, upon payment of a composition in lieu of Stamp Duties thereon*       [19th June 1828]

WHEREAS it is expedient to permit all persons carrying on the business of bankers in England (except within the city of London, or within three miles thereof), to issue their promissory notes payable to bearer on demand, or to order within a limited period after sight, and to draw bills of exchange payable to order on demand, or within a limited period after sight or date, on unstamped paper, upon payment of a composition in lieu of the stamp duties which would otherwise be payable upon such notes and bills respectively, and subject to the regulations hereinafter mentioned: be it therefore enacted by the King's most Excellent Majesty, by and with the advice and consent of the Lords, spiritual and temporal, and

Commons in this present Parliament assembled, and by the authority of the same, that from and after the first day of July One thousand eight hundred and twenty-eight, it shall be lawful for any person or persons carrying on the business of a banker or bankers in England (except within the city of London, or within three miles thereof), having first duly obtained a licence for that purpose, and given security by bond in manner hereinafter mentioned, to issue, on unstamped paper, promissory notes for any sum of money amounting to five pounds or upwards, expressed to be payable to the bearer on demand, or to order, at any period not exceeding seven days after sight; and also to draw and issue, on unstamped paper, bills of exchange, expressed to be payable to order on demand, or at any period not exceeding seven days after sight, or twenty-one days after the date thereof: provided such bills of exchange be drawn upon a person or persons carrying on business of a banker or bankers in London, Westminster, or the borough of Southwark, or provided such bills of exchange be drawn by any banker or bankers at a town or place where he or they shall be duly licensed to issue unstamped notes and bills under the authority of this Act, upon himself or themselves, or his or their copartner or copartners, payable at any other town or place where such banker or bankers shall also be duly licensed to issue such notes and bills as aforesaid.

*Certain bankers may issue unstamped promissory notes and bills of exchange, subject to the regulations herein mentioned.*

II. And be it enacted, that it shall be lawful for any two or more of the commissioners of stamps to grant to all persons carrying on the business of bankers in England (except as aforesaid), who shall require the same, licences authorising such persons to issue such promissory notes, and to draw and issue such bills of exchange as aforesaid, on unstamped paper; which said licences shall be and are hereby respectively charged with a stamp duty of thirty pounds for every such licence.

*Commissioners of stamps may grant licences to issue unstamped notes and bills.*

III. And be it further enacted, that a separate licence shall be taken out in respect of every town or place where any such unstamped promissory notes or bills of exchange as aforesaid shall be issued or drawn: provided always,

*A separate licence to be taken for every place where such notes or*

## APPENDIX

*bills shall be issued, but not to exceed four licences for any number of such places.*

that no person or persons shall be obliged to take out more than four licences in all for any number of towns or places in England; and in case any person or persons shall issue or draw such unstamped notes or bills as aforesaid, at more than four different towns or places, then, after taking out three distinct licences for three of such towns or places, such person or persons shall be entitled to have all the rest of such towns or places included in a fourth licence.

*Regulations respecting licences.*

IV. And be it further enacted, that every licence granted under the authority of this Act shall specify all the particulars required by law to be specified in licences to be taken out by persons issuing promissory notes payable to bearer on demand, and allowed to be re-issued; and every such licence which shall be granted between the tenth day of October and the eleventh day of November in any year shall be dated on the eleventh day of October, and every such licence which shall be granted at any other time shall be dated on the day on which the same shall be granted; and every such licence shall (notwithstanding any alteration which may take place in any copartnership of persons to whom the same shall be granted) have effect and continue in force from the day of the date thereof until the tenth day of October then next following, both inclusive, and no longer.

*Commissioners may cancel licences already taken out, and grant licences under this Act in lieu thereof.*

V. Provided always, and be it further enacted, that where any banker or bankers shall have obtained the licence required by law for issuing promissory notes payable to bearer on demand, at any town or place in England, and during the continuance of such licence shall be desirous of taking out a licence to issue at the same town or place unstamped promissory notes and bills of exchange under the provisions of this Act, it shall be lawful for the commissioners of stamps to cancel and allow as spoiled the stamp upon the said first-mentioned licence, and in lieu thereof to grant to such banker or bankers a licence under the authority of this Act; and every such last-mentioned licence shall also authorise the issuing and re-issuing of all promissory notes payable to the bearer on

VI. Provided always, and be it further enacted, that if any banker or bankers, who shall take out a licence under the authority of this Act, shall issue, under the authority either of this or any other Act, any unstamped promissory notes for payment of money to the bearer on demand, such banker or bankers shall, so long as he or they shall continue licensed as aforesaid, make and issue on unstamped paper all his or their promissory notes for payment of money to the bearer on demand, of whatever amount such notes may be; and it shall not be lawful for such banker or bankers, during the period aforesaid, to issue for the first time any such promissory note as aforesaid on stamped paper.

*Bankers while licensed under this Act shall not issue, for the first time, notes on stamped paper.*

VII. And be it farther enacted, that before any licence shall be granted to any person or persons to issue or draw any unstamped promissory notes or bills of exchange under the authority of this Act, such person or persons shall give security, by bond, to His Majesty, his heirs and successors, with a condition, that if such person or persons do and shall from time to time enter or cause to be entered in a book or books to be kept for that purpose, an account of all such unstamped promissory notes and bills of exchange as he or they shall so as aforesaid issue or draw, specifying the amount or value thereof respectively, and the several dates of the issuing thereof; and in like manner also, a similar account of all such promissory notes as, having been issued as aforesaid, shall have been cancelled, and the dates of the cancelling thereof, and of all such bills of exchange as, having been drawn or issued as aforesaid, shall have been paid, and the dates of the payment thereof; and do and shall from time to time, when thereunto requested, produce and show such accounts to, and permit the same to be examined and inspected by, the said commissioners of stamps, or any officer of stamps appointed under the hands and seals of the said commissioners for that purpose; and also do and shall deliver

*Bankers licensed to issue unstamped notes or bills shall give security, by bond, for the due performance of the conditions herein contained.*

to the said commissioners of stamps half-yearly (that is to say), within fourteen days after the first day of January and the first day of July in every year, a just and true account in writing, verified upon the oaths or affirmations (which any Justice of the Peace is hereby empowered to administer), to the best of the knowledge and belief of such person or persons, and of his or their cashier, accountant, or chief clerk, or of such of them as the said commissioners shall require, of the amount or value of all unstamped promissory notes and bills of exchange issued under the provisions of this or any former Act, in circulation within the meaning of this Act on a given day, that is to say, on Saturday in every week, for the space of half a year prior to the half-yearly day immediately preceding the delivery of such account, together with the average amount or value of such notes and bills so in circulation, according to such account; and also do and shall pay or cause to be paid to the receiver-general of stamp duties in Great Britain, or to some other person duly authorised by the commissioners of stamps, to receive the same, as a composition for the duties which would otherwise have been payable for such promissory notes and bills of exchange issued or in circulation during such half year, the sum of three shillings and sixpence for every one hundred pounds, and also for the fractional part of one hundred pounds, of the said average amount or value of such notes and bills in circulation, according to the true intent and meaning of this Act; and on due performance thereof such bond shall be void, but otherwise the same shall be and remain in full force and virtue.

*For what period notes and bills are to be deemed in circulation.*

VIII. And be it further enacted, that every unstamped promissory note payable to the bearer on demand, issued under the provisions of this Act, shall, for the purpose of payment of duty, be deemed to be in circulation from the day of the issuing to the day of the cancelling thereof, both days inclusive, excepting nevertheless the period during which such note shall be in the hands of the banker or bankers who first issued the same, or by whom the same shall be expressed to be payable; and that every unstamped promissory note payable to order, and every unstamped bill of exchange so as aforesaid issued, shall for the purpose aforesaid be deemed to be in circulation from the day of the issuing to the day of the payment thereof, both days inclusive: provided always, that every such promissory note payable to order, and bill of exchange as aforesaid, which shall be paid in less than seven days from the issuing thereof, shall, for the purpose aforesaid, be included in the account of notes and bills in circulation on the Saturday next after the day of the issuing thereof as if the same were then actually in circulation.

IX. And be it further enacted, that in every bond to be given pursuant to the directions of this Act the person or persons intending to issue or draw any such unstamped promissory notes and bills of exchange as aforesaid, or such and so many of the said persons as the commissioners of stamps shall require, shall be the obligors; and every such bond shall be taken in the sum of one hundred pounds, or in such larger sum as the said commissioners of stamps may judge to be the probable amount of the composition or duties that will be payable from such person or persons, under or by virtue of this Act, during the period of one year; and it shall be lawful for the said commissioners to fix the time or times of payment of the said composition or duties, and to specify the same in the condition to every such bond; and every such bond may be required to be renewed from time to time, at the discretion of the said commissioners, and as often as the same shall be forfeited, or the parties to the same, or any of them, shall die, become bankrupt or insolvent, or reside in parts beyond the seas. *Regulations respecting the bonds to be given pursuant to this Act.*

X. And be it further enacted, that if any alteration shall be made in any copartnership of persons who shall have given any such security by bond as by this Act is directed, whether such alteration shall be caused by the death or retirement of one or more of the partners of the firm, or by the accession of any additional or new partner or partners, a fresh bond shall be given by *Fresh bonds to be given on alterations of copartnerships.*

the remaining partner or partners, or the persons composing the new copartnership, as the case may be, which bond shall be taken as a security for the duties which may be due and owing, or may become due and owing in respect of the unstamped notes and bills which shall have been issued by the persons composing the old copartnership, and which shall be in circulation at the time of such alteration, as well as for duties which shall or may be or become due or owing in respect of the unstamped notes and bills issued or to be issued by the persons composing the new copartnership; provided that no such fresh bond shall be rendered necessary by any such alteration as aforesaid in any copartnership of persons exceeding six in number, but that the bonds to be given by such last-mentioned copartnerships shall be taken as securities for all the duties they may incur so long as they shall exist, or the persons composing the same, or any of them, shall carry on business in copartnership together, or with any other person or persons, notwithstanding any alteration in such copartnership; saving always the power of the said commissioners of stamps to require a new bond in any case where they shall deem it necessary for better securing the payment of the said duties.

*Penalty on bankers neglecting to renew their bonds.*

XI. And be it further enacted, that if any person or persons who shall have given security by bond to His Majesty, in the manner hereinbefore directed, shall refuse or neglect to renew such bond when forfeited, and as often as the same is by this Act required to be renewed, such person or persons so offending shall for every such offence forfeit and pay the sum of one hundred pounds.

*Penalty for post-dating unstamped notes or bills.*

XII. And be it further enacted, that if any person or persons who shall be licensed under the provisions of this Act shall draw or issue, or cause to be drawn or issued, upon unstamped paper, any promissory note payable to order, or any bill of exchange which shall bear date subsequent to the day on which it shall be issued, the person or persons so offending shall, for every such note or bill so drawn or issued, forfeit the sum of one hundred pounds.

APPENDIX

XIII. Provided always, and be it further enacted, that nothing in this Act contained shall extend or be construed to extend to exempt or relieve from the forfeitures or penalties imposed by any Act or Acts now in force, upon persons issuing promissory notes or bills of exchange not duly stamped as the law requires, any person or persons who, under any colour or pretence whatsoever, shall issue any unstamped promissory note or bill of exchange, unless such person or persons shall be duly licensed to issue such note or bill under the provisions of this Act; and such note or bill shall be drawn and issued in strict accordance with the regulations and restrictions herein contained. *This Act not to exempt from penalties any persons issuing unstamped notes or bills not in accordance herewith.*

XIV. And be it further enacted, that all pecuniary forfeitures and penalties which may be incurred under any of the provisions of this Act shall be recovered for the use of His Majesty, his heirs and successors, in His Majesty's Court of Exchequer at Westminster, by action of debt, bill, plaint, or information, in the name of His Majesty's attorney or solicitor-general in England. *Recovery of penalties.*

XV. Provided always, and be it further enacted, that nothing in this Act contained shall extend or be construed to extend to prejudice, alter, or affect any of the rights, powers, or privileges of the governor and company of the Bank of England. *Not to affect the privileges of the Bank of England.*

XVI. And whereas it may happen that bankers who may be desirous to issue unstamped promissory notes payable to bearer on demand, under the provisions of this Act, may have provided themselves with stamps for such notes, which may not have been issued, and which may by this Act be rendered useless or unnecessary, and it is expedient to enable the commissioners of stamps to cancel and allow such stamps in manner hereinafter mentioned: be it therefore enacted, that where any banker or bankers, who shall take out a licence under the authority of this Act, shall have in his or their possession stamps for re-issuable promissory notes payable to the bearer on demand, which shall be rendered useless or unnecessary in con- *Where any bankers taking out licences under the Act shall have stamps in their possession which will become useless, the commissioners may cancel such stamps, and make allowance for the same.*

sequence of such banker or bankers electing to issue such notes on unstamped paper under the provisions of this Act, it shall be lawful for the said commissioners of stamps, and they are hereby authorised and empowered to cancel and allow such stamps so as aforesaid rendered useless or unnecessary, and to repay the amount or value thereof in money, deducting therefrom the sum of one pound ten shillings for every one hundred pounds, and so in proportion for any greater or less sum than one hundred pounds of such amount or value; provided proof be made by affidavit or affirmation, to the satisfaction of the said commissioners, that such stamps have not been issued; and provided application be made for such allowance within six calendar months next after the passing of this Act.

*Act may be altered.* XVII. And be it further enacted, that this Act may be altered, amended, or repealed by any Act or Acts to be passed in this present Session of Parliament.

---

## BANK CHARTER ACT

### 7 & 8 VICT., CAP. 32

*An Act to regulate the issue of Bank Notes, and for giving to the Governor and Company of the Bank of England certain privileges for a limited period*

[19th July 1844]

*3 & 4 W. 4, c. 98.* WHEREAS it is expedient to regulate the issue of bills or notes payable on demand: And whereas an Act was passed in the fourth year of the reign of His late Majesty King William the Fourth, intituled "An Act for giving to the Corporation of the Governor and Company of the Bank of England certain privileges for a limited period, under certain conditions"; and it is expedient that the privileges of exclusive banking therein mentioned should be continued to the said governor and company of the

Bank of England, with such alterations as are herein contained, upon certain conditions: May it therefore please your Majesty that it may be enacted; and be enacted by the Queen's most Excellent Majesty, by and with the advice and consent of the Lords, spiritual and temporal, and Commons, in this present Parliament assembled, and by the authority of the same, that from and after the thirty-first day of August One thousand eight hundred and forty-four the issue of promissory notes of the governor and company of the Bank of England, payable on demand, shall be separated and thenceforth kept wholly distinct from the general banking business of the said governor and company; and the business of and relating to such issue shall be henceforth conducted and carried on by the said governor and company in a separate department to be called "the issue department of the Bank of England," subject to the rules and regulations hereinafter contained; and it shall be lawful for the court of directors of the said governor and company, if they shall think fit, to appoint a committee or committees of directors for the conduct and management of such issue department of the Bank of England, and from time to time to remove the members, and define, alter, and regulate the constitution and powers of such committee, as they shall think fit, subject to any bye-laws, rules, or regulations which may be made for that purpose; provided nevertheless, that the said issue department shall always be kept separate and distinct from the banking department of the said governor and company. *Bank to establish a separate department for the issue of notes.*

II. And be it enacted, that upon the thirty-first day of August One thousand eight hundred and forty-four there shall be transferred, appropriated, and set apart by the said governor and company to the issue department of the Bank of England securities to the value of fourteen million pounds, whereof the debt due by the public to the said governor and company shall be and be deemed a part; and there shall also at the same time be transferred, appropriated, and set apart by the said governor and company to the said issue department so much of the gold coin and gold and silver bullion then held by *Management of the issue by Bank of England.*

the Bank of England as shall not be required by the banking department thereof; and thereupon there shall be delivered out of the said issue department into the said banking department of the Bank of England such an amount of Bank of England notes as, together with the Bank of England notes then in circulation, shall be equal to the aggregate amount of securities, coin, and bullion so transferred to the said issue department of the Bank of England; and the whole amount of Bank of England notes then in circulation, including those delivered to the banking department of the Bank of England as aforesaid, shall be deemed to be issued on the credit of such securities, coin, and bullion so appropriated and set apart to the said issue department; and from thenceforth it shall not be lawful for the said governor and company to increase the amount of securities for the time being in the said issue department, save as hereinafter is mentioned, but it shall be lawful for the said governor and company to diminish the amount of such securities, and again to increase the same to any sum not exceeding in the whole the sum of fourteen million pounds, and so from time to time as they shall see occasion; and from and after such transfer and appropriation to the said issue department as aforesaid it shall not be lawful for the said governor and company to issue Bank of England notes, either into the banking department of the Bank of England, or to any persons or person whatsoever save in exchange for other Bank of England notes, or for gold coin or for gold or silver bullion received or purchased for the said issue department under the provisions of this Act, or in exchange for securities acquired and taken in the said issue department under the provisions herein contained: provided always, that it shall be lawful for the said governor and company in their banking department to issue all such Bank of England notes as they shall at any time receive from the said issue department or otherwise, in the same manner in all respects as such issue would be lawful to any other person or persons.

Proportion   III. And whereas it is necessary to limit the amount

# APPENDIX

of silver bullion on which it shall be lawful for the issue department of the Bank of England to issue Bank of England notes: be it therefore enacted, that it shall not be lawful for the Bank of England to retain in the issue department of the said bank at any one time an amount of silver bullion exceeding one-fourth part of the gold coin and bullion at such time held by the Bank of England in the issue department.

<small>of silver bullion to be retained in the issue department.</small>

IV. And be it enacted, that from and after the thirty-first day of August One thousand eight hundred and forty-four all persons shall be entitled to demand from the issue department of the Bank of England Bank of England notes in exchange for gold bullion, at the rate of three pounds seventeen shillings and ninepence per ounce of standard gold: provided always, that the said governor and company shall in all cases be entitled to require such gold bullion to be melted and assayed by persons approved by the said governor and company, at the expense of the parties tendering such gold bullion.

<small>All persons may demand of the issue department notes for gold bullion.</small>

V. Provided always, and be it enacted, that if any banker who on the sixth day of May One thousand eight hundred and forty-four was issuing his own bank notes shall cease to issue his own bank notes, it shall be lawful for Her Majesty in council, at any time after the cessation of such issue, upon the application of the said governor and company, to authorise and empower the said governor and company to increase the amount of securities in the said issue department beyond the total sum or value of fourteen million pounds, and thereupon to issue additional Bank of England notes to an amount not exceeding such increased amount of securities specified in such order in council, and so from time to time: provided always, that such increased amount of securities specified in such order in council shall in no case exceed the proportion of two-thirds the amount of bank notes which the banker so ceasing to issue may have been authorised to issue under the provisions of this Act; and every such order in council shall be published in the next succeeding *London Gazette*.

<small>Power to increase securities in the issue department, and issue additional notes.</small>

## APPENDIX

*Account to be rendered by the Bank of England.*

VI. And be it enacted, that an account of the amount of Bank of England notes issued by the issue department of the Bank of England, and of gold coin and of gold and silver bullion respectively, and of securities in the said issue department, and also an account of the capital stock, and the deposits, and of the money and securities belonging to the said governor and company in the banking department of the Bank of England, on some day in every week to be fixed by the commissioners of stamps and taxes, shall be transmitted by the said governor and company weekly to the said commissioners in the form prescribed in the schedule hereto annexed marked (A), and shall be published by the said commissioners in the next succeeding *London Gazette* in which the same may be conveniently inserted.

*Bank of England exempted from stamp duty upon their notes.*

VII. And be it enacted, that from and after the said thirty-first day of August One thousand eight hundred and forty-four the said governor and company of the Bank of England shall be released and discharged from the payment of any stamp duty, or composition in respect of stamp duty, upon or in respect of their promissory notes payable to bearer on demand; and all such notes shall thenceforth be and continued free and wholly exempt from all liability to any stamp duty whatsoever.

*Bank to allow £180,000 per annum.*

VIII. And be it enacted, that from and after the said thirty-first day of August One thousand eight hundred and forty-four the payment or deduction of the annual sum of one hundred and twenty thousand pounds, made by the said governor and company, under the provisions of the said Act passed in the fourth year of the reign of his late Majesty King William the Fourth, out of the sums payable to them for the charges of management of the public unredeemed debt, shall cease, and in lieu thereof the said governor and company, in consideration of the privileges of exclusive banking, and the exemption from stamp duties, given to them by this Act, shall, during the continuance of such privileges and such exemption respectively, but no longer, deduct and allow to the

# APPENDIX

public, from the sums now payable by law to the said governor and company for the charges of management of the public unredeemed debt, the annual sum of one hundred and eighty thousand pounds, anything in any Act or Acts of Parliament, or in any agreement, to the contrary notwithstanding: provided always, that such deduction shall in no respect prejudice or affect the rights of the said governor and company to be paid for the management of the public debt at the rate and according to the terms provided in an Act passed in the forty-eighth year of the reign of His late Majesty King George the Third, intituled, "An Act to authorise the advancing for the public service, upon certain conditions, a proportion of the balance remaining in the Bank of England, for payment of unclaimed dividends, annuities, and lottery prizes, and for regulating the allowance to be made for the management of the national debt." *48 G. 3. c. 4.*

IX. And be it enacted, that in case, under the provisions hereinbefore contained, the securities held by the said issue department of the Bank of England shall at any time be increased beyond the total amount of fourteen million pounds, then and in each and every year in which the same shall happen, and so long as such increase shall continue, the said governor and company shall, in addition to the said annual sum of one hundred and eighty thousand pounds, make a further payment or allowance to the public, equal in amount to the net profit derived in the said issue department during the current year from such additional securities, after deducting the amount of the expenses occasioned by the additional issue during the same period, which expenses shall include the amount of any and every composition or payment to be made by the said governor and company to any banker in consideration of the discontinuance at any time hereafter of the issue of bank notes by such banker; and such further payment or allowance to the public by the said governor and company shall, in every year while the public shall be entitled to receive the same, be deducted from the amount by law payable to the said governor *Bank to allow the public the profits of increased circulation.*

and company for the charges of management of the unredeemed public debt, in the same manner as the said annual sum of one hundred and eighty thousand pounds is hereby directed to be deducted therefrom.

<small>No new bank of issue.</small>

X. And be it enacted, that from and after the passing of this Act no person other than a banker who on the sixth day of May One thousand eight hundred and forty-four was lawfully issuing his own bank notes shall make or issue bank notes in any part of the United Kingdom.

<small>Restriction against issue of bank notes.</small>

XI. And be it enacted, that from and after the passing of this Act it shall not be lawful for any banker to draw, accept, make, or issue, in England or Wales, any bill of exchange or promissory note or engagement for the payment of money payable to bearer on demand, or to borrow, owe, or take up, in England or Wales, any sums or sum of money on the bills or notes of such banker payable to bearer on demand, save and except that it shall be lawful for any banker who was on the sixth day of May One thousand eight hundred and forty-four carrying on the business of a banker in England or Wales, and was then lawfully issuing, in England or Wales, his own bank notes, under the authority of a licence to that effect, to continue to issue such notes to the extent and under the conditions hereinafter mentioned, but not further or otherwise; and the right of any company or partnership to continue to issue such notes shall not be in any manner prejudiced or effected by any change which may hereafter take place in the personal composition of such company or partnership, either by the transfer of any shares or share therein, or by the admission of any new partner or member thereto, or by the retirement of any present partner or member therefrom: provided always, that it shall not be lawful for any company or partnership now consisting of only six or less than six persons to issue bank notes at any time after the number of partners therein shall exceed six in the whole.

XII. And be it enacted, that if any banker in any part of the United Kingdom who after the passing of this Act shall be entitled to issue bank notes shall become bankrupt, or shall cease to carry on the business of a banker, or shall discontinue the issue of bank notes, either by agreement with the governor and company of the Bank of England or otherwise, it shall not be lawful for such banker at any time thereafter to issue any such notes. *Bankers ceasing to issue notes may not resume.*

XIII. And be it enacted, that every banker claiming under this Act to continue to issue bank notes in England or Wales shall, within one month next after the passing of this Act, give notice in writing to the commissioners of stamps and taxes at their head office in London of such claim, and of the place and name and firm at and under which such banker has issued such notes during the twelve weeks next preceding the twenty-seventh day of April last; and thereupon the said commissioners shall ascertain if such banker was on the sixth day of May One thousand eight hundred and forty-four carrying on the business of a banker, and lawfully issuing his own bank notes in England or Wales, and if it shall so appear then the said commissioners shall proceed to ascertain the average amount of the bank notes of such banker which were in circulation during the said period of twelve weeks preceding the twenty-seventh day of April last, according to the returns made by such banker in pursuance of the Act passed in the fourth and fifth years of the reign of Her present Majesty, intituled, "An Act to make further provision relative to the returns to be made by banks of the amount of their notes in circulation"; and the said commissioners or any two of them shall certify under their hands to such banker the said average amount, when so ascertained as aforesaid; and it shall be lawful for every such banker to continue to issue his own bank notes after the passing of this Act: provided nevertheless, that such banker shall not at any time after the tenth day of October One thousand eight hundred and forty-four have in circulation upon the average of a period of four weeks, to be ascer- *Existing banks of issue to continue under certain limitations.* *4 & 5 Vict. c. 50.*

244 APPENDIX

tained as hereinafter mentioned, a greater amount of notes than the amount so certified.

*Provision for united banks.*

XIV. Provided always, and be it enacted, that if it shall be made to appear to the commissioners of stamps and taxes that any two or more banks have, by written contract or agreement (which contract or agreement shall be produced to the said commissioners), become united within the twelve weeks next preceding such twenty-seventh day of April as aforesaid, it shall be lawful for the said commissioners to ascertain the average amount of the notes of each such bank in the manner hereinbefore directed, and to certify the average amount of the notes of the two or more banks so united as the amount which the united bank shall thereafter be authorised to issue, subject to the regulations of this Act.

*Duplicate certificate to be published in the Gazette. Gazette to be evidence.*

XV. And be it enacted, that the commissioners of stamps and taxes shall, at the time of certifying to any banker such particulars as they are hereinbefore required to certify, also publish a duplicate of their certificate thereof in the next succeeding *London Gazette* in which the same may be conveniently inserted; and the gazette in which such publication shall be made shall be conclusive evidence in all courts whatsoever of the amount of bank notes which the banker named in such certificate or duplicate is by law authorised to issue and to have in circulation as aforesaid.

*In case banks become united, commissioners to certify the amount of bank notes which each bank was authorised to issue.*

XVI. And be it enacted, that in case it shall be made to appear to the commissioners of stamps and taxes, at any time hereafter, that any two or more banks, each such bank consisting of not more than six persons, have, by written contract or agreement (which contract or agreement shall be produced to the said commissioners), become united subsequently to the passing of this Act, it shall be lawful to the said commissioners, upon the application of such united bank, to certify, in manner hereinbefore mentioned, the aggregate of the amounts of bank notes which such separate banks were previously authorised to issue, and so from time to time; and every such certificate shall be published in manner hereinbefore directed; and from and after such publication the amount therein stated shall be and be deemed to be the limit of the amount of bank notes which such united bank may have in circulation: provided always, that it shall not be lawful for any such united bank to issue bank notes at any time after the number of partners therein shall exceed six in the whole.

XVII. And be it enacted, that if the monthly average circulation of bank notes of any banker, taken in the manner hereinafter directed, shall at any time exceed the amount which such banker is authorised to issue and to have in circulation under the provisions of this Act, such banker shall in every such case forfeit a sum equal to the amount by which the average monthly circulation, taken as aforesaid, shall have exceeded the amount which such banker was authorised to issue and to have in circulation as aforesaid. *Penalty on banks issuing in excess.*

XVIII. And be it enacted, that every banker in England and Wales, who, after the tenth day of October One thousand eight hundred and forty-four, shall issue bank notes, shall, on one day in every week after the nineteenth day of October One thousand eight hundred and forty-four (such day to be fixed by the commissioners of stamps and taxes), transmit to the said commissioners an account of the amount of the bank notes of such banker in circulation on every day during the week ending on the next preceding Saturday, and also an account of the average amount of the bank notes of such banker in circulation during the same week: and on completing the first period of four weeks, and so on completing each successive period of four weeks, every such banker shall annex to such account the average amount of bank notes of such banker in circulation during the said four weeks, and also the amount of bank notes which such banker is authorised to issue under the provisions of this Act; and every such account shall be verified by the signature of such banker or his chief cashier, or, in the case of a company or partnership, by the signature of a *Issuing banks to render accounts.*

managing director or partner or chief cashier of such company or partnership, and shall be made in the form to this Act annexed marked (B); and so much of the said return as states the weekly average amount of the notes of such bank shall be published by the said commissioners in the next succeeding *London Gazette* in which the same may be conveniently inserted, and if any such banker shall neglect or refuse to render any such account in the form and at the time required by this Act, or shall at any time render a false account, such banker shall forfeit the sum of one hundred pounds for every such offence.

*Mode of ascertaining the average amount of bank notes of each banker in circulation during the first four weeks after 10th October 1844.*

XIX. And be it enacted, that for the purpose of ascertaining the monthly average amount of bank notes of each banker in circulation the aggregate of the amount of bank notes of each such banker in circulation on every day of business during the first complete period of four weeks next after the tenth day of October One thousand eight hundred and forty-four, such period ending on a Saturday, shall be divided by the number of days of business in such four weeks, and the average so ascertained shall be deemed to be the average of bank notes of each such banker in circulation during such period of four weeks, and so in each successive period of four weeks, and such average is not to exceed the amount certified by the commissioners of stamps and taxes as aforesaid.

*Commissioners of stamps and taxes empowered to cause the books of bankers containing accounts of their bank notes in circulation to be inspected.*

XX. And whereas, in order to insure the rendering of true and faithful accounts of the amount of bank notes in circulation as directed by this Act, it is necessary that the commissioners of stamps and taxes should be empowered to cause the books of bankers issuing such notes to be inspected, as hereinafter mentioned: be it therefore enacted, that all and every the book and books of any banker who shall issue bank notes under the provisions of this Act in which shall be kept, contained, or entered any account, minute, or memorandum of or relating to the bank notes issued or to be issued by such banker, or of or relating to the amount of such notes in circulation, from time to time, or any account, minute, or memorandum, the sight or inspection whereof may tend to secure the rendering of true accounts of the average amount of such notes in circulation, as directed by this Act, or to test the truth of any such account, shall be open for the inspection and examination, at all seasonable times, of any officer of stamp duties authorised in that behalf by writing, signed by the commissioners of stamps and taxes or any two of them; and every such officer shall be at liberty to take copies of or extracts from any such book or account as aforesaid; and if any banker or other person keeping any such book, or having the custody or possession thereof, or power to produce the same, shall, upon demand made by any such officer, showing (if required) his authority in that behalf, refuse to produce any such book to such officer for his inspection and examination, or to permit him to inspect and examine the same, or to take copies thereof or extracts therefrom, or of or from any such account, minute, or memorandum as aforesaid kept, contained, or entered therein, every such banker or other person so offending shall for every such offence forfeit the sum of one hundred pounds: provided always, that the said commissioners shall not exercise the powers aforesaid without the consent of the commissioners of Her Majesty's Treasury. *Penalty for refusing to allow such inspection.*

XXI. And be it enacted, that every banker in England and Wales who is now carrying on or shall hereafter carry on business as such shall on the first day of January in each year, or within fifteen days thereafter, make a return to the commissioners of stamps and taxes at their head office in London of his name, residence, and occupation, or in the case of a company or partnership, of the name, residence, and occupation of every person composing or being a member of such company or partnership, and also the name of the firm under which such banker, company, or partnership carry on the business of banking, and of every place where such business is carried on; and if any such banker, company, or partnership shall omit or refuse to make such return within fifteen days after the said first day of January, or shall wilfully make other than a true return of the persons as herein required, every banker, *All bankers to return names once a year to the Stamp Office.*

company, or partnership so offending shall forfeit and pay the sum of fifty pounds; and the said commissioners of stamps and taxes shall on or before the first day of March in every year publish in some newspaper circulating within each town or county respectively a copy of the return so made by every banker, company, or partnership carrying on the business of bankers within such town or county respectively, as the case may be.

*Bankers to take out a separate licence for every place at which they issue notes or bills.*

*Proviso in favour of bankers who had four such licences in force on the 6th of May 1844.*

XXII. And be it enacted, that every banker who shall be liable by law to take out a licence from the commissioners of stamps and taxes to authorise the issuing of notes or bills shall take out a separate and distinct licence for every town or place at which he shall, by himself or his agent, issue any notes or bills requiring such licence to authorise the issuing thereof, anything in any former Act contained to the contrary thereof notwithstanding: provided always, that no banker who on or before the sixth day of May, one thousand eight hundred and forty-four, had taken out four such licences, which on the said last-mentioned day were respectively in force, for the issuing of any such notes or bills at more than four separate towns or places, shall at any time hereafter be required to take out or to have in force at one and the same time more than four such licences to authorise the issuing of such notes or bills at all or any of the same towns or places specified in such licences in force on the said sixth day of May, one thousand eight hundred and forty-four, and at which towns or places respectively such bankers had on or before the said last-mentioned day issued such notes or bills in pursuance of such licences or any of them respectively.

*Compensation to certain bankers named in the schedule.*

XXIII. And whereas the several bankers named in the schedule hereto annexed marked (C) have ceased to issue their own bank notes under certain agreements with the governor and company of the Bank of England; and it is expedient that such agreements should cease and determine on the thirty-first day of December next, and that such bankers should receive by way of compensation such composition as hereafter mentioned; and a list of such bankers, and a statement of the maximum sums in respect of which each such banker is to receive compensation, hath been delivered to the commissioners of stamps and taxes, signed by the chief cashier of the Bank of England: be it therefore enacted, that the several agreements subsisting between the said governor and company and the several bankers mentioned in the schedule hereto relating to the issue of Bank of England notes, shall cease and determine on the thirty-first day of December next; and from and after that day the said governor and company shall pay and allow to the several bankers named in the schedule hereto marked (C), so long as such bankers shall be willing to receive the same, a composition at and after the rate of one pound per centum per annum on the average amount of the Bank of England notes issued by such bankers respectively and actually remaining in circulation, to be ascertained as follows; (that is to say), on some day in the month of April One thousand eight hundred and forty-five, to be determined by the said governor and company, an account shall be taken of the Bank of England notes delivered to such bankers respectively by the said governor and company within three months next preceding, and of such of the said Bank of England notes as shall have been returned to the Bank of England, and the balance shall be deemed to be the amount of the Bank of England notes issued by such bankers respectively and kept in circulation; and a similar account shall be taken at intervals of three calendar months; and the average of the balances ascertained on taking four such accounts shall be deemed to be the average amount of Bank of England notes issued by such bankers respectively and kept in circulation during the year One thousand eight hundred and forty-five, and on which amount such bankers are respectively to receive the aforesaid composition of one per centum for the year One thousand eight hundred and forty-five; and similar accounts shall be taken in each succeeding year; but in each year such accounts shall be taken in different months from those in which the accounts of the last preceding year were taken, and on different days of the month, such months and days to be determined by the said governor and company; and the amount of the composition payable as aforesaid shall be paid by the said governor and company out of their own funds; and in case any difference shall arise between any of such bankers and the governor and company of the Bank of England in respect of the composition payable as aforesaid, the same shall be determined by the Chancellor of the Exchequer for the time being, or by some person to be named by him, and the decision of the Chancellor of the Exchequer, or his nominee, shall be final and conclusive: provided always, that it shall be lawful for any banker named in the schedule hereto annexed marked (C) to discontinue the receipt of such composition as aforesaid, but no such banker shall by such discontinuance as aforesaid thereby acquire any right or title to issue bank notes.

*Bank of England to be allowed to compound with issuing banks.*

XXIV. And be it enacted, that it shall be lawful for the said governor and company to agree with every banker who, under the provisions of this Act, shall be entitled to issue bank notes, to allow to such banker a composition at the rate of one per centum per annum on the amount of Bank of England notes which shall be issued and kept in circulation by such banker, as a consideration for his relinquishment of the privilege of issuing his own bank notes; and all the provisions herein contained for ascertaining and determining the amount of composition payable to the several bankers named in the schedule hereto marked (C) shall apply to all such other bankers with whom the said governor and company are hereby authorised to agree as aforesaid; provided that the amount of composition payable to such bankers as last aforesaid shall in every case in which an increase of securities in the issue department shall have been authorised by any order in council be deducted out of the amount payable by the said governor and company to the public under the provisions herein contained:

*Limitation of compositions.*

provided always, that the total sum payable to any banker, under the provisions herein contained, by way of composition as aforesaid, in any one year, shall not exceed, in case of the bankers mentioned in the schedule hereto marked (C), one per centum per annum on the several sums set against the names of such bankers respectively in the list and statement delivered to the commissioners of stamps as aforesaid, and in the case of other bankers shall not exceed one per centum on the amount of bank notes which such bankers respectively would otherwise be entitled to issue under the provisions herein contained.

XXV. And be it enacted, that all the compositions payable to the several bankers mentioned in the schedule hereto marked (C), and such other bankers as shall agree with the said governor and company to discontinue the issue of their own bank notes as aforesaid, shall, if not previously determined by the Act of such banker as hereinbefore provided, cease and determine on the first day of August One thousand eight hundred and fifty-six, or on any earlier day on which Parliament may prohibit the issue of bank notes. *Compositions to cease on 1st August 1856.*

XXVI. And be it enacted, that from and after the passing of this Act it shall be lawful for any society or company or any persons in partnership, though exceeding six in number, carrying on the business of banking in London, or within sixty-five miles thereof, to draw, accept, or endorse bills of exchange, not being payable to bearer on demand, anything in the hereinbefore recited Act passed in the fourth year of the reign of his said Majesty King William the Fourth, or in any other Act, to the contrary notwithstanding. *Banks within sixty-five miles of London may accept, etc., bills.*

XXVII. And be it enacted, that the said governor and company of the Bank of England shall have and enjoy such exclusive privilege of banking as is given by this Act, upon such terms and conditions, and subject to the termination thereof at such time and in such manner, as is by this Act provided and specified; and all and every the powers and authorities, franchises, privileges, and advantages, given or recognised by the said recited Act passed in the fourth year of the reign of His Majesty King William the Fourth as belonging to or *Bank to enjoy privileges, subject to redemption.*

enjoyed by the said governor and company of the Bank of England, or by any subsequent Act or Acts of Parliament, shall be, and the same are hereby declared to be, in full force and continued by this Act, except so far as the same are altered by this Act; subject, nevertheless, to redemption upon the terms and conditions following; (that is to say), at any time upon twelve months' notice to be given after the first day of August One thousand eight hundred and fifty-five, and upon repayment by Parliament to the said governor and company or their successors of the sum of eleven million fifteen thousand and one hundred pounds, being the debt now due from the public to the said governor and company, without any deduction, discount, or abatement whatsoever, and upon payment to the said governor and company and their successors of all arrears of the sum of one hundred thousand pounds per annum, in the last-mentioned Act mentioned, together with the interest or annuities payable upon the said debt or in respect thereof, and also upon repayment of all the principal and interest which shall be owing unto the said governor and company and their successors upon all such tallies, Exchequer orders, Exchequer bills, or Parliamentary funds which the said governor and company or their successors shall have remaining in their hands or to be entitled to at the time of such notice to be given as last aforesaid, then and in such case, and not till then, the said exclusive privileges of banking granted by this Act shall cease and determine at the expiration of such notice of twelve months; and any vote or resolution of the House of Commons, signified under the hand of the Speaker of the said House in writing, and delivered at the public office of the said governor and company, shall be deemed and adjudged to be a sufficient notice.

Interpretation clause.

XXVIII. And be it enacted, that the term "Bank Notes" used in this Act shall extend and apply to all bills or notes for the payment of money to the bearer on demand other than bills or notes to the governor and company of the Bank of England; and that the term "Bank of England Notes" shall extend and apply to

APPENDIX 253

the promissory notes of the governor and company of the Bank of England payable to bearer on demand; and that the term "Banker" shall extend and apply to all corporations, societies, partnerships, and persons, and every individual person carrying on the business of banking, whether by the issue of bank notes or otherwise, except only the governor and company of the Bank of England; and that the word "Person" used in this Act shall include corporations; and that the singular number in this Act shall include the plural number, and the plural number the singular, except where there is anything in the context repugnant to such construction: and that the masculine gender in this Act shall include the feminine, except where there is anything in the context repugnant to such construction.

XXIX. And be it enacted, that this Act may be amended or repealed by any Act to be passed in the present session of Parliament.

*Act may be amended.*

---

### SCHEDULE (B)

Name and title as set forth in the licence . . . . _____ Bank.
Name of the firm . . . _____ Firm.
Insert head office or principal place of issue . . . _____ Place.

An Account pursuant to the Act 7 and 8 Vict., cap. of the notes of the said bank in circulation during the week ending Saturday the        day of        18   .

Monday . . . .
Tuesday . . . .
Wednesday . . . .
Thursday . . . .
Friday . . . .
Saturday . . . .

(6)

Average of the week       .

[*To be annexed to this Account at the end of each period of four weeks*]

Amount of notes authorised by law . £
Average amount in circulation during
the four weeks ending as above . £

I, being [the banker, chief cashier, managing director, or partner of the          bank, *as the case may be*], do hereby certify, that the above is a true account of the notes of the said bank in circulation during the week above written.

(Signed)

Dated the          day of          18

---

## BANK INCORPORATION ACT

### 7 & 8 VICT., CAP. 113.

*An Act to regulate Joint-Stock Banks in England*

[5th September 1844]

No joint-stock bank established after 6th May last to carry on business unless by virtue of letters-patent granted according to this Act; but companies previously established not restrained from carrying on business until letters-patent have been granted.

WHEREAS the laws in force for the regulation of copartnerships of bankers in England need to be amended: be it enacted by the Queen's most Excellent Majesty, by and with the advice and consent of the Lords, spiritual and temporal, and Commons, in this present Parliament assembled, and by the authority of the same, that it shall not be lawful for any company of more than six persons to carry on the trade or business of bankers in England, after the passing of this Act, under any agreement or covenant or copartnership made or entered into on or after the sixth day of May last passed, unless by virtue of letters-patent to be granted by Her Majesty according to the provisions of this Act; but nothing herein contained shall be construed to restrain any such company established before the said sixth day of May for the purpose of carrying on the said trade or business of bankers in England from continuing to carry on the same trade and business as legally as they might have done before the passing of this Act, until letters-patent have been granted to them severally on their application, as hereinafter provided, to be made subject to the provisions of this Act.

II. And be it enacted, that before beginning to exercise the said trade or business every such company shall present a petition to Her Majesty in Council, praying that Her Majesty will be graciously pleased to grant to them letters-patent under this Act; and every such petition shall be signed by seven at least of the said company, and shall set forth the following particulars: (that is to say), *[margin: Company to petition for charter.]*

> First, The names and additions of all the partners of the company, and the name of the street, square, or other place where each of the said partners reside:
>
> Second, The proposed name of the bank:
>
> Third, The name of the street, square, or other local description of the place or places where the business of the bank is to be carried on:
>
> Fourth, The proposed amount of the capital stock, not being in any case less than one hundred thousand pounds, and the means by which it is to be raised:
>
> Fifth, The amount of capital stock then paid up, and where and how invested:
>
> Sixth, The proposed number of shares in the business:
>
> Seventh, The amount of each share, not being less than one hundred pounds each.

III. And be it enacted, that every such petition shall be referred by Her Majesty to the committee of privy council for trade and plantations, and so soon as the Lords of the said committee shall have reported to Her Majesty that the provisions of this Act have been complied with on the part of the said company, it shall thereupon be lawful for Her Majesty, if Her Majesty shall so think fit, with the advice of her privy council, to grant the said letters-patent. *[margin: Charter to be granted on report of Board of Trade.]*

IV. And be it enacted, that the deed of partnership of every such banking company shall be prepared according to a form to be approved by the Lords of the said committee, and shall, in addition to any other provisions *[margin: Deed of settlement.]*

which may be contained therein, contain specific provisions for the following purposes: (that is to say),

First, For holding ordinary general meetings of the company once at least in every year, and at an appointed time and place:

Second, For holding extraordinary general meetings of the company, upon the requisition of nine shareholders or more, having in the whole at least twenty-one shares in the partnership business:

Third, For the management of the affairs of the company, and the election and qualification of the directors:

Fourth, For the retirement of at least one fourth of the directors yearly, and for preventing the re-election of the retiring members for at least twelve calendar months:

Fifth, For preventing the company from purchasing any shares or making advances of money, or securities for money, to any person on the security of a share or shares in the partnership business:

Sixth, For the publication of the assets and liabilities of the company once at least in every calendar month:

Seventh, For the yearly audit of the accounts of the company by two or more auditors chosen at a general meeting of the shareholders, and not being directors at the time:

Eighth, For the yearly communication of the auditors' report, and of a balance sheet, and profit and loss account, to every shareholder:

Ninth, For the appointment of a manager or other officer to perform the duties of manager:

And such deed, executed by the holders of at least one half of the shares in the said business, on which not less than ten pounds on each such share of one hundred pounds, and in proportion for every share of larger amount, shall have been then paid up, shall be annexed to the petition; and the provisions of such deed, with such others as to Her Majesty shall seem fit, shall be set forth in the letters-patent.

## APPENDIX

V. Provided always, and be it enacted, that it shall not be lawful for any such company to commence business until all the shares shall have been subscribed for, and until the deeds of partnership shall have been executed personally, or by some person duly authorised by warrant of attorney to execute the same on behalf of such holder or holders, by the holders of all the shares in the said business, until a sum of not less than one half of the amount of each share shall have been paid up in respect of each such share; and it shall not be lawful for the company to repay any part of the sum so paid up without leave of the Lords of the said committee.

*No company to commence business till deed executed and all the shares subscribed for, and at least half the amount paid up.*

VI. And be it enacted, that it shall be lawful for Her Majesty in and by such letters-patent to grant that the persons by whom the said deed of partnership shall have been executed, and all other persons who shall thereafter become shareholders in the said banking business, their executors, administrators, successors, and assigns respectively, shall be one body, politic and corporate, by such name as shall be given to them in and by the said letters-patent, for the purpose of carrying on the said banking business, and by that name shall have perpetual succession and a common seal, and shall have power to purchase and hold lands of such annual value as shall be expressed in such letters-patent; and such letters-patent shall be granted for a term of years not exceeding twenty years, and may be made subject to such other provisions and stipulations as to Her Majesty may seem fit.

*Company to be incorporated.*

VII. Provided always, and be it enacted, that, notwithstanding such incorporation, the several shareholders for the time being in the said banking business, and those who shall have been shareholders therein, and their several executors, administrators, successors, and assigns, shall be and continue liable for all the dealings, covenants, and undertakings of the said company, subject to the provisions hereinafter contained, as fully as if the said company were not incorporated.

*Incorporation not to limit the liability of the shareholders.*

VIII. And be it enacted, that no action or suit by or

*Actions by*

258 APPENDIX

*or against shareholders.*

against the company shall be in anywise affected by reason of the plaintiff or defendant therein being a shareholder or former shareholder of the company; but any such shareholder, either alone or jointly with another person as against the company, or the company as against any such shareholder, either alone or jointly with any other person, shall have the same action and remedy in respect of any cause of action or suit whatever which such shareholder or company might have had if such cause of action or suit had arisen with a stranger.

*Decree or judgment to be enforced against company and shareholders.*

IX. And be it enacted, that every judgment, decree, or order of any court of justice in any proceeding against the company may be lawfully executed against and shall have the like effect on the property and effects of the company, and also, subject to the provisions hereinafter contained, upon the person, property, and effects of every shareholder and former shareholder thereof, as if every individual shareholder and former shareholder had been by name a party to such a proceeding.

*Execution against company to precede execution against present or former shareholders.*

X. And be it enacted, that it shall be lawful for the plaintiff to cause execution upon any judgment, decree, or order obtained by him in any such action or suit against the company to be issued against the property and effects of the company; and if such execution shall be ineffectual to obtain satisfaction of the sums sought to be recovered thereby, then it shall be lawful for him to have execution in satisfaction of such judgment, decree, or order against the person, property, and effects of any shareholder, or, in default of obtaining satisfaction of such judgment, decree, or order from any shareholder, against the person,

*Extent of liability of former shareholders.*

property, and effects of any person who was a shareholder of the company at the time when the cause of action against the company arose: provided always, that no person having ceased to be a shareholder of the company, shall be liable for the payment of any debt for which any such judgment, decree, or order shall have been so obtained, for which he would not have been liable as a partner in case a suit had been originally brought against him for the same, or for which judgment shall have been obtained, after the expiration of three years from the time when he shall have ceased to be a shareholder of such company; nor shall this Act be deemed to enable any party to a suit to recover from any individual shareholder of the company, or any other person whomsoever, any other or greater sum than might have been recovered if this Act had not been passed.

XI. And be it enacted, that every person against whom or against whose property or effects any such execution shall have issued shall be reimbursed out of the property and effects of the company for all monies paid, and for all damages, costs, and expenses incurred by him by reason of such execution, or of the action or suit in which the same shall have issued, or, in default of such reimbursement, by contribution from the other shareholders of the company. *Reimbursement of individual shareholders.*

XII. And be it enacted, that if any such execution be issued against any present or former shareholder of the company, and if, within fourteen days next of the levying of such execution, he be not reimbursed, on demand, out of the property and effects of the company, all such monies, damages, costs, and expenses as he shall have paid or incurred in consequence of such execution, it shall be lawful for such shareholder, or his executors or administrators, to have execution against the property and effects of the company in satisfaction of such monies, damages, costs, and expenses; and the amount of such monies, damages, costs, and expenses shall be ascertained and certified by one of the masters or other officer of the court out of which such execution shall issue. *Individuals paying under execution to recover against the company.*

XIII. And be it enacted, that in the cases provided by this Act for the execution of any judgment, decree, or order in any action or suit against the company, to be issued against the person or against the property and effects of any shareholder or former shareholder of such company, or against the property and effects of the company at the suit of any shareholder or former shareholder, in satisfaction of any monies, damages, costs, and *How such execution is to be had.*

expenses paid or incurred by him as aforesaid in any action or suit against the company, such execution may be issued by leave of the court or of a judge of the court in which such judgment, decree, or order shall have been obtained, upon motion or summons for a rule to show cause, or other motion or summons consistent with the practice of the court, without any suggestion or *scire facias* in that behalf, and that it shall be lawful for such court or judge to make absolute, or discharge such rule, or allow or dismiss such motion (as the case may be), and to direct the costs of the application to be paid by either party, or to make such order therein as to such court or judge shall seem fit; and in such cases such form of writs of execution shall be sued out of the courts of law and equity respectively, for giving effect to the provision in that behalf aforesaid, as the judges of such courts respectively shall from time to time think fit to order, and the execution of such writs shall be enforced in like manner as writs of execution are now enforced; provided that any order made by a judge as aforesaid may be discharged or varied by the court, on application made thereto by either party dissatisfied with such order; provided also, that no such motion shall be made nor summons granted for the purpose of charging any shareholder or former shareholder until ten days' notice thereof shall have been given to the person sought to be charged thereby.

*Contribution to be recovered from other shareholders.*

XIV. And be it enacted, that if such shareholder be not by the means aforesaid fully paid all such monies, with interest, damages, costs, and expenses, as he shall have paid or incurred by reason of any such execution, it shall be lawful for him, his executors or administrators, to divide the amount thereof, or so much thereof as he shall not have been reimbursed, into as many equal parts as there shall then be shares in the capital stock of the company (not including shares then under forfeiture); and every shareholder for the time being of the company, and the executors or administrators of every deceased shareholder, shall, in proportion to the number of shares which they may hold in the company, pay one or more of such parts, upon demand, to the shareholder against whom such execution shall have been issued, or to his executors or administrators; and upon neglect or refusal so to pay, it shall be lawful for such shareholder, his executors or administrators, to sue for and recover the same against the shareholder, or the executors or administrators of any shareholder, who shall so neglect or refuse as aforesaid, in any of Her Majesty's courts of record at Westminster, or in any other court having jurisdiction in respect of such demand.

XV. And be it enacted, that if the shareholder or former shareholder against whom any such execution shall have issued, his executors or administrators, shall by reason of the bankruptcy or insolvency of any shareholder, or from any other cause, but without any neglect or wilful default on his own part, be prevented from recovering any proportion of the monies, costs, or expenses which he shall have so paid, it shall be lawful for him, his executors or administrators, again to divide the amount of all such monies, costs, and expenses as shall not have been recovered by him or them into as many equal parts as there shall be shares in the capital stock of the company (not including the shares then under forfeiture), except the shares in respect of which such default shall have happened; and every shareholder for the time being of the company, and the executors or administrators of every deceased shareholder, except as aforesaid, shall rateably, according to the number of shares which they shall hold in the company, upon demand, pay one or more such last-mentioned parts to the shareholder against whom such execution shall have issued, his executors or administrators; and in default of payment he or they shall have the same remedies in all respects for the recovery thereof as under the provisions hereinbefore mentioned are given in respect of the original proportions of such monies, damages, costs, and expenses; and if any proportion of the said monies, damages, costs, and expenses shall remain unpaid by reason of any such bankruptcy, insolvency, or other cause as aforesaid, such shareholder, his executors or administrators, shall have in like manner, from time to time, and by way of accumulative remedy, the same

*Further remedy in case of bankruptcy, etc., of company's shareholders.*

powers, according to the circumstances of the case, of again dividing and enforcing payment of the amount of such proportion, until he or they shall, in the end, if a former shareholder, be fully reimbursed the whole of the said monies, costs, and expenses, and if then a shareholder, the whole excepting the portions belonging to the shares held by him.

*Memorial to be registered.*

XVI. And be it enacted, that within three months after the grant of the said letters-patent, and before the company shall begin to carry on their business as bankers, an account or memorial shall be made out, according to the form contained in the schedule marked (A) to this Act annexed, wherein shall be set forth the true title or firm of the company, and also the names and places of abode of all the members of such company, as the same respectively shall appear on the books of such company, and also the name and place of abode of every director and manager or other like officer of the company, and the name or firm of every bank or banks established or to be established by such company, and also the name of every town or place where the business of the said company shall be carried on; and a new account or memorial of the same particulars shall be made by the said company in every year, between the twenty-eighth day of February and the twenty-fifth day of March, while they shall continue to carry on their business as bankers; and every such memorial shall be delivered to the commissioners of stamps and taxes at the stamp office in London, who shall cause the same to be filed and kept in the said stamp office, and an entry or registry thereof to be made in a book or books to be there kept for that purpose by some person or persons to be appointed by the said commissioners in that behalf, which book or books any person or or persons shall from time to time have liberty to search and inspect on payment of the sum of one shilling for every search; and the company shall from time to time cause to be printed and kept, in a conspicuous place accessible to the public in their office or principal place of business, a list of the registered names and places of abode of all the members of such company for the time being.

XVII. Provided also, and be it enacted, that the manager or one of the directors of every such company shall, from time to time as occasion shall require, make out in manner hereinbefore directed, and cause to be delivered to the commissioners of stamps and taxes as aforesaid, a further account or memorial, according to the form contained in the schedule marked (B) to this Act annexed, of the name and place of abode of every new director, manager, or other like officer of such company, and also of the name or names of any person or persons who shall have ceased to be members of such company, and also of the name or names of any person or persons who shall have become a member or members of such company, either in addition to or instead of any former member or members thereof, and of the name or names of any new or additional town or towns, place or places, where the business of the said company is carried on; and such further account or memorial shall from time to time be filed, and kept and entered and registered at the Stamp Office in London in like manner as is hereinbefore required with respect to the original or annual acocunt or memorial hereinbefore directed to be made. *Memorials of occasional changes.*

XVIII. And be it enacted, that the several memorials aforesaid shall be signed by the manager or one of the directors of the company, and shall be verified by a declaration of such manager or director before a justice of the peace, or a master or master extraordinary of the High Court of Chancery, made pursuant to the provisions of an Act passed in the sixth year of His late Majesty's reign, intituled, "An Act to repeal an Act of the present session of Parliament, intituled, 'An Act for the more effectual abolition of oaths and affirmations taken and made in various departments of the State, and to substitute declarations in lieu thereof, and for the more entire suppression of voluntary and extra-judicial oaths and affidavits;' and to make other provisions for the abolition of unnecessary oaths;" and if any declaration so made shall be false in any material particular the person wilfully making such false declaration shall be guilty of a misdemeanour. *Form of memorials.* 5 & 6 W. 4, c. 62.

*Evidence of memorials.*

XIX. And be it enacted, that a true copy of any such memorial, certified under the hand of one of the commissioners of stamps and taxes for the time being, upon proof made that such certificate has been signed with the handwriting of the person certifying the same, whom it shall not be necessary to prove to be a commissioner of stamps and taxes, shall be received in evidence as proof of the contents of such memorial, and proof shall not be required that the person by whom the memorial shall purport to be verified was, at the time of such verification, the manager or one of the directors of the company.

*Commissioners of stamps to give certified copies on payment of ten shillings.*

XX. And be it enacted, that the said commissioners of stamps and taxes for the time being shall, upon application made to them by any person or persons requiring a copy, certified according to this Act, of any such account or memorial as aforesaid, in order that the same may be produced in evidence, or for any other purpose, deliver to the person or persons so applying for the same such certified copy, he, she, or they paying for the same the sum of ten shillings and no more.

*Existing liabilities to continue till new memorials.*

XXI. And be it enacted, that the persons whose names shall appear from time to time in the then last delivered memorial, and their legal representatives, shall be liable to all legal proceedings under this Act, as existing shareholders of the company, and shall be entitled to be reimbursed, as such existing shareholders only, out of the funds or property of the company, for all losses sustained in consequence thereof.

*Bills and notes to be signed by one director or manager.*

XXII. And be it enacted, that all bills of exchange or promissory notes made, accepted, or endorsed on behalf of the said company, may be made, accepted, or endorsed (as the case may be) in any manner provided by the deed of partnership, so that they be signed by one of the managers or directors of the company, and be by him expressed to be so made, accepted, or endorsed by him

*Manager not personally liable.*

on behalf of such company: provided always, that nothing herein contained shall be deemed to make any such manager or director liable upon any such bill of exchange or promissory note to any greater extent or in a different manner than upon any other contract signed by him on behalf of any such company; and that every such company on whose behalf any bill of exchange or promissory note shall be made, accepted, or endorsed in manner and form as aforesaid may sue and be sued thereon as fully as in the case of any contract made and entered into under their common seal.

XXIII. And be it enacted, that, subject to the regulations herein contained, and to the provisions of the deed of settlement, every shareholder may sell and transfer his shares in the said company by deed duly stamped, in which the consideration shall be truly stated; and such deed may be according to the form in the schedule marked (C) annexed to this Act, or to the like effect; and the same (when duly executed) shall be delivered to the secretary, and be kept by him; and the secretary shall enter a memorial thereof in a book, to be called the "Register of Transfers," and shall endorse such entry on the deed of transfer, and for every such entry and endorsement the company may demand any sum not exceeding two shillings and sixpence; and until such transfer have been so delivered to the secretary as aforesaid the purchaser of the share shall not be entitled to receive any share of the profits of the said business, or to vote in respect of such share. *Transfers of shares to be registered, etc.*

XXIV. And be it enacted, that no shareholder shall be entitled to transfer any share until he shall have paid all calls for the time being due on every share held by him. *Transfer not to be made until all calls paid.*

XXV. And be it enacted, that the directors may close the register of transfers for a period not exceeding fourteen days previous to each ordinary meeting, and may fix a day for the closing of the same, of which seven days' notice shall be given by advertisement in some newspaper, as after-mentioned; and any transfer made during the time when the transfer books are so *Closing of transfer books.*

closed shall, as between the company and the party claiming under the same, but not otherwise, be considered as made subsequently to such ordinary meeting.

*Transmission of shares by other means than transfer to be authenticated by a declaration.*

XXVI. And with respect to the registration of shares the interest in which may have become transmitted in consequence of the death or bankruptcy or insolvency of any shareholder, or in consequence of the marriage of a female shareholder, or by any other legal means than by a transfer according to the provisions of this Act: be it enacted, that no person claiming by virtue of any such transmission shall be entitled to receive any share of the profits of the said business, or to vote in respect of any such share as the holder thereof, until such transmission have been authenticated by a declaration in writing as hereinafter mentioned, or in such other manner as the directors shall require; and every such declaration shall state the manner in which and the party to whom such share shall have been so transmitted, and shall be made and signed by some credible person before a justice of the peace, or before a master or master extraordinary in the High Court of Chancery; and such declaration shall be left with the secretary, and thereupon he shall enter the name of the person entitled under such transmission in the register book of shareholders of the company; and for every such entry the company may demand any sum not exceeding two shillings and sixpence.

*Proof of transmission by marriage, will, &c.*

XXVII. And be it enacted, that if such transmission be by virtue of the marriage of a female shareholder, the said declaration shall contain a copy of the register of such marriage, or other particulars of the celebration thereof, and shall declare the identity of the wife with the holder of such share; and if such transmission have taken place by virtue of any testamentary instrument, or by intestacy, the probate of the will or letters of administration, or an official extract therefrom, shall, together with such declaration, be produced to the secretary; and upon such production, in either of the cases aforesaid, the secretary shall make an entry of the declaration in the said register of transfers.

XXVIII. And be it enacted, that with respect to any share to which several persons may be jointly entitled, all notices directed to be given to the shareholders shall be given to such of the said persons whose name shall stand first in the register of shareholders; and notice so given shall be sufficent notice to all the proprietors of such share. Notices to joint proprietors of shares.

XXIX. And be it enacted, that if any money be payable to any shareholder, being a minor, idiot, or lunatic, the receipt of the guardian of such minor, or the receipt of the committee of such idiot or lunatic, shall be a sufficient discharge to the company for the same. Receipts for money payable to minors, &c.

XXX. And be it enacted, that the company shall not be bound to see to the execution of any trust, whether express, implied, or constructive, to which any of the said shares may be subject; and the receipt of the party in whose name any such share shall stand in the books of the company shall from time to time be a sufficient discharge to the company for any dividend or other sum of money payable in respect of such share, notwithstanding any trusts to which such share may then be subject, and whether or not the company have had notice of such trusts; and the company shall not be bound to see to the application of the money paid upon such receipt. Company not bound to regard trusts.

XXXI. And be it enacted, that from time to time the directors may make such calls of money upon the respective shareholders, in respect of the amount of capital stock respectively subscribed by them, as they shall think fit; and whenever execution upon any judgment against the company shall have been taken out against any shareholder, the directors, within twenty-one days next after notice shall have been served upon the company of the payment of any money by such shareholder, his executors or administrators, in or towards satisfaction of such judgment, shall make such calls upon all the shareholders as will be sufficient to reimburse to Power to make calls.

such shareholder, his executors or administrators, the money so paid by him or them, and all his or their damages, costs, and expenses by reason of such execution, and shall apply the proceeds of such calls accordingly; and every shareholder shall be liable to pay the amount of every call, in respect of the shares held by him, to the persons and at the times and places from time to time appointed by the directors.

*Interest on calls unpaid.*

XXXII. And be it enacted, that if, before or on the day appointed for payment, any shareholder do not pay the amount of any call to which he may be liable, then such shareholder shall be liable to pay interest for the same at the yearly rate of five pounds in the hundred from the day appointed for the payment thereof to the time of the actual payment.

*Enforcement of calls by action.*

XXXIII. And be it enacted, that if at the time appointed by the directors for the payment of any call the holder of any share fail to pay the amount of such call, the company may sue such shareholder for the amount thereof in any court of law or equity having competent jurisdiction, and may recover the same, with interest at the yearly rate of five pounds in the hundred from the day on which such call may have been payable.

*Declaration in action for calls.*

XXXIV. And be it enacted, that any action to be brought by the company against any shareholder to recover any money due for any call it shall not be necessary to set forth the special matter, but it shall be sufficient for the company to declare that the defendant is a holder of one share or more in the company (stating the number of shares), and is indebted to the company in the sum of money to which the calls in arrear shall amount, in respect of one call or more upon one share or more (stating the number and amount of each of such calls), whereby an action hath accrued to the company by virtue of this Act.

*Matter to be*

XXXV. And be it enacted, that on the trial of such

action it shall not be necessary to prove the appointment of the directors who made such call, or any other matter, except that the defendant at the time of making such was a holder of one share or more in the company, and that such call was in fact made, and such notice thereof given, as is directed by this Act; and thereupon the company shall be entitled to recover what shall be due upon such call, with interest thereon.

*proved in action for calls.*

XXXVI. And be it enacted, that the production of the register book of shareholders of the company shall be evidence of such defendant being a shareholder, and of the number and amount of his shares.

*Proof of proprietorship.*

XXXVII. And be it enacted, that if the holder of any share fail to pay a call payable by him in respect thereof, with the interest, if any, that shall have accrued thereon, the directors, at any time after the expiration of six calendar months from the day appointed for payment of such call, may declare such share forfeited, and that whether the company have sued for the amount of such call or not; but the forfeiture of any such share shall not relieve any shareholder, his executors or administrators, from his and their liability to pay the calls made before such forfeiture.

*Forfeiture of shares for non-payment of calls.*

XXXVIII. And be it enacted, that before declaring any share forfeited the directors shall cause notice of such intention to be left at the usual or last place of abode of the person appearing by the register book of shareholders to be the proprietor of such share; and if the holder of any such share be not within the United Kingdom, or if the interest in any such share shall be known by the directors to have become transmitted otherwise than by transfer, as hereinbefore mentioned, but a declaration of such transmission shall not have been registered as aforesaid, and so the address of the parties to whom the same may have been transmitted shall not be known to the directors, the directors shall give public notice of such intention in the *London Gazette;* and the several notices aforesaid shall be given twenty-

*Notice of forfeiture to be given before declaration thereof.*

one days at least before the directors shall make such declaration of forfeiture.

*Forfeiture to be confirmed by a general meeting.*

XXXIX. And be it enacted, that such declaration of forfeiture shall not take effect, so as to authorise the sale or other disposition of any share, until such declaration have been confirmed at some general meeting of the company, to be held after the expiration of two calendar months at the least from the day on which such notice of intention to make such declaration of forfeiture shall have been given; and it shall be lawful for the company to confirm such forfeiture at any such meeting, and by an order at such meeting, or at any subsequent general meeting, to direct the share so forfeited to be sold or otherwise disposed of; and after such confirmation the directors shall sell the forfeited share, either by public auction or private contract, within six calendar months next after the confirmation of the forfeiture, and if there be more than one such forfeited share, then either separately or together, as to them shall seem fit; and any shareholder may purchase any forfeited share so sold.

*Sale of forfeited shares.*

*Evidence as to forfeiture of shares.*

XL. And be it enacted, that a declaration in writing by some credible person not interested in the matter, made before any justice of the peace, or before any master or master extraordinary in the High Court of Chancery, that the call in respect of a share was made, and notice thereof given, and that default in payment of the call was made, and that the forfeiture of the share was declared and confirmed in manner hereinbefore required, shall be sufficient evidence of the facts therein stated; and such declaration, and the receipt of a director or manager of the company for the price of such share, shall constitute a good title to such share, and thereupon such purchaser shall be deemed the holder of such share discharged from all calls made prior to such purchase; and a certificate of proprietorship shall be delivered to such purchaser, and he shall not be bound to see to the application of the purchase money, nor shall his title to such share be effected by any irregularity in the proceedings in reference to any such sale.

XLI. And be it enacted, that the company shall not sell or transfer more of the shares of any such defaulter than will be sufficient, as nearly as can be ascertained at the time of such sale, to pay the arrears then due from such defaulter on account of any calls, together with interest, and the expenses attending such sale and declaration of forfeiture; and if the money produced by the sale of any such forfeited share be more than sufficient to pay all arrears of calls, and interest thereon, due at the time of such sale, and the expenses attending the declaration of forfeiture and sale thereof, the surplus shall, on demand, be paid to the defaulter. *No more shares to be sold than sufficient for payment of calls.*

XLII. And be it enacted, that if payment of such arrears of calls, and interest and expenses, be made before any share so forfeited and vested in the company shall have been sold, such share shall revert to the party to whom the same belonged before such forfeiture, in such manner as if such calls had been duly paid. *On payment of calls, forfeited shares to revert.*

XLIII. And be it enacted, that in all cases wherein it may be necessary for any person to serve notice, writ, or other proceeding at law or in equity, or otherwise, upon the company, service thereof respectively on the manager or any director for the time being of the company, by leaving the same at the principal office of the company, or, if the company have suspended or discontinued business, by serving the same personally on such manager or director, or by leaving the same with some inmate at the usual or last abode of such manager or director, shall be deemed good service of the same on the company. *Service of notice on the company.*

XLIV. Provided always, and be it enacted, that every company of more than six persons, for the formation or establishment of which proceedings had been begun or taken before the sixth day of May last, and which before the fourth day of July then next following was registered at the Stamp Office, and on the fourth day of July actually carried on the said trade or business of bankers in England, although under a covenant or agreement of co-partnership *Existing companies may continue their trades until twelve months after the passing of this Act.*

made or entered into on or after the sixth day of May last, may continue to carry on the said trade or business under any such agreement or covenant of co-partnership for any time not exceeding twelve calendar months next after the passing of this Act, in the same manner in all respects as they legally might have done before the passing of this Act, and after the expiration of the said twelve calendar months, in case the company shall not be incorporated under this Act, shall have, for the purpose of closing their trade or business, but for no other purpose, the same powers and privileges which they would have had if this Act had not been passed.

Existing companies may be brought under this Act.

XLV. And be it enacted, that it shall be lawful for any company of more than six persons carrying on the trade or business of bankers in England before the said sixth day of May, or any company which by the provision hereinbefore in that behalf contained is enabled to carry on the said trade or business of bankers in England for a time not exceeding twelve calendar months next after the passing of this Act, to present a petition to Her Majesty, praying that Her Majesty will be pleased to grant to them letters-patent under this Act; and if, upon their compliance with the provisions hereinbefore contained with respect to companies formed after the said sixth day of May, Her Majesty shall be pleased to grant to them letters-patent under this Act as aforesaid, it shall be lawful for them thereafter to carry on their trade and business of bankers as aforesaid according to this Act, and not otherwise: provided always, that a majority of the directors of any such company for the time being, with the consent of three-fourths in number and value of the shareholders present at a general meeting of the company to be specially called for the purpose, may resolve to make any alterations in the constitution of such company, or otherwise, which may be deemed necessary or expedient for enabling such company to come within the provisions of this Act; and the majority of the directors of such company may, in pursuance of the resolution of such meeting as aforesaid, execute a new deed of partnership on behalf of such company, and it shall not be necessary for such deed to be executed by any other shareholder of such company; and it shall thereupon be lawful for such company to present such petition as aforesaid, and a copy of such resolution and of such new deed of partnership so executed by a majority of the directors of the company as aforesaid shall be annexed to such petition; and if Her Majesty shall thereupon grant letters-patent to such company under this Act, all the shareholders of such company at the time of the grant of such letters-patent shall be deemed to be incorporated under such letters-patent, and to be the first shareholders in such incorporated company; and the said new deed of partnership so executed by a majority of the directors as aforesaid shall have such and the same effect, to all intents and purposes, as if it had been executed by all the shareholders.

XLVI. And be it enacted, that, notwithstanding the incorporation of any company under this Act, all contracts and agreements entered into by and with such company shall continue in force as between such incorporated company and the parties with which the company entered into such contracts and agreements before the incorporation thereof, and may be enforced in like manner as if the company had been incorporated before the making of any such contract or agreement, and that no suit at law or in equity by or against such company shall be abated by reason of such incorporation, but, on the application of either of the parties to such suit to the court in which such suit is pending, at any time before execution on any judgment in such suit shall have issued, it shall be lawful for the court to order that the corporate name of such company be entered on the record, instead of the name of the plaintiff or defendant representing such company before the incorporation thereof, and thereupon such suit may be prosecuted and defended in the same manner as if the same had been originally instituted by or against the said incorporated company; and where execution on any judgment in such suit shall have issued before such application, execution of such judgment may be had as if such company were not incorporated as if this Act had not been passed.

*Agreements entered into with companies after their incorporation to be enforced as if made before incorporation.*

XLVII. And be it enacted, that after the passing of this Act every company of more than six persons established on the said sixth day of May for the purpose of carrying on the said trade or business of bankers within the distance of sixty-five miles from London, and not within the provisions of this Act, shall have the same powers and privileges of suing and being sued in the name of any one of the public officers of such co-partnership as the nominal plaintiff, petitioner, or defendant on behalf of such co-partnership; and that all judgments, decrees, and orders made and obtained in any such suit may be enforced in like manner as is provided with respect to such companies carrying on the said trade or business at any place in England exceeding the distance of sixty-five miles from London under the provisions of an Act passed in the seventh year of the reign of King George the Fourth, intituled "An Act for the better regulating Co-partnerships of certain Bankers in England;" and for amending so much of an Act of the thirty-ninth and fortieth years of the reign of His late Majesty King George the Third, intituled "An Act for establishing an Agreement with the Governor and Company of the Bank of England, for advancing the Sum of Three Millions towards the Supply for the Service of the year One thousand eight hundred," as relates to the same; provided that such first-mentioned company shall make out and deliver from time to time to the commissioners of stamps and taxes the several accounts or returns required by the last-mentioned Act; and all the provisions of the last-recited Act as to such accounts or returns shall be taken to apply to the accounts or returns so made out and delivered by such first-mentioned companies, as if they had been originally included in the provisions of the last-recited Act.

*Existing companies to have the powers of suing and being sued.*

*7 G. 4, c. 46.*

XLVIII. And be it declared and enacted, that every company of more than six persons carrying on the trade or business of bankers in England shall be deemed a trading company within the provisions of an Act passed in this session, intituled "An Act for facilitating the winding up the Affairs of Joint-Stock Companies unable to meet their pecuniary Engagements."

*Banking companies to be deemed trading companies.*

XLIX. And be it enacted, that in this Act the following words and expressions shall have the several meanings hereby assigned to them, unless there be something in the subject or context repugnant to such construction; (that is to say), *Interpretation of Act.*

> Words importing the singular number shall include the plural number, and words importing the plural number shall include the singular number:
> Words importing the masculine gender shall include females:
> The word "plaintiff" shall include pursuer and petitioner.
> The word "defendant" shall include defender and respondent:
> The word "execution" shall include diligence or other proceeding proper for giving effect to any judgment, decree, or order of a court of justice.

L. And be it enacted, that this Act may be amended or repealed by any Act to be passed in this Session of Parliament. *Act may be amended.*

## LEEMAN'S ACT

### 30 & 31 VICT., CAP. 29

*An Act to Amend the Law in Respect of the Sale and Purchase of Shares in Joint-Stock Banking Companies*
[17th June 1867]

WHEREAS it is expedient to make provision for the prevention of contracts for the sale and purchase of shares and stock in joint-stock banking companies, of which the sellers are not possessed or over which they have no control:

May it therefore please Your Majesty that it may be enacted; and be it enacted by the Queen's most Excellent Majesty, by and with the advice and consent of the Lords, spiritual and temporal, and Commons, in this present Parliament assembled, and by the authority of the same:

## APPENDIX

*Contracts for sale, etc., of shares to be void unless the numbers by which such shares are distinguished are set forth in contract.*

I. That all contracts, agreements, and tokens of sale and purchase which shall, from and after the first day of July One thousand eight hundred and sixty-seven, be made or entered into for the sale or transfer, or purporting to be for the sale or transfer, of any share or shares, or of any stock or other interest, in any joint-stock banking company in the United Kingdom of Great Britain and Ireland constituted under or regulated by the provisions of any Act of Parliament, Royal Charter, or Letters-Patent, issuing shares or stock transferable by any deed or written instrument, shall be null and void to all intent and purposes whatever, unless such contract, agreement, or other token shall set forth and designate in writing, such shares, stock, or interest by the respective numbers by which the same are distinguished at the making of such contract, agreement, or token on the register or books of such banking company as aforesaid, or where there is no such register of shares or stock by distinguishing numbers, then unless such contract, agreement, or other token shall set forth the person or persons in whose name or names such shares, stock, or interest shall at the time of making such contract stand as the registered proprietor thereof in the books of such banking company; and every person, whether principal, broker, or agent, who shall wilfully insert in any such contract, agreement, or other token any false entry of such numbers, or any name or names other than that of the person or persons in whose name such shares, stock, or interest shall stand as aforesaid, shall be guilty of a misdemeanour, and be punished accordingly, and, if in Scotland, shall be guilty of an offence punishable by fine or imprisonment.

*Registered shareholders may see lists.*

II. Joint-stock banking companies shall be bound to show their list of shareholders to any registered shareholder during business hours, from ten of the clock to four of the clock.

*Extent of Act limited.*

III. This Act shall not extend to shares or stock in the Bank of England or the Bank of Ireland.

# COINAGE ACT 1870

## 33 & 34 Vict., cap. 10

*An Act to consolidate and amend the Law relating to the Coinage and Her Majesty's Mint*

[4th April 1870]

WHEREAS it is expedient to consolidate and amend the law relating to the coinage and Her Majesty's Mint:

Be it enacted by the Queen's most Excellent Majesty, by and with the advice and consent of the Lords, spiritual and temporal, and Commons, in this present Parliament assembled, and by the authority of the same, as follows:

I. This Act may be cited as "The Coinage Act 1870." Short title.

II. In this Act— Definitions of terms.

The term "Treasury" means the Lord High Treasurer for the time being, or the commissioners or any two of them;

The term "the Mint" means, except as expressly provided, Her Majesty's Royal Mint in England;

The term "British possession" means any colony, plantation, island, territory, or settlement within Her Majesty's dominions and not within the United Kingdom; and

The term "person" includes a body corporate.

III. All coins made at the Mint of the denominations mentioned in the first schedule to this Act shall be of the weight and fineness specified in that schedule, and the standard trial plates shall be made accordingly. Standard of coins.

If any coin of gold, silver, or bronze, but of any other denomination than that of the coins mentioned in the first schedule to this Act, is hereafter coined at the Mint, such coin shall be of a weight and fineness bearing the same proportion to the weight and fineness specified in that schedule as the denomination of such coin bears to the denominations mentioned in that schedule.

Provided that in the making of coins a remedy (or variation from the standard weight and fineness specified in the said first schedule) shall be allowed of an amount not exceeding the amount specified in that schedule.

*Legal tender.*

IV. A tender of payment of money, if made in coins which have been issued by the Mint in accordance with the provisions of this Act, and have not been called in by any proclamation made in pursuance of this Act, and have not become diminished in weight, by wear or otherwise, so as to be of less weight than the current weight; that is to say, that the weight (if any) specified as the least current weight in the first schedule to this Act, or less than such weight as may be declared by any proclamation made in pursuance of this Act, shall be a legal tender,—

> In the case of gold coins for a payment of any amount:
> In the case of silver coins for a payment of an amount not exceeding forty shillings, but for no greater amount:
> In the case of bronze coins for a payment of an amount not exceeding one shilling, but for no greater amount.

Nothing in this Act shall prevent any paper currency which under this Act or otherwise is a legal tender from being a legal tender.

*Prohibition of other coins and tokens.*

V. No piece of gold, silver, copper, or bronze, or of any metal or mixed metal, of any value whatever, shall be made or issued, except by the Mint, as a coin or a token for money, or as purporting that the holder thereof is entitled to demand any value denoted thereon. Every person who acts in contravention of this section shall be liable on summary conviction to a penalty not exceeding twenty pounds.

*Contracts, etc., to be made in currency.*

VI. Every contract, sale, payment, bill, note, instrument, and security for money, and every transaction, dealing, matter, and thing whatever relating to money, or involving the payment of or the liability to pay any money, which is made, executed, or entered into, done or had, shall be made, executed, entered into, done and had according to the coins which are current and legal tender in pursuance of this Act, and not otherwise, unless the same be made, executed, entered into, done or had according to the currency of some British possession or some foreign state.

VII. Where any gold coin of the realm is below the current weight as provided by this Act, or where any coin is called in by any proclamation, every person shall, by himself or others, cut, break, or deface any such coin tendered to him in payment, and the person tendering the same shall bear the loss. *Defacing light gold coin.*

If any coin cut, broken, or defaced in pursuance of this section is not below the current weight, or has not been called in by any proclamation, the person cutting, breaking, or defacing the same shall receive the same in payment according to its denomination. Any dispute which may arise under this section may be determined by a summary proceeding.

VIII. Where any person brings to the Mint any gold bullion, such bullion shall be assayed and coined, and delivered out to such person, without any charge for such assay or coining, or for waste in coinage: *Coining of bullion taken to the Mint.*

Provided that—
- (1.) If the fineness of the whole of the bullion so brought to the Mint is such that it cannot be brought to the standard fineness under this Act of the coin to be coined thereout, without refining some portion of it, the master of the Mint may refuse to receive, assay, or coin such bullion:
- (2.) Where the bullion so brought to the Mint is finer than the standard fineness under this Act of the coin to be coined thereout, there shall be delivered to the person bringing the same such additional amount of coin as is proportionate to such superior fineness.

No undue preference shall be shown to any person under this section, and every person shall have priority according to the time at which he brought the bullion to the Mint.

**Purchase of bullion.**

IX. The Treasury may from time to time issue to the master of the Mint, out of the growing produce of the consolidated fund, such sums as may be necessary to enable him to purchase bullion in order to provide supplies of coin for the public service.

**Payment of profits, etc., to Exchequer.**

X. All sums received by the master of the Mint, or any deputy-master or officer of the Mint, in payment for coin produced from bullion purchased by him, and all fees and payments received by the master or any deputy-master or officer of the Mint as such, shall (save as otherwise in the case of any branch mint in a British possession by a proclamation respecting such branch mint) be paid into the receipt of the Exchequer, and carried to the consolidated fund.

**Regulations by proclamation.**

XI. It shall be lawful for Her Majesty, with the advice of her Privy Council, from time to time by proclamation to do all or any of the following things, namely :—

(1.) To determine the dimension of and design for any coin :

(2.) To determine the denominations of coins to be coined at the Mint :

(3.) To diminish the amount of remedy allowed by the first schedule to this Act in the case of any coin :

(4.) To determine the weight (not being less than the weight, if any, specified in the first schedule to this Act) below which a coin, whether diminished in weight by wear or otherwise, is not to be a current or a legal tender :

(5.) To call in coins of any date or denomination, or any coins coined before the date in the proclamation mentioned :

(6.) To direct that any coins, other than gold,

silver, or bronze, shall be current and be a legal tender for the payment of any amount not exceeding the amount specified in the proclamation, and not exceeding five shillings:

(7.) To direct that the coins coined in any foreign country shall be current, and be a legal tender, at such rates, up to such amounts, and in such portion of Her Majesty's dominions as may be specified in the proclamation; due regard being had in fixing those rates to the weight and fineness of such coins, as compared with the current coins of this realm:

(8.) To direct the establishment of any branch of the Mint in any British possession, and impose a charge for the coinage of gold thereat; determine the application of such charge: and determine the extent to which such branch is to be deemed part of the Mint, and to which the coins issued therefrom are to be current and be a legal tender, and to be deemed to be issued from the Mint:

(9.) To direct that the whole or any part of this Act shall apply to and be in force in any British possession, with or without any modifications contained in the proclamation:

(10.) To regulate any matters relative to the coinage and the Mint within the present prerogative of the Crown which are not provided for by this Act:

(11.) To revoke or alter any proclamation previously made.

Every such proclamation shall come into operation on the date therein in that behalf mentioned, and shall have effect as if it were enacted in this Act.

XII. For the purpose of ascertaining that coins issued from the Mint have been coined in accordance with this Act, a trial of the pyx shall be held at least once in every year in which coins have been issued from the Mint.

It shall be lawful for Her Majesty, with the advice of

*Trial of the pyx.*

her Privy Council, from time to time, by order, to make regulations respecting the trial of the pyx and all matters incidental thereto, and in particular respecting the following matters, viz. :—

(1.) The time and place of the trial :

(2.) The setting apart out of the coins issued by the Mint certain coins for the trial :

(3.) The summoning of a jury of not less than six out of competent freemen of the mystery of goldsmiths of the city of London or other competent persons :

(4.) The attendance at the trial of the jury so summoned, and of the proper officers of the Treasury, the Board of Trade, and the Mint, and the production of the coins so set apart, and of the standard trial plates and standard weights :

(5.) The proceedings at and conduct of the trial, including the nomination of some person to preside thereat, and the swearing of the jury, and the mode of examining the coins :

(6.) The recording and the publication of the verdict, and the custody of the record thereof, and the proceedings (if any) to be taken in consequence of such verdict.

Every such order shall come into operation on the date therein in that behalf mentioned, and shall have effect as if it were enacted in this Act, but may be revoked or altered by any subsequent order under this section.

*Regulations by Treasury.* XIII. The Treasury may from time to time do all or any of the following things :

(1.) Fix the number and duties of the officers of and persons employed in the Mint :

(2.) Make regulations and give directions (subject to the provisions of this Act and any proclamation made thereunder) respecting the general management of the Mint, and revoke and alter such regulations and directions.

## Master and Officers of Mint

XIV. The Chancellor of the Exchequer for the time being shall be the master, worker, and warden of Her Majesty's Royal Mint in England, and governor of the Mint in Scotland. <small>Master of Mint.</small>

Provided that nothing in this section shall render the Chancellor of the Exchequer incapable of being elected to or of sitting or voting in the House of Commons, or vacate the seat of the person who at the passing of this Act holds the office of Chancellor of the Exchequer.

All duties, powers, and authorities imposed on or vested in or to be transacted before the master of the Mint may be performed and exercised by or transacted before him or his sufficient deputy.

XV. The Treasury may from time to time appoint deputy-masters and other officers and persons for the purpose of carrying on the business at the Mint in the United Kingdom or elsewhere, and assign them their duties, and award them their salaries. <small>Deputy-masters and officers.</small>

The master of the Mint may from time to time promote, suspend, and remove any such deputy-masters, officers, and persons.

## Standard Trial Plates and Weights

XVI. The standard trial plates of gold and silver used for determining the justness of the gold and silver coins of the realm issued from the Mint, which now exist or may hereafter be made, and all books, documents, and things used in connection therewith or in relation thereto, shall be in the custody of the Board of Trade, and shall be kept in such places and in such manner as the Board of Trade may from time to time direct; and the performance of all duties in relation to such trial plates shall be part of the business of the standard weights and measures department of the Board of Trade. <small>Custody, etc., of standard trial plates.</small>

The Board of Trade shall from time to time, when necessary, cause new standard trial plates to be made and duly verified, of such standard fineness as may be in conformity with the provisions of this Act.

<small>Standard weights for coin.</small>

XVII. The standard weights for weighing and testing the coin of the realm shall be placed in the custody of the Board of Trade, and be kept in such places and in such manner as the Board of Trade may from time to time direct; and the performance of all duties in relation to such standard weights shall be part of the business of the standard weights and measures department of the Board of Trade.

The Board of Trade shall from time to time cause weights of each coin of the realm for the time being, and of multiples of such of those weights as may be required, to be made and duly verified; and those weights, when approved by Her Majesty in Council, shall be the standard weights for determining the justness of the weight of and for weighing such coin.

The master of the Mint shall from time to time cause copies to be made of such standard weights, and once at least in every year the Board of Trade and the master of the Mint shall cause such copies to be compared and duly verified with the standard weights in the custody of the Board of Trade.

All weights which are not less in weight than the weight prescribed by the first schedule to this Act for the lightest coin, and are used for weighing coin, shall be compared with the said standard weights, and if found to be just shall, on payment of such fee, not exceeding five shillings, as the Board of Trade from time to time prescribe, be marked by some officer of the standard weights and measures department of the Board of Trade with a mark approved of by the Board of Trade, and notified in the *London Gazette*, and a weight which is required by this section to be so compared, and is not so marked, shall not be deemed a just weight for determining the weight of gold and silver coin of the realm.

If any person forges or counterfeits such mark, or any weight so marked, or wilfully increases or diminishes any weight so marked, or knowingly utters, sells, or uses any weight with such counterfeit mark, or any weight so increased or diminished, or knowingly uses any weight declared by this section not to be a just weight, such person shall be liable to a penalty not exceeding fifty pounds.

All fees paid under this section shall be paid into the Exchequer, and carried to the consolidated fund.

### Legal Proceedings.

XVIII. Any summary proceeding under this Act may be taken, and any penalty under this Act may be recovered,— *Summary procedure.*

In England, before two justices of the peace in manner directed by the Act of the session of the eleventh and twelfth years of the reign of Her present Majesty, chapter forty-three, intituled "An Act to facilitate the performance of the Duties of Justices of the Peace out of Sessions within England and Wales with respect to summary Convictions and Orders," and any Act amending the same.

In Scotland, in manner directed by "The Summary Procedure Act, 1864."

In Ireland, so far as respects Dublin, in manner directed by the Acts regulating the powers of justices of the peace or the police of Dublin metropolis, and elsewhere in manner directed by The Petty Sessions (Ireland) Act 1851, and any Act amending the same.

In any British possession, in the courts, and before such justices or magistrates, and in the manner in which the like proceedings and penalties may be taken and recovered by the law of such possession, or as near thereto as circumstances admit, or in such other courts, or before such other justices or magistrates, or in such other manner as any Act or Ordinance having the force of law in such possession may from time to time provide.

### Miscellaneous.

XIX. This Act, save as expressly provided by this Act, or by any proclamation made thereunder, shall not extend to any British possession. *Extent of Act.*

*Repeal of Acts and parts of Acts in second schedule.*

XX. The Acts mentioned in the first part of the second schedule to this Act are hereby repealed to the extent in the third column of such schedule mentioned, and those mentioned in the second part of the same schedule are hereby repealed entirely.

Provided that—

(1.) This repeal shall not affect anything already done or suffered, or any right already acquired or accrued:

(2.) All weights for weighing coin which have before the passing of this Act been marked at the Mint or by any proper officer shall be deemed to have been marked under this Act:

(3.) Every branch of the Mint which at the passing of this Act issues coins in any British possession shall, until the date fixed by any proclamation made in pursuance of this Act with respect to such branch Mint, continue in all respects to have the same power of issuing coins and be in the same position as if this Act had not passed, and coins so issued shall be deemed for the purpose of this Act to have been issued from the Mint:

(4.) The said Acts (unless relating to a branch Mint and unless in the said schedule expressly otherwise mentioned) are not repealed so far as they apply to any British possession to which this Act does not extend until a proclamation directing that this Act or any part thereof, with or without any modification contained in the proclamation, shall be in force in such British possession comes into operation.

APPENDIX

## FIRST SCHEDULE

| Denomination of Coin. | Standard Weight. | | Least Current Weight. | | Standard Fineness. | Remedy Allowance. | | |
|---|---|---|---|---|---|---|---|---|
| | Imperial Weight. Grains. | Metric Weight. Grams. | Imperial Weight. Grains. | Metric Weight. Grams. | | Weight per piece. | | Millesimal Fineness. |
| | | | | | | Imperial Grains. | Metric Grams. | |
| GOLD— | | | | | Eleven-twelfths fine gold, one-twelfth alloy; or millesimal fineness 916·66. | | | |
| Five Pound | 616·37239 | 39·94028 | 612·50000 | 39·68935 | | 1·00000 | 0·06479 | |
| Two Pound | 246·54895 | 15·97611 | 245·00000 | 15·87574 | | 0·40500 | 0·02592 | 0·002 |
| Sovereign | 123·27447 | 7·98805 | 122·50000 | 7·93787 | | 0·20000 | 0·01296 | |
| Half Sovereign | 61·63723 | 3·99402 | 61·12500 | 3·96083 | | 0·10000 | ·00648 | |
| SILVER— | | | | | Thirty-seven-fortieths fine silver, three-fortieths alloy; or millesimal fineness 925. | | | |
| Crown | 436·36363 | 28·27590 | — | — | | 1·81818 | 0·11781 | |
| Half Crown | 218·18181 | 14·13795 | — | — | | 0·90909 | 0·05890 | |
| Florin | 174·54545 | 11·31036 | — | — | | 0·72727 | 0·04712 | |
| Shilling | 87·27272 | 5·65518 | — | — | | 0·36363 | 0·02356 | 0·004 |
| Sixpence | 43·63636 | 2·82759 | — | — | | 0·18181 | 0·01178 | |
| Groat or Fourpence | 29·09090 | 1·88506 | — | — | | 0·12121 | 0·00785 | |
| Threepence | 21·81818 | 1·41379 | — | — | | 0·09090 | 0·00589 | |
| Twopence | 14·54545 | 0·94253 | — | — | | 0·06060 | 0·00392 | |
| Penny | 7·27272 | 0·47126 | — | — | | 0·03030 | 0·00196 | |
| BRONZE— | | | | | Mixed metal, copper, tin, and zinc. | | | |
| Penny | 145·83333 | 9·44084 | — | — | | 2·91666 | 0·18890 | |
| Halfpenny | 87·50000 | 5·66990 | — | — | | 1·75000 | 0·11339 | None. |
| Farthing | 43·75000 | 2·83495 | — | — | | 0·87500 | 0·05669 | |

The weight and fineness of the coins specified in this schedule are according to what is provided by the Act fifty-six George the Third, chapter sixty-eight, that the gold coin of the United Kingdom of Great Britain and Ireland should hold such weight and fineness as were prescribed in the then existing Mint indenture (that is to say), that there should be nine hundred and thirty-four sovereigns and one ten shilling piece contained in twenty pounds weight troy of standard gold, of the fineness at the trial of the same of twenty-two carats of fine gold and two carats of alloy in the pound weight troy; and further, as regards silver coin, that there should be sixty-six shillings in every pound troy of standard silver of the fineness of eleven ounces two pennyweights of fine silver and eighteen pennyweights of alloy in every pound weight troy.

## BANKERS' BOOKS EVIDENCE ACT 1879

### 42 & 43 VICT., CAP. 11

*An Act to amend the Law of Evidence with respect to Bankers' Books*

[23rd May 1879]

BE it enacted by the Queen's most Excellent Majesty, by and with the advice and consent of the Lords, spiritual and temporal, and Commons, in this present Parliament assembled, and by the authority of the same, as follows:

*Short title.*

I. This Act may be cited as "The Bankers' Books Evidence Act 1879."

*Repeal of 39 & 40 Vict. c. 48.*

II. "The Bankers' Books Evidence Act 1876" shall be repealed as from the passing of this Act, but such repeal shall not affect anything which has been done or happened before such repeal takes effect.

*Mode of proof of entries in banker's book.*

III. Subject to the provisions of this Act, a copy of any entry in a banker's book shall in all legal proceedings be received as *primâ facie* evidence of such entry, and of the matters, transactions, and accounts therein recorded.

*Proof that book is a banker's book.*

IV. A copy of an entry in a banker's book shall not be received in evidence under this Act unless it be first proved that the book was at the time of the making of the entry one of the ordinary books of the bank, and that the entry was made in the usual and ordinary course of business, and that the book is in the custody or control of the bank.

Such proof may be given by a partner or officer of the bank, and may be given orally or by an affidavit sworn before any commissioner or person authorised to take affidavits.

*Verification of copy*

V. A copy of an entry in a banker's book shall not be

received in evidence under this Act unless it be further proved that the copy has been examined with the original entry and is correct.

Such proof shall be given by some person who has examined the copy with the original entry, and may be given either orally or by an affidavit sworn before any commissioner or person authorised to take affidavits.

VI. A banker or officer of a bank shall not, in any legal proceeding to which the bank is not a party, be compellable to produce any banker's book the contents of which can be proved under this Act, or to appear as a witness to prove the matters, transactions, and accounts therein recorded, unless by order of a judge made for special cause. *Case in which banker, etc., not compellable to produce book, etc.*

VII. On the application of any party to a legal proceeding a court or judge may order that such party be at liberty to inspect and take copies of any entries in a banker's book for any of the purposes of such proceedings. An order under this section may be made either with or without summoning the bank or any other party, and shall be served on the bank three clear days before the same is to be obeyed, unless the court or judge otherwise directs. *Court or judge may order inspection, etc.*

VIII. The costs of any application to a court or judge under or for the purposes of this Act, and the costs of anything done or to be done under an order of a court or judge made under or for the purposes of this Act shall be in the discretion of the court or judge, who may order the same or any part thereof to be paid to any party by the bank, where the same have been occasioned by any default or delay on the part of the bank. Any such order against a bank may be enforced as if the bank was a party to the proceeding. *Costs.*

IX. In this Act the expressions "bank" and "banker" mean any person, persons, partnership, or company carrying on the business of bankers and having duly made a return to the commissioners of Inland Revenue, and also *Interpretation of "bank," "banker," and "bankers' books."*

any savings bank certified under the Acts relating to savings banks, and also any post-office savings bank.

The fact of any such bank having duly made a return to the commissioners of Inland Revenue may be proved in any legal proceeding by production of a copy of its return verified by the affidavit of a partner or officer of the bank, or by the production of a copy of a newspaper purporting to contain a copy of such return published by the commissioners of Inland Revenue; the fact that any such savings bank is certified under the Acts relating to savings banks may be proved by an office or examined copy of its certificate; the fact that any such bank is a post-office savings bank may be proved by a certificate purporting to be under the hand of Her Majesty's Postmaster-General or one of the secretaries of the post-office.

Expressions in this Act relating to "bankers' books" include ledgers, day books, cash books, account books, and all other books used in the ordinary business of the bank.

*Interpretation of "legal proceeding," "court," "judge."*

X. In this Act—

The expression "legal proceeding" means any civil or criminal proceeding or inquiry in which evidence is or may be given, and includes an arbitration:

The expression "the court" means the court, judge, arbitrator, persons, or person before whom a legal proceeding is held or taken:

The expression "a judge" means with respect to England a judge of the High Court of Justice, and with respect to Scotland a Lord Ordinary of the Outer House of the Court of Session, and with respect to Ireland a judge of the High Court of Justice in Ireland:

The judge of a county court may with respect to any action in such court exercise the powers of a judge under this Act.

*Computation of time.*

XI. Sunday, Christmas Day, Good Friday, and any bank holiday shall be excluded from the computation of time under this Act.

## COMPANIES ACT 1879

### 42 & 43 Vict., cap. 76

#### ARRANGEMENT OF SECTIONS

Section.
1. Short title.
2. Act not to apply to Bank of England.
3. Act to be construed with 25 & 26 Vict., c. 89, 30 & 31 Vict., c. 131, and 40 & 41 Vict., c. 26.
4. Registration anew of company.
5. Reserve capital of the company, how provided.
6. 25 & 26 Vict., c. 89 s. 182 repealed, and liability of bank of issue unlimited in respect of notes.
7. Audit of accounts of banking companies.
8. Signature of balance-sheet.
9. Application of 25 & 26 Vict., c. 89, 30 & 31 Vict., c. 131, and 40 & 41 Vict., c. 26.
10. Privileges of Act available notwithstanding constitution of company.

---

*An Act to amend the Law with respect to the Liability of Members of Banking and other Joint-Stock Companies; and for other purposes* [15th August 1879]

BE it enacted by the Queen's most Excellent Majesty, by and with the advice and consent of Lords, spiritual and temporal, and Commons, in this present Parliament assembled, and by the authority of the same, as follows:—

I. This Act may be cited as the Companies Act 1879. *Short title.*

II. This Act shall not apply to the Bank of England. *Act not to apply to Bank of England.*

III. This Act shall, so far as is consistent with the tenor thereof, be construed as one with the Companies Acts 1862, 1867, and 1877, and those Acts together *Act to be construed with 25 & 26 Vict. c. 89,*

## APPENDIX

**30 & 31 Vict. c. 131, and 40 & 41 Vict. c. 26.**

with this Act may be referred to as the Companies Acts 1862 to 1879.

**Registration anew of company.**
**25 & 26 Vict. c. 89.**
**30 & 31 Vict. c. 131.**
**40 & 41 Vict. c. 76.**
**42 & 43 Vict. c. 76.**

IV. Subject as in this Act mentioned, any company registered before or after the passing of this Act as an unlimited company may register under the Companies Acts 1862 to 1879 as a limited company, or any company already registered as a limited compay may re-register under the provisions of this Act.

The registration of an unlimited company as a limited company in pursuance of this Act shall not affect or prejudice any debts, liabilities, obligations, or contracts incurred or entered into by, to, with, or on behalf of such company prior to registration; and such debts, liabilities, contracts, and obligations may be enforced in manner provided by Part VII. of the Companies Act

**25 & 26 Vict. c. 89.**

1862 in the case of a company registering in pursuance of that part.

**Reserve capital of company, how provided.**
**25 & 26 Vict. c. 89.**
**30 & 31 Vict. c. 131.**
**40 & 41 Vict. c. 26.**
**42 & 43 Vict. c. 76.**

V. An unlimited company may, by the resolution passed by the members when assenting to registration as a limited company under the Companies Acts 1862 to 1879, and for the purpose of such registration or otherwise, increase the nominal amount of its capital by increasing the nominal amount of each of its shares.

Provided always, that no part of such increased capital shall be capable of being called up, except in the event of and for the purposes of the company being wound up.

And, in cases where no such increase of nominal capital may be resolved upon, an unlimited company may, by such resolution as aforesaid, provide that a portion of its uncalled capital shall not be capable of being called up, except in the event of and for the purposes of the company being wound up.

A limited company may by a special resolution declare that any portion of its capital which has not been already called up shall not be capable of being called up, except in the event of and for the purpose of the company being wound up; and thereupon such portion of capital shall not be capable of being called up, except in the event of and for the purposes of the company being wound up.

VI. Section one hundred and eighty-two of the Companies Act 1862 is hereby repealed, and in place thereof it is enacted as follows:—A bank of issue registered as a limited company, either before or after the passing of this Act, shall not be entitled to limited liability in respect of its notes; and the members thereof shall continue liable in respect of its notes in the same manner as if it had been registered as an unlimited company; but in case the general assets of the company are, in the event of the company being wound up, insufficient to satisfy the claims of both the noteholders and the general creditors, then the members, after satisfying the remaining demands of the noteholders, shall be liable to contribute towards payment of the debts of the general creditors a sum equal to the amount received by the noteholders out of the general assets of the company.

For the purpose of this section the expression "the general assets of the company" means the funds available for payment of the general creditor as well as the noteholder.

It shall be lawful for any bank of issue registered as a limited company to make a statement on its notes to the effect that the limited liability does not extend to its notes, and that the members of the company continue liable in respect of its notes in the same manner as if it had been registered as an unlimited company.

*25 & 26 Vict. c. 89, s. 182, repealed, and liability of bank of issue unlimited in respect of notes.*

VII. (1.) Once at the least in every year the accounts of every banking company registered after the passing of this Act as a limited company shall be examined by an auditor or auditors, who shall be elected annually by the company in general meeting.

(2.) A director or officer of the company shall not be capable of being elected auditor of such company.

(3.) An auditor on quitting office shall be re-eligible.

(4.) If any casual vacancy occurs in the office of any auditor the surviving auditor or auditors (if any) may act, but if there is no surviving auditor, the directors

*Audit of accounts of banking companies.*

shall forthwith call an extraordinary general meeting for the purpose of supplying the vacancy or vacancies in the auditorship.

(5.) Every auditor shall have a list delivered to him of all books kept by the company, and shall at all reasonable times have access to the books and accounts of the company; and any auditor may, in relation to such books and accounts, examine the directors or any other officer of the company: provided that if a banking company has branch banks beyond the limits of Europe, it shall be sufficient if the auditor is allowed access to such copies of and extracts from the books and accounts of any such branch as may have been transmitted to the head office of the banking company in the United Kingdom.

(6.) The auditor or auditors shall make a report to the members on the accounts examined by him or them, and on every balance-sheet laid before the company in general meeting during his or their tenure of office; and in every such report shall state whether, in his or their opinion, the balance-sheet referred to in the report is a full and fair balance-sheet properly drawn up, so as to exhibit a true and correct view of the state of the company's affairs, as shown by the books of the company; and such report shall be read before the company in general meeting.

(7.) The remuneration of the auditor or auditors shall be fixed by the general meeting appointing such auditor or auditors, and shall be paid by the company.

<small>Signature of balance-sheet.</small>  VIII. Every balance-sheet submitted to the annual or other meeting of the members of every banking company registered after the passing of this Act as a limited company shall be signed by the auditor or auditors, and by the secretary or manager (if any), and by the directors of the company, or three of such directors at the least.

<small>Application of 25 & 26 Vict. c. 89.</small>  IX. On the registration, in pursuance of this Act, of a company which has been already registered, the registrar shall make provision for closing the former

registration of the company, and may dispense with the delivery to him of copies of any documents with copies of which he was furnished on the occasion of the original registration of the company; but, save as aforesaid, the registration of such a company shall take place in the same manner and have the same effect as if it were the first registration of that company under the Companies Acts 1862 to 1879, and as if the provisions of the Acts under which the company was previously registered and regulated had been contained in different Acts of Parliament from those under which the company is registered as a limited company. 30 & 31 Vict. c. 13, and 49 & 41 Vict. c. 26. 25 & 26 Vict. c. 89. 30 & 31 Vict. c. 131. 40 & 41 Vict. c. 26, and 42 & 43 Vict. c. 76.

X. A company authorised to register under this Act may register thereunder and avail itself of the privileges conferred by this Act, notwithstanding any provisions contained in any Act of Parliament, royal charter, deed of settlement, contract of copartnery, cost book, regulations, letters-patent, or other instrument constituting or regulating the company. Privileges of Act available notwithstanding constitution of company.

---

# COMPANIES ACT 1862

## 25 & 26 VICT., CAP. 89

*An Act for the Incorporation, Regulation, and Winding Up of Trading Companies and other Associations*

[7th August 1862]

### FORM D

*Form of Statement referred to in Part 3 of the Act*

[1] The capital of the Company is    ,
divided into    shares of    each.
   The number of shares issued is
   Calls to the amount of    pounds per share

[1] If the company has no capital divided into shares the portion of the statement relating to capital and shares must be omitted.

have been made, under which the sum of pounds has been received.

The liabilities of the company on the first day of January (or July) were :—
Debts owing to sundry persons by the company.
On judgment, £
On specialty, £
On notes or bills, £
On simple contracts, £
On estimated liabilities, £

The assets of the company on that day were—
Government securities [*stating them*], £
Bills of exchange and promissory notes, £
Cash at the bankers, £
Other securities, £

---

## STAMP DUTIES ACT.

### 33 & 34 VICT., CAP. 97

*An Act for granting certain Stamp Duties in lieu of Duties of the same kind now payable under various Acts, and consolidating and amending provisions relating thereto*      [10th August 1870]

BANK NOTE—

| | | | | £ | s. | d. |
|---|---|---|---|---|---|---|
| For money not exceeding £1 | | | . | £0 | 0 | 5 |
| Exceeding £1 and not exceeding £2 | | | | 0 | 0 | 10 |
| ,, | £2 | ,, | £5 | 0 | 1 | 3 |
| ,, | £5 | ,, | £10 | 0 | 1 | 9 |
| ,, | £10 | ,, | £20 | 0 | 2 | 0 |
| ,, | £20 | ,, | £30 | 0 | 3 | 0 |
| ,, | £30 | ,, | £50 | 0 | 5 | 0 |
| ,, | £50 | ,, | £100 | 0 | 8 | 6 |

And *see* sections 45, 46, and 47.

# INDEX

ACCOUNTS, demand for publicity of, 41, 42
 in pass-book, 71-73
 mistakes in, 59, 60
 not conclusive, 59, 60
 of bank notes in circulation, 23, 24
 of branch banks, 53, 58
 of customer at different branches, 58, 59
  how far to be kept secret, 64, 65
 under Companies Act 1862, 40
  1879, 40, 41
Advances to agent, 88, 89
 usual form of, 3
Agent, advances to, 88, 89
 director is, 46
 indorsement of cheque by, 96
 London joint-stock banks free to act as, 12
 manager is, 47
 mercantile defined, 180, 181
  dispositions by, 180-184
 signature of bill by, 165
Appropriation, arrangement with third person as to, 78
 by banker, 75
 by customer, 56, 57, 75
 implied from course of dealing, 75, 76
 under rule in Clayton's case, 76-78
Audit, under Companies Act 1879, 14, 40, 41

BANK Charter Act, bills at less than six months under, 11, 12
 loss of right of issue under, 11
 no new bank of issue after, 11
 provisions as to Bank of England, 11
 restricts issue of private banks, 11
 right to exchange bullion under, 16
 scope of, 11
Bank mortgages, 185-187
Bank-notes, accounts of, in circulation, 23, 24
 altered, 26, 27, 35, 36
 amount of issue of, by Bank of England, 22
 are money, 15, 16
 attain their modern form, 10
 cases on, 29-32
 characteristics of English, 17
 conditions of issue by private bank, 23
 defined, 17
 dishonoured, 32
 duty to present or circulate, 28, 29
 earliest form of, 1
 forged, 26, 27, 35
 how differ from promissory notes, 26
 how transferable, 27
 included in Bills of Exchange Act, 27

## INDEX

Bank-notes, issue of, by private banks, restricted, 11
  discontinued by London banks, 2, 7
  issued against bullion, 22, 23
  liability of limited company as to, 13, 14, 21, 22
  licence for issue of, 24
  loss of right of issue of, 11, 18, 19
  lost, 33, 34
  may be cut in halves, 26
  payment of debt by, 28
  presentment to issuer of, 28
  provisions of Stamp Act as to, 24, 25
  purchase of goods by, 28
  right of issue of, how transmitted, 18-21
  rights of mutual holders of, 33
  set off of, 32, 33
  stolen, 33, 34
  stopped, 34, 35
  time for presentment, 28, 29
  unstamped, 23, 24
  when legal tender, 25, 26
  who may issue, 18
Bank of England, Act of 1708 as to, 5, 6
  altered note of, 35, 36
  business restricted, 4, 5
  custom of, as to dividend warrants, 168
  established, 4
  first exclusive privilege, 5
  how affected by Bank Charter Act, 11
  issue of notes by, against bullion, 22, 23
    without licence, 23
    without stamps, 23
  notes of, when a legal tender, 25, 26
  privileges curtailed, 8
Bank of issue, accounts to be kept by, 23, 24

Bank of issue, commercial aspect of, 2, 3
  extent of issue of, 23
  how loses its rights, 4
  no new, after Bank Charter Act, 11
  notes of, when a legal tender, 26
Bank post bills, 120, 121
Banker, appropriation by, 75
  as bailee, 93, 94
  as collector of bills, 116, 117
    cheques, 108-110
    dividend warrants, 168, 169
  as discounter of bills, 118
  as mortgagee, 185-189
  bound to know customers' signature, 95
  characteristic of debt of, to customer, 59
  complex duties of, 1
  duty of, to honour customer's cheque, 60-62
  earliest, 1
  general relation to customer, 56
  liability for trust money, 68-70
  may rectify mistakes, 56, 60, 112, 113
  must not be party to breach of trust, 60, 61, 88
  must pay person entitled, 101
  not bound to know signature of payee, 95, 96
  not bound to pay bills, 100
  not liable to drawer of bill, 103
    third persons, 67, 68
  not officer of company, 84
  not trustee for customer, 56
  rights of, to cheque paid into account, 108
  right to charge compound interest, 65, 66
    cross cheques, 115
    make charges, 65
    use clearing-house, 109, 110
  simplest functions of, 15

# INDEX

Banker, various functions of, 3
 what is receipt of money by, 110
 when put on inquiry, 100
Bankers' books, as evidence, 73
 entries in not conclusive, 59, 60
 mistakes in, 73
 pass-book, 71–73
 production of, 73, 74
Bankers' lien, applies to what securities, 62
 exceptions to, 62–64
Banking, basis of, 1
 becomes lucrative trade, 2
 second stage of, 2
Banking companies, etc., duties of directors of, 46, 47
 introduced, 12
 nature of, 12
 possible forms of, 38
 powers of, 43–46
 powers of directors of, 46
 under Companies Act, 1862, formation of, 39, 40
  list of members of, 40
  registration of, 39, 40
  accounts of, 40
 1879, 40, 41
Banking partnerships, after Companies Act 1862, 13, 40
 clergymen in, 37, 38
 extended, 8, 38
 how execute instruments, 9
 how may sue and be sued, 8, 9
 how regulated, 38
 liability of members of, 9
 nature of, 8, 9
 not corporations, 8
 registration of members of, 37, 38
 restricted, 6
Banks with limited liability, introduced, 13
 under Companies Act 1862, 13
 1879, 14, 21, 22
Bill-broker, arrangement with, 92

Bill of Exchange, acceptance of, 148, 149, 159
 for honour, 161, 162
 accepted payable at bank, 100
 alteration of, 160, 161
 at less than six months, 11, 12
 banker as collector of, 116, 117
  not liable to drawer of, 103
 capacity to contract by, 149
 cancellation of, 160, 161
 conflict of laws as to, 163, 164
 consideration for, 150
 damages on dishonour of, 160
 definition of, 146, 147
 definition of holder in due course, 150, 151
 delivery of, 149
 discharge of, 160, 161
 discount of, 118
 dishonoured, 152, 153
 drawn in sets, 163
 dual capacity towards, 147
 effect of acceptance of, 159
  drawing of, 159
  indorsing, 159
 fictitious payee of, 104–107
 foreign, 118
 forged indorsement of, 100, 101
 funds not assigned by, 159
 history of, 146
 indorsement of, 151, 152, 159
 inland, 147
 lost, 163
 lost, protest of, 158
 material alteration, 102
 non-acceptance of, 154
 non-payment of, 156
 notice of dishonour of, 156–158
 overdue, 152, 153
 payment of, 160, 161
  for honour, 162, 163
  through correspondent, 101, 102
 position of acceptor of, 158, 159
 presentment of for acceptance, 153, 154

Bill of Exchange, presentment of, for payment, 154, 155
 presumptions of faith and good value, 151
 protest of, 158
 qualified acceptance of, 154
 right of customer to recover in specie, 116
 rights of holder of, 153
 short, 117
 signature of, 149, 150
  by agent, 165
  by stranger, 160
 special directions as to, 102, 103
 sum payable under, 147, 148
 time of payment of, 148
 transference of, 151, 160
 under Bills of Exchange Act, 146 165
 waiver of, 160, 161
 when negotiable, 147
 with marginal notes, 119
Bill of Lading, conditional on acceptance of bills, 174
 contract under, assignable by statute, 175, 176
 definition of, 171
 drawn in sets, 172, 174, 175
 history of, 171
 holder for value of, 172, 173
 not negotiable, 173, 174
 stoppage *in transitu* under, 172
 transfer of without authority, 173, 174
 who liable for freight under, 176
Bond, given as security, 129, 130, 131
 how revocable, 132
 when effects merger, 129
Branch banks, independent of main bank, 54, 55
 part of main bank, 53, 54
 statement under Companies Act 1862, 54, 55
Brokers and agents, as customers, 88-92

Broker and agent, notice that customer is, 89-92

CHARGES, acquiescence in by customer, 65
 right of banker to make, 65
Cheques, advantages of use of, 6
 banker as collector of, 108-110
 banker must know customer's signature of, 95
  need not know payee's indorsement, 95, 96
 countermand of payment of, 100
 crossed, 114-116
 first adopted, 2, 6
 material alteration of, 97
 negligence of customer as to, 98, 99
 negotiable, 138
 operation of, 99
 paid into account, 108
 paying and collecting bank the same, 108, 109
 payment of, at branch bank, 54, 55
 what is, 99, 110
 property in, 99
Circular notes, 127, 128
Clearing-house, banker may use, 108, 109
 country, 110, 111
 London, 111, 113, 114
 provincial, 111, 112
Coins, issue of notes against in Ireland, 210
 Scotland, 207
 under Coinage Act 1870, 16, 17
 when legal tender, 16, 17
Companies and corporations, as customers, 81-84
 banker not officer of, 84, 202
 form of instruments of, 84
 mode of borrowing, 83, 84, 200-202
 power to borrow, 81, 82, 200

# INDEX

Correspondent, payment of bills through, 101, 102
  relation to customer, 117, 118
Criminal law, 203-206
Customer, accounts of, at different branches, 58, 59
  acquiescence in banker's charges, 65
  appropriation by, 56, 57, 75
  banker not trustee for, 56
  brokers and agents as, 88-92
  corporations and companies as, 80-84
  duty to honour cheque of, 60-62
  effect of bankruptcy of, 66
    death of, 66, 100
    payment in by, 56, 57
  executors as, 87, 88
  general relation of to banker, 56
  how far entitled to secrecy, 64, 65
  husband and wife as, 80
  liquidator as, 84, 85
  married woman as, 79, 80
  negligence of, as to cheque, 98, 99
  no right to separate accounts, 57, 58
  onus on, to distinguish trust money, 68, 69
  partners as, 85
  relation to correspondent, 117, 118
  right to recover bills in specie, 116
  shareholder as, 80, 81
  trustee as, 87
  trustee in bankruptcy as, 84, 85

DEBENTURES, estoppel of assigner of, 250
  issuer of, 199, 200
  issue of, formalities as to, 200-202
  to bearer, 199

Debentures, when subject to equities, 198, 199
Delivery order, 177-179
Deposit bank, commercial aspects of, 2, 3
  joint-stock, declared lawful, 10
  origin of, 6
  originally thought illegal, 2
Directors, duty of, 46, 47
  powers of, 46
Dividend warrants, 167-169
Dock warrants, 176, 177

ESTOPPEL, by negligence, 98, 106, 107
  by representation of holder, 143-145
  issuer, 141-143
  under Bills of Exchange Act, 159, 160
Exchequer bills, form of, 166
  negotiable, 166, 167
Executor, as customer, 87, 88
  insufficiently stamped probate of, 87
  powers of, 87
  residuary legatee, 88
  revocation of probate, 87
  transfer of account to, 87, 88
  when personally liable, 87

FACTOR, defined, 180
  persons in position of, 180-184

GOLD bullion, notes issued against, 22, 23
  right to exchange, 16
  right to have coined, 16
Guarantee, by bond, etc., 129-131
  how revoked, 131, 132
  illusory, given by manager, 49, 50
  in writing, 129

HUSBAND and wife, as customers, 80

## 302 INDEX

IRISH law, 210
Iron warrants, 170, 171

JOINT accounts, 86, 87

LETTER of credit, containing conditions, 126, 127
  documentary, 123, 124
  failure of issuer of, 127
  for acceptance of bills, 112, 123
  for transmission of money, 121, 122
  object of, 121
  open and documentary, 123
  power of liquidator to accept bills under, 127
  privity of bill-holder and bank through, 124
  rights of bill-holder under, 124-126
Liquidator, as customer, 84, 85
  when may accept bills under letter of credit, 127
London banks, discontinue note issue, 2, 7

MANAGER, false representation by, 50
  fraud of, 50, 51
  general agent, 47
  illusory guarantee by, 49, 50
  liability of bank for, 47, 48
  to bank, 51, 52
  payment of money to, 48, 49
  power of, to arrest and prosecute, 51
Married woman, as customer, 79, 80
  without separate estate, 80
Money, includes bank notes, 15, 16
  kinds of, 15

NEGOTIABILITY, by estoppel, 140-145
  defined, 137, 138
  not known to Common Law, 137

Negotiable instruments, English, 138
  foreign, 138-140
  payment of debt by, 27, 28
Notice of change of firm in pass-book, 73
  that customer is agent, 89-92
  to banker that money is trust money, 69
  to branch banks, 53-55

PARTNERS, as customers, 85, 86
  powers of, 85, 86
  under Partnership Act, 1890, 85, 86
Pass-book, nature of, 71-73
Payment, countermand of by death, 100
  of bill for honour, 162, 163
  mode of, 101
  through correspondent, 101, 102
  time for, 148
  of cheque by branch bank, 54, 55
  to collecting bank, what is, 110
  what is, 99, 100
  presentment of bill for, 154, 155
  to manager, 48, 49
  under special directions, 102, 103
Post-office orders, 169, 170
Presentment, of bank note to issuer, 32
  transferor, 28, 29
  of bill for acceptance, 153, 154
  payment, 154, 155
Promissory notes, are negotiable, 138
  bank notes, a form of, 26
  given as security, 130, 131
  nature of settled, 5
  under Bills of Exchange Act, 164, 165

RESERVE capital, under Act of 1879, 40, 41

# INDEX

Rule in Clayton's case, defined, 76
  examples of, 77
  when no power to borrow, 83, 84
  when security given, 131
  when trust money involved, 77, 78

SCOTCH LAW, bank agents, 208
  bank notes, 207
  banker's lien, 209
  bills and cheques, 209
  cash credits, 208, 209
  history of, 207, 208
Shareholder of bank, as customer, 80, 81
Shares, advances on security of, 188, 189
  are choses in action, 190
  blank transfers of, 191-193
    attached to certificates, 195-197
  conflict of equitable titles to, 193, 194
  forged transfer of, 191, 197
  in banking company, purchase of, 42
  notice of claim to, 194
  pledged, bank as owner of, 190
  reputed ownership of, 194
Statutes, Bank Charter Act 1844, 11, 12, 16
  Bank Incorporation 1844, 12
  Bank Notes (Licence, etc.) 1828, 10
  Bank of England 1708, 5, 6
  Bank Partnerships 1826, 8
  Banks with limited liability 1858, 13

Statutes, Bankers' Books Evidence Act 1876, 73
  1879, 73, 74
  Bills of Exchange Act 1882, 26, 27, 34, 35, 36, 64, 100, 101, 104-107, 114-116, 146-165
  Bills of Lading Act 1856, 175, 176
  Coinage Act 1870, 16, 17
  Companies Act 1862, 13, 39, 40, 54, 55
  1879, 14, 21, 22, 40, 41
  1890, 39, 45, 46
  Deposit Banks 1833, 10
  Factors Act 1823, 180
  1842, 180
  1847, 180
  1889, 177, 180-184
  Indorsement of Cheques 1854, 96, 97
  Leeman's Act 1879, 42
  Limitations, 59, 130
  Partnership Act 1890, 38, 85
  Stamp Act 1870, 24, 25
Surety, death of, 132, 133
  discharge of, 133-136
  principal shown to be, 135, 136

TRUSTEE, as customer, 87
Trustee in bankruptcy, as customer, 84, 85
Trust money, appropriation of, 77, 78
  customer must distinguish, 68, 69
  notice that money is, 69

www.ingramcontent.com/pod-product-compliance
Lightning Source LLC
Chambersburg PA
CBHW022042230426
43672CB00008B/1042